Social Policy in Britain

Also by Pete Alcock

Welfare Law and Order (with P. Harris)
Poverty and State Support
Understanding Poverty

Social Policy in Britain

Themes and Issues

Pete Alcock

Consultant editor: Jo Campling

First published in Great Britain 1996 by
MACMILLAN PRESS LTD
Houndmills, Basingstoke, Hampshire RG21 6XS
and London
Companies and representatives
throughout the world

A catalogue record for this book is available
from the British Library.

ISBN 0–333–62544–7 hardcover
ISBN 0–333–62545–5 paperback

First published in the United States of America 1996 by
ST. MARTIN'S PRESS, INC.,
Scholarly and Reference Division,
175 Fifth Avenue,
New York, N.Y. 10010

ISBN 0–312–16201–4

Library of Congress Cataloging-in-Publication Data
Alcock, Peter, 1951–
Social policy in Britain : themes and issues / Pete Alcock :
consultant editor: Jo Campling.
p. cm.
Includes bibliographical references and index.
ISBN 0–312–16201–4
1. Great Britain—Social policy.   I. Campling, Jo.   II. Title.
HN385.5.A43   1996
361.6'1'0941—dc20   96–7687
                                                           CIP

10   9   8   7   6   5   4   3   2   1
05   04   03   02   01   00   99   98   97   96

Printed and bound in Great Britain by
Antony Rowe Ltd, Chippenham, Wiltshire

For my Mother and Father

Contents

List of Figures

Preface

This book is intended to provide a general introduction to social policy for students studying the discipline at all levels of further and higher education. The main intended readership is students in higher education on the first year – or at the first level – of undergraduate degree courses in social policy. However, the book will be equally valuable to students studying social policy as part of a broader undergraduate programme in the social sciences, as part of NVQ or BTEC courses in further education or as part of professional education courses in areas such as social work or nursing. It also aims to provide a comprehensive and up-to-date guide to the discipline for students first encountering social policy at postgraduate level, or wishing to re-examine previous studies as part of a new postgraduate course.

The book adopts a comprehensive, and topical, approach to social policy – focusing on the major structure, context and issues that inform both study and research within the discipline. Unlike other established introductory texts, such as Hill (1993a), there is no extensive discussion of the detailed content of specific areas of social policy. Students seeking this could use Hill as a supplement, or could go to one of the many specialist texts covering each of the major areas. Unlike Cahill (1994), however, the approach remains rooted firmly within the traditional debates and empirical foci of the discipline. The overall aim, therefore, is to avoid duplication of existing texts, and yet to provide a clear and comprehensive guide to all the major issues that are likely to be covered in the study of social policy.

The primary focus of this text is on Britain and on the development and analysis of British social policy. Its primary intended readership, therefore, is students in British universities and colleges. However, as is argued in the text, it is no longer feasible to restrict the study of social policy to the context and actions of only one nation state. The international context of British social policy is thus discussed, and in particular the growing impact of the European Union (EU) upon policy development in Britain. This provides a framework for the coverage of British policy development, however – rather than an extensive focus on comparative study or on the EU in particular detail. Students seeking a textbook on comparative social policy or on social policy in the EU should look to some of the increasing numbers of specialist texts now focusing on these aspects of the study of social policy, such as Ginsburg (1991) or Hantrais (1995).

This is not to suggest, however, that this book is likely only to be of interest to students of social policy in Britain. Because the book situates the debates and concerns of British social policy within a broader international and theoretical context, it is likely to be of interest, too, to students in other countries, who wish to find a comprehensive and accessible guide to the development and analysis of policy within the UK that could provide a basis for comparative study with other countries.

Students studying social policy are, of course, studying an academic discipline; and, as the book explains in Chapter 1, social policy is such a discipline, just like economics, sociology or law. However, the term *social policy* is also used to refer to the political changes and reforms that take place in the real world as governments, or other powerful agents, seek to bring about social improvement through the provision or regulation of welfare. For instance, we talk about a cut or an increase in social security benefit entitlement as a 'change in social policy'. The same term is used, therefore, to refer both to the academic discipline and to the object of its study. This is perhaps misleading, although it is understandable, and is well established. Most commentators do use the term interchangeably to refer to both, leaving the reader to determine the appropriate meaning in each case – and we will do so here, too, in the hope that the real meaning is generally fairly clear.

Readers of this book may start at the beginning and carry on through to the end; however, many students of social policy following a course, or courses, of study will probably want to move backwards and forwards between the sections and chapters in order to find out about the specific themes or issues that they are studying at any particular time. With this in mind, the contents of the book have been carefully divided between sections and chapters addressing different issues, and have been written so that any one chapter could be read in isolation from those around it – but in the expectation that the others would probably be used or referred to at another time. This is a book, therefore, that can either be read or used as a source of reference – or, perhaps most commonly, both.

The chapters have also been divided into subsections, with subheadings listed in the contents. These are intended to help the reader to find quickly the particular issue on which they want to focus at any one time. However, where issues – or particular terms or concepts – are not listed in the contents, readers should use the index at the end. This provides page references to the detailed coverage of all specific concepts and empirical policy developments and is perhaps the quickest way of all to gain access to the book in order to find the answer to a particular question. What follows here, however, is a summary of major sections and chapters of the book, for those who want a little more general guidance than is provided in the contents and index.

- **Section One** provides an introduction to the discipline of social policy, setting it in the context of its historical development and of the major empirical concerns of policy development in Britain. The changes in the way social policy has been conceived and studied are discussed in **Chapter 1**, and the major influences behind these changes are identified. These are set within broad themes looking at the shift from social *administration* to social *policy*, and the widening of the focus of the discipline from Britain to Europe and beyond. **Chapter 2** provides brief summaries of the development of the major areas of welfare provision in Britain. These are often each the focus of separate study within social policy courses, and of separate textbooks that cover each in much more detail. What is provided here is an introduction to each, which can then set the scene for further study.
- **Section Two** addresses the structure of the welfare mix in Britain, looking separately at the four major sectors of welfare provision – the state, the market, the voluntary sector and the informal

sector. Each of these is dealt with in a separate chapter which emphasises the strengths and weaknesses of that particular form of provision. However, in reality these different sectors of welfare overlap – and even duplicate or contradict each other. These general features, and the problems to which they may give rise, are also discussed; and each chapter concludes that one sector of welfare provision cannot alone be expected to meet all of the wide range of needs and preferences for social protection that are found in complex modern socieities.

- **Section Three** examines some of the major contextual influences upon policy development and policy analysis, and seeks to explain how these have been addressed in the study of social policy. **Chapter 7** explains the importance of ideology and theory in shaping our perceptions of welfare, and examines the major ideological frameworks that have influenced the study and development of social policy in Britain in recent times. **Chapter 8** explores the economic context within which social policy is developed, explaining how, and why, economic policy in Britain has changed in the fifty years since the end of the Second World War. One of the important lessons of the study of economic policy is the recognition that policy changes in one country are influenced more and more by changes and developments on an international scale. In Britain, this international context is shaped by our membership of the European Union; and the structure and influence of Europe and the EU on policy change in Britain is discussed in **Chapter 9**. While Chapter 9 looks 'above' the national level to Europe, **Chapter 10** looks 'below' it to the important role played in policy development and implementation by local govern-ment in this country. This includes description of the history of local authority involvement in the control and delivery of social policy and explanation of the conflicts between central and local government to which this has sometimes given rise.
- **Section Four** focuses upon some issues that now occupy a central place in the analysis of the operation of social policies – although they have sometimes been absent from policy debate and academic discussion in the past. Of particular importance in the recent development of social policy study has been recognition of the important role played by social divisions in structuring both the development and delivery of welfare services. Divisions of social class have widely been recognised and debated within social

science; but it is now clear that societies are also structured by the diverse circumstances and experiences that result from differences of gender, race, age and disability too – and indeed from the impact of other social divisions. These major divisions and their impact on social policy are explored in **Chapter 11**. **Chapters 12** and **13** take up more specific issues to do with the production and consumption of welfare services within modern society. The focus here is on how we pay for the welfare services that we provide in Britain, and on how we ensure that those services that are provided are actually available to, and used by, the people for whom they are intended – although the evidence reviewed suggests that in some cases this does not happen successfully.

- **Section Five** is an overview and conclusion of the themes and issues covered in the book. This overview is approached in **Chapter 14** through an appraisal of the likely future development of the discipline, in terms of its relations with other academic disciplines, its geographical boundaries locally, nationally and internationally, and its major ideological debates and differences. The chapter, and the book, conclude that, while the study of social policy is now characterised by a wider range of perspectives, debates and issues than ever before, there is still a clear and considerable consensus on its importance as an academic discipline – and as a force for social change.

Throughout the text, therefore, the aim of the book is to provide an accessible, and yet comprehensive, guide to what is in practice a wide-ranging and contested field of study. The intention is to use the themes that inform current academic debate and research to present the major issues in a form which simplifies them – without treating them as simplistic. Obviously students wishing to look in more detail at particular issues or debates, or at particular areas of service development or delivery, will need to move on to more specialist texts within the discipline; and indeed it is likely that they will be directed to do so. So, although this could be the first – and most comprehensive – text that students of social policy use – it will almost certainly not be the only one.

Acknowledgements

I should like to take this opportunity to thank a few people who have helped in the production of this book, although I should say at the outset that no-one other than myself can take any responsibility for its final content. Jo Campling encouraged me to begin the project and assured me of its value; having finished it I am now, finally, convinced that she was right in her belief that a new approach to introductory study could be developed. Alan Deacon at the University of Leeds and Robert Page at the University of Nottingham, together with two anonymous readers selected by Macmillan, read the whole text and provided me with a range of valuable comments and suggestions. Most, though not all, of these I have followed; and for all I am most grateful – it is a better book for their assistance in it. Sheffield Hallam University provided me with some space, or should I say time, to work on the text – without this support I could not have completed it. Finally, and most importantly, I am grateful to Sandra Cooke for her support, help and encouragement throughout, and for suffering my preoccupations and my frustrations with fortitude and understanding.

I should also like to thank David Billis for permission to reproduce his diagram as Figure 5.1.

List of Abbreviations

ASI	Adam Smith Institute
CAB	Citizens Advice Bureau
CDP	Community Development Project
COS	Charity Organisation Society
CPAG	Child Poverty Action Group
CSA	Child Support Agency
CSE	Certificate of School Education
CSP	Critical Social Policy
DG	Directorate General
DLA	Disability Living Allowance
DSS	Department of Social Security
EAPN	European Anti-Poverty Network
EEC	European Economic Community
EC	European Community
ECU	European Currency Unit
EMS	European Monetary System
ERDF	European Regional Development Fund
ERM	Exchange Rate Mechanism
ESF	European Social Fund
ESRC	Economic and Social Research Council
EU	European Union
GCE	General Certificate of Education
GCSE	General Certificate of School Education

GDP	Gross Domestic Product
GLC	Greater London Council
GNP	Gross National Product
GP	General Practitioner
GREA	Grant Related Expenditure Assessment
ICA	Invalid Care Allowance
IEA	Institute of Economic Affairs
IMF	International Monetary Fund
JSP	Journal of Social Policy
LEA	Local Education Authority
LETS	Local Exchange and Trading Schemes
LSE	London School of Economics
MP	Member of Parliament
MSC	Manpower Services Commission
NACAB	National Association of Citizens Advice Bureaux
NCC	National Consumer Council
NHS	National Health Service
NI	National Insurance
NIC	National Insurance Contribution
NSPCC	National Society for the Prevention of Cruelty to Children
OPCS	Office of Population Censuses and Surveys
OPEC	Organisation of Petroleum Exporting Countries
PSBR	Public Sector Borrowing Requirement
QUANGO	Quasi-Autonomous Non-Government Organisation
SPA	Social Policy Association
SSA	Standard Spending Assessment
SSD	Social Services Department
TEC	Training and Enterprise Council
UK	United Kingdom
USA	United States of America
VAT	Value Added Tax
WRVS	Women's Royal Volunteer Service
YTS	Youth Training Scheme

SECTION ONE

Introduction

1

The Discipline of Social Policy

What is social policy?

It is probably true that there will always be argument and debate about what constitutes an academic discipline and how to define particular disciplines. In the area of social science, in particular, there has been debate about the overlap between disciplines like sociology, economics and politics – and social policy, and about what should be the core concerns of each. This debate has not just been an academic one; it has a political significance too. For instance, in the early 1980s the Conservative Government in Britain, under the influence of the Secretary of State for Education and Science, Sir Keith Joseph, required the major state body providing research funding for the social sciences to change its name from the *Social Science Research Council* (SSRC) to the *Economic and Social Research Council* (ESRC) in a direct attempt to shift the focus of research in the field towards economic issues and applied policy research.

Students of social science must recognise therefore that what they study, and how they study it, is consequently the subject of continual academic and political debate – and indeed disagreement. Of course in general this is no bad thing. We cannot, and should not, take for granted that we are working only within a limited field where we alone are experts and everyone is agreed what it is we are experts on. If this were the case academic knowledge would not advance very far, and it would not have much impact on the broader social world.

However, recognition that the boundaries of our study are never closed and that the focus of our concern is subject to external influences does not mean that we cannot find distinctive features of research and debate within social policy that make it possible, and desirable, to separate out this work from the different, although related, concerns of sociology, economics, politics and other social sciences. If we examine the development of the discipline of social policy, we can see clearly how the attempt to provide a specific focus for study was embarked upon, how this led to boundary disputes with other disciplines, how it was subject to external political influence – and to internal theoretical debate, and how these events changed the nature of social policy itself. In fact, debates over the nature of social policy even resulted in a change in name for the discipline from *social administration* to *social policy* – symbolised by the change of the professional association to the Social Policy Assocation in 1987. It was a change, however, that was not without conflict and disagreement (Glennerster, 1988; Smith, 1988; Donnison, 1994); many university departments and qualifications are still called social administration, and the ESRC only recently changed its description of research in the field from social administration to social administration and policy.

As we shall shortly discuss, the shift from social administration to social policy signified important changes within the discipline; it also opened up once again boundary disputes with other disciplines such as sociology, economics and politics that the advocates of a narrow view of social administration had sought to close. The change also raised the perennial question of whether social policy, or social administration, was a *discipline* – with an established theoretical tradition and a discreet focus for study – or merely a *field* of study – where academics from other disciplines took a specialist interest in a particular area of study.

Perhaps this is really a question which need not detain us for long, however, for the difference between a discipline and a field is more one of semantic debate for academics than of practical relevance for students. It is of most consequence, in practice, in the arguments conducted within universities and research institutes about the academic recognition – or more pragmatically the political power and financial resources – to be accorded to a discipline as opposed to a field. In universities an academic discipline may be the focus of work of a department or the subject of a degree qualification, whereas a field of study may be the specialism or particular interest of someone whose main base is elsewhere in a separate discipline. For students of either a field or a discipline even this may be of limited importance, although it does have some important pragmatic implications; for, practically speaking at least, a field of activity clearly comes out as second best to a discipline in terms of organisational status – whatever the academic merits of its practitioners or students.

In most British universities social policy in fact often shares departmental status with other cognate social sciences or professional education, such as sociology or social work; and in research institutes specialists in social policy often work alongside sociologists, economists and even lawyers. However, there is sufficient institutional recognition and academic support for social policy to claim to be a *discipline* alongside sociology, economics and other social sciences; and for the boundary disputes, the theoretical arguments, and even the change of title, to be regarded as evidence of healthy self-criticism and self-reflection – rather than self-doubt. There are undergraduate and postgraduate degrees in social policy, academic journals publishing the findings of social policy research, and a professional association representing social policy practitioners (now the Social Policy Association [SPA]). As a history of the development of the discipline reveals, social policy has an important and unique contribution to make to our understanding of the social world and its future development.

From social administration to social policy

Where social policy differs from sociology is in its specific focus upon the development and implementation of policy measures in order to influence the social circumstances of individuals rather than the more general study of those social circumstances themselves. Where it differs from economics is in its focus upon welfare policies, or policies impacting upon the welfare of citizens, rather than those seeking to influence the production of goods, materials and services. Although, as we have suggested, both of these boundaries are moveable and porous.

Within the British social policy tradition in particular, what has also distinguished social policy from some other social science disciplines has been in its specific, and driving, concern not merely to understand the world, but also to change it. In this tradition social policy is not only a *descriptive* discipline, it is also a *prescriptive* one. This is in large part because the early academic development of social policy in Britain was closely allied to the political development of *Fabianism*. The Fabians were both academics and politicians and they wanted to utilise academic research and analysis in order to influence government welfare policy. Throughout much of the early part of this century the development of British social policy was almost synonomous with the concerns and perspectives of the Fabians; the discipline largely shared Fabianism's benign view of the role of state provision within welfare policy. Social policy also shared the empirical focus of Fabianism, in particular its concern to measure the need for, and the impact of, state welfare provision.

The ideological and empirical alliances with Fabianism were, however, associated most closely with the social administration perspective of the discipline, and with a concern with *what* is done by policy action, and *how* it is done – rather than *why* this is done, or indeed *whether* it should be done. In the last two decades or so this perspective, and its Fabian alliances, has come under increasing criticism and attack from a range of different perspectives which have sought to widen the questions asked by the discipline and to challenge the assumption about the benign role of the state in welfare provision. Furthermore, the narrow focus and assumptions of the social administration tradition have also been called into question by the increasing academic and political concern with *international* comparisons of welfare policy. For what international comparisons quickly reveal is that welfare policies have not developed elsewhere as they have done in Britain; that different political assumptions in different countries have led to different patterns of provision and, therefore, that different political assumptions could lead to different patterns of provision in Britain too.

The cumulative effect of these questions and challenges has been to bring about a significant shift in the focus of academic debate and political influence within the discipline, which has been represented by the change in title from administration to policy. This has resulted in a shift from a discipline that was, in Mishra's (1989, p. 80) terms, 'pragmatic, Britain-centred, socially concerned and empirical', to one that is characterised by ideological division, theoretical pluralism, and a growing internationalism. However, this shift, significant though it is, should not deter us from recognising the continuities, as well as the discontinuities, in the development of social policy that, in particular, its concern with policies for welfare provides.

Fabianism

The concern of social policy to contribute to the development of political change – as well as to analyse it – is generally credited with providing for its birth as a discipline in Britain, at a time when state policy towards the welfare of citizens was undergoing a radical revision and Fabian politics were seeking both to understand and to influence this. The Fabian Society was formed in 1885, under the leading guidance of Sydney and Beatrice Webb. The Webbs were firm believers that collective provision for welfare through the state was an essential, and inevitable, development within British capitalist society; Sydney Webb also held strong views on the moral values of social (or socialist) provision (Headlam, 1892; Ball, 1896).

The Webbs were both members of the Royal Commission on the Poor Laws and the Relief of Distress. The Commission was established by the government, in 1905, to review the old Victorian approach to support for the poor. It signified a recognition by government of the need to overhaul welfare policies and of the importance of social policy debate in shaping this process, and it increased the pressure on government to bring about the major changes in social security and other policies that were introduced in the ten years before the First World War.

Debate about the future direction of welfare policy was a central concern of the work of the Commission, and when it reported in 1909 the Commission produced both a Majority and Minority Report, as the members could not all agree about the role that the state should play as provider of welfare services. The Webbs, as authors of the *Minority* Report, argued for an extensive role for state provision. The *Majority* Report envisaged a greater, continuing, role for charitable and voluntary action. Nevertheless, both argued for significant reform, and in retrospect there was as much in common across the two reports as there was in conflict between them.

Influential in the drafting of the Majority Report were Bernard and Helen Bosanquet, leading organisers of the Charity Organisation Society (COS), which coordinated the voluntary sector provision of social work and social services and the training of social workers. In December 1912, however, the COS's School of Sociology was merged with the London School of Economics (LSE), founded by the Webbs, to form the LSE's new Department of Social Science and Administration. This was arguably the first academic base for the discipline of social policy and it provided a significant academic forum for the debates rehearsed in the deliberations of the Poor Law Commission to be continued and developed. The first lecturer to be appointed to the new department in 1913 was Clement Attlee, demonstrating almost immediately the close link that the Fabians were concerned to secure between academic analysis and political change. For, after the Second World War, Attlee became the Prime Minister of the Labour government which introduced many of the far-reaching state welfare reforms that the Fabian reformers had been calling for throughout the intervening period.

During the early part of the twentieth century the LSE Department of Social Science and Administration also received significant financial support from the private trusts of an Indian millionaire, Ratan Tata. This money was specifically tied to support for empirical research on policies for the prevention and relief of poverty and destitution. It therefore provided an impetus for the development of another significant aspect of the discipline; its concern with empirical work on the need for, and impact of, social policy. In particular, the research funding supported the work of academics such as Tawney, and Bowley and Burnett Hurst, who were early pioneers in the theoretical and empirical investigation of poverty and inequality in Britain (Harris, 1989).

During the period following the First World War, therefore, the department at the LSE contained the main themes of the discipline of social policy in its early form. The department was informed, and directed, by a strong ideological commitment to Fabianism, in particular the use of academic knowledge and research on social problems to create pressure on the state to introduce welfare reforms. The continuing influence of the old COS, however, also maintained a concern with the role of the voluntary sector in social service and, although diminished by the statism of the Fabian approach, this broader concern with non-state welfare provision has always remained a vital feature of political as well as academic debate in social policy. Teaching at the LSE, although also informed by sociology and economics, remained firmly tied to the education and training of social services workers; research work focused on the detailed investigation of the problem of poverty.

Despite the high-profile political context of its birth in the early twentieth century, when the Webbs and the Bosanquets were influential in shaping the reform of Victorian welfare policy in Britain, social policy soon became more concerned with the pragmatic issues of education for practice and empirical research on established social problems – the social administration tradition.

In the period following the Second World War and the publication in 1942 of his report on social insurance by Beveridge (himself Director of the LSE during the interwar period), this tradition reached its high-water mark; many of the goals of the Fabian leaders of social policy appeared to be realised with the introduction of the widespread welfare reforms in the 'creation' of the *welfare state*. The National Health Service, state education to fifteen, the National

Insurance scheme, public housing and local authority Children's Departments appeared to embody the comprehensive state provision for the prevention of social deprivation within a capitalist economy that the academics and researchers had argued for so eloquently.

The head of the LSE Department of Social Science and Administration during this period was T H Marshall. In a famous treatise on citizenship (1950) he argued that the earlier development of *civil* and *political* citizenship in British society had been complemented in the mid-twentieth century by the creation of *social* citizenship. This involved the use of state policy intervention to meet basic social needs and to guarantee basic social rights for all. The welfare state of the postwar period appeared to be the embodiment of social citizenship and to have created the basic framework for a new role for the state as the provider of social services – a role that we will return to discuss in more detail in Chapter 3.

Furthermore, the postwar welfare state appeared to have widespread political and ideological support. Although the reforms were introduced by the Labour government elected in 1945 (with the exception of the education reforms which had been a product of the coalition National Government in power during the war), when Labour were replaced by the Conservatives in 1951, the state welfare services were maintained in almost exactly the same form. The general assumption was that there was a political consensus over the desirability of state welfare provision within a capitalist economy. In 1954 *The Economist* magazine coined the phrase *Butskellism* to refer to this consensus – an amalgamation of the names of the Labour Chancellor of the Exchequer, Gaitskell, and his Conservative successor, Butler (also the author of the 1944 education reform) (Dutton, 1991, Ch. 2). This consensus seemed to represent an accommodation in Conservative thinking to the role of state intervention, referred to by Macmillan as *The Middle Way* (1938), and a recognition in Labour thinking of the abandonment of the need for a future socialist revolution (Crosland, 1956 [see also Chapter 7]; Addison, 1975; and Hill, 1993b, Ch. 1).

The welfare state and the postwar consensus may be seen as significant achievements for social policy but they also presented the discipline with something of a challenge, for in a sense they removed the need for further academic and ideological debate and therefore the main basis for future political influence. In the period following the introduction of the welfare state, social work practice and training became more and more concerned with the individualistic, psychoanalytical approach to social problems; voluntary sector activity began relatively to decline; and policy research became restricted to the narrow role of gathering facts to support the case for the gradual expansion and greater effectivity of the now-established agencies of state welfare.

Fabianism continued to dominate social policy during this period. But it was a Fabianism that had lost both its political drive – the creation of the welfare state had apparently been achieved and all that remained was to make this work better – and its academic controversy – now the only role for academic enquiry was empirical research to provide information for the better administration of state welfare. Of course, the supposed consensus on welfare had not in practice completely stifled academic debate (Lowe, 1990); within the consensual framework there were, nevertheless, some questioning voices. Titmuss, who succeeded Marshall at the LSE, challenged the narrow conception of state welfare and its assumed egalitarian consequences by pointing out that the state also provided welfare support to the rich (Titmuss, 1956). Townsend, a former student and colleague of Titmuss, conducted research which showed that, despite the welfare reforms, many people continued to be living in poverty in Britain in the 1950s and 60s (Abel-Smith and Townsend, 1965; Townsend, 1979).

Influential though these criticisms were in questioning the success of the welfare state in meeting all the goals of its Fabian protagonists, they remained contained within the overall Fabian framework of academic and political debate which continued to dominate social policy. Both Titmuss and Townsend were staunch supporters of the British welfare state and their criticisms were intended to create pressure to improve it, not to question its basic desirability or its fundamental structures. By the 1970s, however, changes in Britain's *welfare capitalist* economy were beginning to create the climate for a challenge to the assumed desirability of the maintenance and gradual expansion of the postwar welfare state; critical voices were beginning to develop within the discipline of social policy to challenge the Fabian domination of debate and research.

The New Left

Towards the end of the 1960s and the beginning of the 1970s, the rapid expansion of higher education saw social policy becoming established as an academic subject in most British universities and expanding its research base with increased state and charitable support for an ever wider range of projects on the implementation of state welfare. In 1967 the professional association (then the Social Administration Association) was established, and in 1971 a major academic journal for the discipline was launched – the *Journal of Social Policy* (JSP).

However, the expansion of social policy also brought into the discipline a wider range of academics and practitioners, not all of whom shared the Fabian perspective (and LSE roots) of its earlier leaders. The late 1960s and early 1970s was a period of the renaissance of Marxist and other radical debate within the social sciences in most welfare capitalist countries, referred to by many of the leading protagonists as the *New Left*. The expanding base of social policy brought this debate into the politics and ideology of welfare too.

Marxist theorising covered a range of different, and disputed, approaches to social structure and social policy but, in general, there was agreement among many that the achievement of the welfare state in postwar Britain and the Fabian-supported consensus on the gradual and unilinear growth of welfare protection were neither as successful, nor as desirable, as had been assumed. Pointing to the empirical work of Titmuss, Townsend and others, the Marxists argued that the welfare state had not succeeded in solving the social problems of the poor and the broader working class and, in practice, operated to *support* capitalism rather than to *challenge* it (Ginsburg, 1979). They argued, therefore, for a rejection of the consensual, Fabian, approach to the understanding of, and support for, state welfare and its replacement with a *political economy of the welfare state* (Gough, 1979), which situated the explanation of the growth of state welfare in the needs of the capitalist economy for healthy and educated workers and the struggle of the working class for concessions from the capitalist state (sometimes referred to as the *social wage*).

By the 1980s the influence of the left was no longer a 'new' feature of the discipline; theoretical debate between Marxists and Fabians about the desirability, or the compatibility, of their different approaches to the subject ranged widely (Taylor-Gooby and Dale, 1981; Lee and Raban, 1988). In 1981 a new journal, *Critical Social Policy* (CSP), was launched to provide a forum for such debates and for other alternative approaches to theory and research in social policy.

The New Left critics challenged the theoretical assumptions of the postwar consensus approach to state welfare, arguing for a conflict model that saw welfare reforms as the product of struggle and compromise rather than gradual enlightenment (Saville, 1983). They also challenged the assumed desirability of state welfare services, arguing that for many working-class people welfare services such as council housing or social security were experienced as oppressive and stigmatising. These criticisms were not only informed by Marxism. The pages of CSP, in particular, were also filled with academics and practitioners arguing that state welfare was also failing women, ethnic minorities and other oppressed or marginalised social groups, an issue to which we shall return in Chapter 11.

It is perhaps no coincidence that the New Left challenge to the Fabian domination of social policy was occurring at more or less the same time as Fabianism's great achievements in the welfare state were also under threat from Britain's changing economic and political fortunes. The failure of economic growth in the 1970s to continue to provide a platform for expanding state welfare was argued by Marxists to be an inevitable consequence of the inability to reform capitalism from within and was evidence that the process was beginning to experience a 'crisis' in which stark choices would have to be faced by social policy planners and politicians. However, the crisis – if crisis it was – in state welfare of the 1970s did not only attract a critical reappraisal of the Fabian domination of social policy from the left, it also provoked a counter-attack from right-wing theorists too.

The New Right

Despite the overriding influence of Fabianism within social policy, especially during the immediate postwar period, right-wing critics of state welfare had always argued against the interference of state provision with the workings of a capitalist market economy (Hayek, 1944). During the 1950s, through the work of organisations like the Institute of Economic Affairs (IEA), the appeal for a 'return' to the classic liberal values of a *laissez-faire* state and self-protecting families and communities had been kept alive – if rather marginalised from mainstream social policy debate. In the 1970s, however, the crisis in the welfare state created circumstances in which such right-wing critics of state welfare could present a more cogent attack on the 'middle way'. What is more, this academic attack was accompanied by a shift to the right in politics too, exemplified by the election of Margaret Thatcher as leader of the Conservative Party in 1975. Together these changes provided an opportunity at the end of the century for a new liberalism (neo-liberalism) to rise to a prominence in academic and political debate that it had not achieved at any time in the previous eighty years.

Drawing on the work of right-wing American theorists such as Friedman (1962) and Murray (1984), the IEA and others began to develop a neo-liberal critique of state welfare and Fabian politics that both they, and their left-wing critics, began to refer to as the *New Right.* Not of course that these views were that new – as we shall discuss in Chapter 7; they drew on classical liberal thinking from the nineteenth century and before. Their main argument was that state intervention to provide welfare services, and the gradual expansion of these which Fabianism sought, merely drove up the cost of public expenditure to a point at which it began to interfere with the effective operation of a market economy. They claimed that this was a point that had already been reached in Britain in the 1970s as the high levels of taxation needed for welfare services had reduced profits, crippled investment and driven capital overseas.

Like the (not so) New Left, the New Right also challenged the desirability of state welfare in practice, arguing that free welfare services only encouraged feckless people to become dependent upon them and provided no incentive for individuals and families to protect themselves through savings or insurance. Furthermore, right-wing theorists claimed that state monopoly over welfare services reduced the choices available to people to meet their needs in a variety of ways and merely perpetuated professionalism and bureaucracy (Green, 1987). After 1979, once the Conservative Party under Thatcher's leadership came into power, these academic arguments found a sympathetic hearing from government ministers such as Keith Joseph and Rhodes Boyson.

Critical perspectives

By the 1980s, therefore, the domination that Fabianism had enjoyed over social policy had been overturned from two contradictory directions and, at the same time, its influence on government through support for the Butskellite consensus had been displaced by a political climate in which controversy was widely preached and the value of academic analysis and empirical research openly questioned.

However, it was not just those from the left and right of the political spectrum who were challenging the consensual approach to welfare by the 1980s – other critical perspectives too were questioning the central role of Fabianism and the benign view of the state welfare. Feminist writers began to question what they claimed was the male domination of academic social policy and the assumptions about unequal gender roles that were contained in much practical social policy provision (Dale and Foster, 1986; Pascall, 1986); and the women's movement more generally began to take the politics of gender onto the national policy agenda. Other critical perspectives drew attention to the racism inherent in much of British social policy provision, and to the failure of past students and academics to recognise the divisive nature of the supposedly universal welfare state (Williams, 1989).

That the new theorists from the left and the right, and elsewhere, should be successful in challenging the Fabian domination of social policy was, of course, no bad thing for the discipline itself. It opened up teaching and research to a wider range of ideas and issues; it stimulated theoretical enquiry and debate; and it broadened the base of academic scholarship and social service practice. The new critical perspectives on welfare also challenged the narrow national focus of existing social policy debate on the development of welfare policy in Britain. Critics of state welfare drew on ideas and examples from other countries in their criticisms of British welfare capitalism, and thus effectively provided a further challenge to the existing traditions of the discipline by opening up a concern with the comparative analysis of welfare.

Comparative perspectives

Throughout most of its development social policy had remained, like many other academic disciplines in the social sciences, concerned almost exclusively with policy change and policy implementation in Britain. This is perhaps understandable, for Britain has had a more or less self-contained social and legal order with a government with the power to introduce policies affecting the lives of all people in Britain. Description of, and prescription for, welfare policy has therefore focused primarily on Britain and its government.

However, as we are all now very much aware, the lives of people in Britain are affected not only by the decisions and actions of the British government. Economic trends and economic decisions, affecting people in many countries, are taken on an international scale by bodies largely outside the control of the British government, such as the World Bank and the International Monetary Fund – a point to which we will return in more detail in Chapter 8. Furthermore, Britain is now a member of the European Union (EU) along with other Western European countries and, increasingly, decisions taken by the representative bodies of the EU have an impact upon policy development in its members' nations, as we shall discuss in Chapter 9. Social policies in Britain are thus no longer exclusively British – if indeed they ever really were – and the discipline of social policy has been required to recognise, and to analyse, this broader international dimension.

As we said above, the left- and right-wing critics of Fabian social policy were quick to point to the lessons that could be learned from policy development in other countries. Those on the left looked to the socialist countries of the Soviet block, although, even before the collapse of Soviet socialism, others were drawing attention instead to the social democratic countries of Scandinavia as models for welfare reform in Britain. Those on the right used the Soviet block as a negative example, and argued rather for policy changes modelled on the market-oriented welfare provisions found in the USA. What all seemed agreed on was that the welfare policies, or the welfare states, of other countries demonstrated that social policies did not *have* to be as they were in Britain.

Recognition of the importance of international comparison radically changes the focus of debate within social policy; but it, too, is not without its problems and disagreements. For a start, much of the early development of social policy in Britain had been presented as a gradual extension of state welfare, as if driven by a kind of inexorable law of progress, and tempered only by questions of speed – not direction. International comparisons initially tended to be dominated by similar assumptions. The expectation was that other countries would be following the same pattern of state welfare growth as Britain – albeit perhaps at a different pace. This assumption of international congruity is sometimes called a *convergence thesis*, because all nations are assumed to be converging towards one common goal.

Although it is true to argue that most capitalist and socialist countries have developed policies to make some provision for the welfare of citizens, this convergence thesis can, however, only be sustained at a level of massive simplification. More detailed study of the welfare policies of other countries, even of Britain's nearby neighbours in the EU, reveals significant differences in the form, and the extent, of social policies – and in the political pressures that have given rise to them (Spicker, 1993).

By the 1980s social policy scholars in Britain and elsewhere were increasingly concerned to make such international comparisons, not merely in order to argue for the importation into Britain of models of welfare provision from other countries, but rather to demonstrate, at a more general theoretical and empirical level, the widespread diversity within welfare states. They sought, in effect, to challenge the convergence thesis with a celebration of difference – or a *divergence* thesis (Mishra, 1990; Ginsburg, 1991). Perhaps the most influential contribution to the comparative perspective in social policy, and to the divergence thesis, came from a Swedish academic, Esping-Andersen (1990), who carried out a detailed study of the welfare states of a number of developed welfare capitalist countries, from which he concluded that the different developments could be roughly grouped into three types of *welfare regime*. Esping-Andersen identified three major welfare regimes:

- the *Liberal* – exemplified by the USA
- the *Corporatist* – exemplified by Germany and the rest of continental Western Europe
- the *Social Democratic* – exemplified by Scandinavia, in particular Sweden.

Critics have argued that Esping-Andersen's *Three Worlds of Welfare Capitalism* (the title of his book), although demonstrating divergence in the international development of social policy, are even themselves something of a simplification of a range of differences within and between the regimes. For instance, as we discuss in Chapter 9, some have argued that there may be additional types of regime to be identified if other countries are also studied. But Esping-Andersen's approach remains a central example of the importance of international comparison and analysis to the study of social policy, and of the greater understanding to be gained when study and research looks beyond narrow national boundaries.

Welfare pluralism

The different forms of welfare regime to be found in other countries thus reveal that welfare policies develop in different ways in different social, economic and political contexts. These differences also reveal a varying balance within different regimes between the role of the state in the provision of welfare, for example with public welfare playing a major role in social democratic regimes like Sweden and the private market playing a major role in liberal regimes like the USA. It is not, however, only the balance between the state and the market which varies between different regimes. In corporatist regimes like Germany, considerable emphasis is placed on the informal role of family structures in providing welfare support, for instance in the care of children or the long-term chronically sick. In other regimes, for example the 'welfare societies' of some Mediterranean countries like Greece and Spain, many welfare services are provided by voluntary agencies such as churches and other religious organisations.

In other words, in different welfare states there is a variation between the roles of different *sectors* in the provision of welfare services. We shall return in Section 2 to look at the roles of these different sectors, in Britain in particular, in more detail. However, it is important to recognise here that it is not just that the balance between the different sectors varies between different welfare states, or welfare regimes, but also that this balance may vary within any one welfare state over time – especially, of course, if that welfare state is experiencing a move from one regime to another. Indeed, it is primarily upon the balance between the roles of the different sectors of welfare that the nature of the welfare regime in any one country at any one time can be determined. In all regimes there will inevitably be such a balance.

Despite the success of the Fabian tradition of social policy and political reform in establishing state welfare in Britain in the 1940s and, despite the criticisms of right-wing, left-wing and other critics of the problems resulting from this apparent state monopoly over welfare services, in practice welfare services in this country have always been delivered by a mixture of state, market, voluntary and informal means. Furthermore, the balance of this mixture has changed over time – for instance with the role of the voluntary sector declining in the early part of the twentieth century, especially after the Second World War, and rising again in the later part of the century. The general point is, however, that there has always been a balance between the providers of services – or what some commentators have called a *mixed economy* of welfare. What is more, criticism of state welfare provision in the last two decades or so, and the attempt by the Conservative government of the 1980s to reduce the role of the state in the provision of welfare, have made the importance of the mixed economy of welfare in Britain ever more clear.

Theoretical debate within social policy is increasingly an academic debate about the appropriate structure for welfare services and has focused upon what the balance between the different sectors should be – rather than whether one (state welfare) or the other (market welfare) should be pursued exclusively. This question of balance has been referred to as the issue of the *welfare mix*, and a recognition of the value of mixed provision within academic debate is also called a *welfare pluralist* approach. This has been supported by some as a means of challenging and attacking the apparent state monopoly over welfare provision, and the bureaucracy and professional control associated with this (Hadley and Hatch, 1981). It has also been associated in the 1980s with attempts to reduce state expenditure on welfare and support a shift towards the privatisation of welfare services (Johnson, 1987).

Of course, the promotion of welfare pluralism does challenge the idea that any one sector should monopolise welfare provision. However, although it has been invoked by critics such as Hadley and Hatch (1981) to challenge state welfare, the concept itself is not essentially an anti-state one. Some of those associated more recently with support for welfare pluralism may be seeking primarily rather to shift the balance of provision *between* the different sectors of welfare in Britain in the 1980s and 90s. In practice, however, this is really only what all welfare reformers and welfare critics have been doing throughout the history of social policy – and the welfare state.

Welfare services in Britain, and in all other welfare capitalist societies, are delivered in different measure by different means. Social policy focuses on the study of these measures and these means and, through argument and prescription, seeks to influence them. As we shall see in the rest of this book this requires:

- a knowledge of the role and structure of these different sectors;
- an analysis of the ideological, economic and international context within which they are situated, and
- an understanding of important issues affecting use of services such as social divisions and inequalities, the costs of providing services and the means of ensuring access to them.

Furthermore, as we shall discuss in the next chapter, these debates about structures, contexts and issues determine in practice the shape of provision within the major features of welfare policy – what we might call the *content* of social policy.

2

The Content of Social Policy

The provision of social services

In trying to define the scope of social policy in his Inaugural Lecture of 1951 Titmuss (1958, p. 14) suggested that it was concerned with those

> services, both statutory and voluntary, with the moral values implicit in their action, with the roles and functions of the services, with their economic aspects, and with the part they play in meeting certain needs in the social process.

Thus, although social policy is about values and how needs are met within economic constraints, it is also about services and the roles that welfare services play within the social process. Indeed, to some extent the study of social policy has concentrated traditionally, and even sometimes exclusively, on the description and analysis of welfare services – for instance identifying the major service areas and looking at each one in turn. Social policy in practice is concerned with the provision of services such as health, education or housing; and students of social policy need to examine each of these major areas of provision in some detail.

However, the adoption of such a service-based approach varies in practice, and there is some debate about what to include within the list of welfare services to be studied as social policy. Hill's (1993a) introductory text, for instance, focuses on traditional areas of welfare but also includes those services that are the subject of economic analysis, such as housing or employment, or the basis of sociological concern, such as family support or community development. Courses in social policy also frequently permit students to select particular areas of welfare, such as health or social security, for more detailed study; however, the range and scope of these selections varies.

Of course, at this level, some debate and disagreement about the scope and structure of the content of social policy is inevitable, and is perhaps to be welcomed as evidence of a continued concern to review the development and scope of the discipline. Nevertheless, at any one time we all have to take some practical decisions about what to include within the scope of our study of social policy. So here we will review those most commonly adopted in social policy courses (social security, health, education, personal social services and housing) but we will also include some others that feature less frequently (employment and family policy).

Social security

The major concern of the early pioneers of twentieth-century social policy, such as the Webbs and Tawney, was with the problem of poverty within Britain's affluent capitalist society. Poverty, and the broader deprivation that is associated with it, is arguably the most serious of social problems because it is the most pervasive; and, if social policy is concerned with the meeting of needs, it should be concerned most of all with the prevention, or the relief, of poverty.

Whether social policies should aim to prevent or to relieve poverty is in fact a matter of some considerable debate. Policies aimed at the relief of poverty, such as the Poor Law which we discuss below, have tended to focus provision upon those who are proved to be already in need of state support, with the aim of raising them (just) above the poverty level; whereas poverty prevention measures aim to predict the social circumstances that might give rise to poverty, such as unemployment or retirement, and to make provision available in such circumstances, so that no-one in these groups falls into poverty in the first place. These differences are also reflected in debates about how to define the problem of poverty in the first place as a product either of personal failing needing state relief or of social change that could be protected against (Alcock, 1993). However, that there should be some policy response to the problem of poverty is nevertheless widely accepted; the question of what to do about poverty has thus always been one of the main questions facing students of social policy.

By far the most important aspect of anti-poverty policy has been the redistribution of resources (usually money) between people in order to provide an adequate income for those who would otherwise be poor. The mechanism for this redistribution is referred to as *social security*. This has now become a technical term for policies designed to ensure the subsidisation or protection of incomes for individuals and families in designated circumstances. In Britain there is a government Department of Social Security to oversee the operation of this and, with an annual budget of almost £90 billion in the mid 1990s, it is by far the largest part of state social policy provision. However, the notion of 'social security' also has a more general meaning that reflects important aspects of this area of social policy – the concern with a collective (social) approach and the aim to guarantee protection (security) through this.

All welfare capitalist countries have social security systems, designed to redistribute resources between individuals, families or households. In most there is a mixture of *state* provision (such as Child Benefit or Unemployment Benefit in Britain), *private* provision (such as private pension schemes), *voluntary* activity (such as charities and handouts) and *informal* support (such as loans or gifts from family or friends). The transfer of resources involved in social security also operates to provide both *horizontal* redistribution – transfer between people across different stages of their lifecycle, for instance Child Benefit and pensions, and *vertical* redistribution – transfer from the better-off to those currently in need, for instance Income Support and Family Credit. This is an issue to which we shall return in more detail in Chapter 12.

Social security benefits may be provided on a *universal* basis to all people. Child Benefit is a universal benefit paid in Britain for all children to their parents, although such universal provision is limited in most welfare capitalist countries. More generally, social security benefits are either paid on an *insurance* basis – to those who have previously made some contribution into the social security scheme; or on a *means-tested* basis – to those who can establish through an examination of their means that they do not have enough resources to provide for themselves.

Private social security protection is generally insurance based, and most voluntary and informal support is in effect means-tested – albeit rather arbitrarily in most cases. State social security provision in Britain contains a mixture of insurance and means-tested provisions, together with universal Child Benefit, although the development of the different schemes is contradictory and overlapping, and the operation of all of them is both complex and confusing for administrators and claimants alike (Hill, 1990).

In Britain social security policy has been a central feature of state welfare policy at least since the days of the Poor Law of the nineteenth century and before. The Poor Law was first established in Elizabethan times as a means of providing relief from local funds for those unable to provide for themselves. In the nineteenth centrury it became a national system of state support under which those who could prove that they were destitute could receive public assistance, on the condition that this assistance included a direct incentive to seek alternative self-support and was provided on a more punitive (or 'less eligible') basis than the conditons enjoyed by those in the worst paid employment (Thane, 1982, Ch. 2; Hill, 1990, Ch. 2). This early form of social security often took the form of residence in a state institution (the workhouse) where conditions were indeed harsh, although Poor Law support could also take the form of financial support for destitution.

The introduction of new forms of insurance-based financial protection in the early part of the twentieth century gradually replaced the role of the Poor Law in the relief of poverty; it was finally formally abolished in the 1940s when the current structure of social security provision was introduced, modelled in large part on the proposal of the Beveridge Report (1942). Beveridge's aim was to prevent poverty by guaranteeing social security payments to certain categories of people, such as the unemployed and the sick. However, the postwar National Insurance scheme did not in fact provide comprehensive coverage for all at risk of poverty. Thus, in practice, a mixture of insurance protection and means-tested benefits aiming to relieve poverty has continued to dominate state social security provision in Britain (Hill, 1990); private and voluntary social security protection have also remained, although their importance has fluctuated (Finlayson, 1994).

Social security policy has been by far the most important feature of welfare policy responses to the problem of poverty; but it has not been the only response. As some critics have often pointed out, the persistence of poverty in countries with well-developed social security systems such as Britain provides evidence that these systems have not succeeded in preventing or removing the problem. In recent decades in particular, alternative anti-poverty strategies have been developed, aimed at targeting additional resources on a local basis onto the poor people or poor communities that social security provision has failed to provide for, in order to help people to develop the means to escape both poverty and dependency upon social security support. These strategies, too, have their problems and limitations, in particular because, by focusing resources upon certain social groups or geographical areas, they inevitably exclude from their scope many, if not most, of the poor and at the same time run the risk of labelling those on whom they do concentrate as deprived and dependant (Alcock, 1993, Ch. 15). Despite their growth in scope and importance, they have not displaced social security from its central role in anti-poverty policy – nor, arguably, have they been any more successful in combating poverty.

Health

Concern with individual and public health within social policy also dates from the nineteenth century; this, too, has been based upon a mixture of state, private, voluntary and informal provision, with state provision occupying a more and more central and dominating role, especially after the 1940s welfare reforms. In the nineteenth century the major focus of public policy was with attempts to secure general levels of sanitation and cleanliness in order to contain the spread of disease. In the twentieth century, however, concern began to focus on individual ill-health and on the provision of measures to cure those suffering from it. This shift from a *preventive* to a *curative* model of health care was the result, in particular, of the growing power and influence of the medical professions – most notably the doctors – in academic and scientific development and policy debate. Through drugs, operations, therapies and other forms of treatment doctors can now cure many illnesses; the concern of health policy has become dominated by the means of making these treatments available to the people who need them.

A comprehensive state National Health Service (NHS) was introduced in Britain in 1948, based on legislation passed in 1946, in order to secure the provision of such health services to the whole of the population (Klein, 1995). The aim was that the NHS would be funded out of general taxation and would be free to users at the point of demand. It also contained a wide range of services: the most important of these were the provision of General Practitioners (GPs) – to provide a local contact point for all people experiencing ill-health; and the establishment of state-run hospitals – to provide treatment for more serious conditions requiring operations or intensive care. Today, people who are ill can thus go to a doctor or a hospital and receive treatment provided by the state.

Such a comprehensive state health service also exists in a number of other welfare capitalist countries – but not in all. In the USA, for instance, the provision of treatment for ill-health has remained largely within a private market of health providers from whom services are purchased by patients who need them, usually through the use of private health insurance packages. In fact, even the USA does have a small public health sector and, in practice, in most other countries – including Britain – there is in reality a mix of state and private health services.

Because the NHS operates by and large in response to individual requests for treatment it has sometimes been described as an 'illness service' rather than a health service – it responds to illness rather than promoting health. However, health promotion and a range of other general measures to prevent illness have always been included within the NHS; in recent years the profile of these aspects of the service has been enhanced by government – for example through the 1992 'Health of the Nation' initiative (Department of Health, 1992). Nevertheless, the vast majority of state expenditure on health policy is still geared to the provision of GP and hospital services for ill people, and the study of health policy has largely focused on these aspects of the NHS (Ham, 1993; Klein, 1995).

The NHS is rightly regarded by most as the major feature of health policy in Britain. However, at the time of its introduction there was a fierce debate between the government and the doctors over whether the NHS should replace private provision for the treatment of illness. In part as a concession to the doctors, a private health sector was therefore maintained; and in recent years with government encouragement this has grown in scope and importance – in particular because of the incorporation of private health protection into the occupational benefit packages offered to some employees. Furthermore, the NHS is also no longer a free service for users. Charges for prescriptions for drugs were introduced in 1951, not long after the NHS itself had been established. These prescription charges have risen significantly since, in particular in the 1980s when they increased over ten times. Charges for other services, such as optical and dental checks, have also been introduced.

The structure of the NHS has also undergone a series of re-examinations and reforms since the 1940s. In the late 1980s and early 1990s the government introduced what it called a system of 'internal markets' into the service in order to import market-based allocation criteria into the distribution of public health services. In simple terms this means that state financing for health services is provided in the form of fixed budgets to 'purchasers' (such as GPs) who use these to buy treatments for their patients from major 'providers' of services (such as hospitals). Resources are thus transferred from the purchasers to the providers within the system in order to meet the needs of patients, as we shall discuss in more detail in Chapter 4.

Despite the introduction, and reform, of the NHS, illness and the need for treatment of course continues to exist. Indeed, and somewhat ironically, the continued success of researchers and professionals in developing new forms of treatment for a wider range of illnesses has operated to expand the need, and the demand, for health services rather than to reduce these. Such growing demand has also been compounded by the success of public health measures in prolonging people's lives – people live longer and so they have a greater need of health services. There has thus been a growing demand for health services, which has meant an inevitable expansion in the cost of the NHS. As a result of this, much of the concern of social policy debate in recent years has been on the need for rationing of health services and on the different measures, overt and covert, used to achieve this. The introduction of the purchaser–provider model of the 1990s was in a sense, therefore, only an attempt to put this rationing onto a more explicit and market-oriented basis.

Whether by design or default, however, the rationing of health services has not impacted equally on all people in Britain. Studies of the distribution of ill-health have consistently shown that it is not distributed equally across the social spectrum, and in particular that poor health is closely associated with lower social class (Townsend *et al.*, 1988). Whether, and how, health policy should seek to redress these inequalities in health remains a central issue for social policy. In contrast to this inequality, however, studies of the use of health services, in particular the NHS, have also demonstrated that middle-class people appear to make greater, and more successful, use of available services (Le Grand, 1982). A service that is available on demand will of course be most used by those who are best able to demand it most often. Policy planners must, therefore, also address the management and the promotion of demand for health services if they are to secure equal benefit of such services for all. As we shall discuss in Chapter 13, these issues of equality of use and equality of benefit are important ones for students of all aspects of social policy.

Education

As in the case of health, the provision of education in Britain is based largely upon a comprehensive state education service much of which was introduced during the period of welfare reform of the 1940s. Similarly, this comprehensive state service exists alongside a continuing private sector of education provision – sometimes confusingly referred to as 'public schools'. What is more, evidence also suggests that inequalities exist in educational achievement and in the use of education services. In addition, educational provision was subject to significant structural reform in the late 1980s. Like health services, therefore, state education is comprehensive but it is not a monopoly and, despite its achievements, it still has its critics.

Most discussion of education policy in social policy focuses upon the education of children in schools. This is certainly the most important aspect because there is near universal agreement that all children should undergo a period of school-based education – indeed, this is compulsory in Britain and in all other welfare capitalist countries. However it is not the only aspect of education provision. There is nursery education for children under school age. There is also further education, either in schools or more commonly in separate colleges, providing a mixture of A levels and vocational or skills training for those over the school leaving age of 16 and for adults. There is higher education for degrees and postgraduate qualifications in universities and colleges. And there is a range of optional, non-specific, adult education provision including such things as language training and leisure skills. Although the focus on compulsory education for children remains central, therefore, education policy is now increasingly focused on the provision of learning opportunities throughout the lifecycle, for those who are willing and able to take advantage of them.

Commitment to nursery education in Britain, however, is very limited, especially compared to the situation in many of our European neighbour-states where the majority of children receive preschool education from a very early age. In this country only a minority of children receive preschool education outside the home and, to a large extent, the provision that does exist is geared more to the needs of childcare than education as such. In other words, provision is for nursery care rather than nursery education. This is certainly true of the growing number of occupational or work-based nurseries and many of the private nurseries used by parents who are both in full-time paid employment. It is also to some extent true of the limited public provision which many local authorities make, which is often focused specifically upon the needs of families with particular problems. Of course children do learn things before they begin to attend school on a compulsory basis, and they do learn in nursery schools; but it is probably true to say that they do not receive any systematic education.

Formal education begins in Britain at the age of five, and children are required to attend school from this age until 16, unless they can obtain special exemption for home-based learning. Education for children from age 5 until 11 to 13, sometimes referred to as *primary* education, began in the nineteenth century in local schools run by locally elected School Boards. In 1902 these were transferred to democratically elected local authorities. *Secondary* education for children over the school leaving age which was then set at twelve was provided in private 'grammar' schools used mainly by the children of wealthy middle-class parents, although local authorities could provide financial assistance to enable other children to attend them. In the early part of the twentieth century, however, fewer than ten per cent of children went on to secondary schools, less than in some other countries such as the USA.

During the interwar years there was increasing pressure for the extension of secondary education to all, both as a result of Fabian pressures to extend equality of opportunity to children from all social classes and as a product of the increasing recognition that a growing industrial economy required a better educated workforce. Politicians both on the right and the left had reasons to support the introduction of compulsory secondary education; and the Education Act which provided for this, the first of the welfare state reforms, was introduced in 1944 by a Conservative member of the wartime

Coalition Government, R A B Butler, although with support from Labour's Chuter Ede.

Following the 1944 reforms, compulsory school education was extended to the age of 15 (later extended in 1973 to 16) for all children. However, this secondary education, as with primary education, was to be provided by local authorities within a *tripartite* system of grammar, technical and secondary-modern schools according to the ability and aptitude of pupils as assessed by a standard examination taken at the end of primary school (the 'eleven plus') – although in practice few technical schools were developed and the system mainly consisted of grammar and secondary-modern schools. However, the private provision in the 'public' grammar schools remained alongside local authority education, as did the possibility of state-funded places in these schools for some children from poorer families and a small number of 'direct grant' schools which were funded by the state but based outside local authority control.

Labour had initially supported the (supposedly) tripartite system of secondary education in the 1940s and 1950s, but in the 1960s the Labour Government introduced reforms to require local authority secondary education to move towards a system of *comprehensive* schools, which took children of all abilities and prepared them for national assessment at age 16 in GCE 'O levels', and provided education to 'A level' at age 18 for those pupils willing and able to stay on for further study.

Despite the comprehensive ideal, however, assessment at O and A level revealed significant inequalities in education achievements in schools. Middle-class children, especially those attending schools in predominantly middle-class areas, on average did better in exams than did working-class children; white children tended to do better than those from ethnic minorities; and, at A level in particular, boys tended to do better than girls. These patterns of inequality suggested that comprehensive schooling was not able entirely to counteract broader societal disadvantages. However, concern with their persistence did lead to government reports on 'under achievement' (for example, Newsom, 1963; Swann, 1985) and to attempts to extend additional priority funding to educational provision in deprived areas. They also resulted in a restructuring of assessment at age 16. Initially, separate examinations (CSEs) were introduced for children with lesser academic ability but these were later merged with O levels to become GCSEs, with different levels of assessment within one common qualification.

In the 1970s, however, the government became concerned not just with differentials but with the overall levels of educational achievement in schools. Labour Prime Minister James Callaghan initiated a 'Great Debate' on the need to link school education more closely to the needs of economic development; this eventually resulted in the late 1980s in the introduction of a 'core curriculum' for all schools with regular testing of pupils' standards of achievement at particular ages.

The late 1980s also saw the beginning of the break-up of the local authority monopoly control of state education. All schools within local authority control were given local control over the management of their budgets; and schools, whose governing bodies wanted to, were given the power to 'opt out' of local authority control altogether and receive funding direct from the Department for Education. At the same time there was support for the greater expansion of private provision within school education, with more state-financed ('assisted') places being provided in private schools, and business and industry being encouraged to provide resources for their local schools or colleges. In the 1980s, too, expenditure on non-educational provision within schools, for instance on free milk, school meals or subsidised clothing, was largely curtailed. Such provision had initially been seen as a means of ensuring that children from all families were able to spend a full day at school but this assistance is now largely restricted to the provision of free school meals for the children of parents on Income Support.

Further education was also initially provided by local authorities. It was closely linked to apprenticeships and industrial training with local further education colleges providing courses, mainly for school-leavers, leading to qualifications recognised by particular trades or professional bodies. In the 1970s and 80s the high levels of unemployment among school-leavers severely undermined this basis of further education; but the development of alternative schemes for youth education, such as the Youth Training Scheme (YTS) – with government funding from the Department of Employment – revitalised provision within colleges. Today vocational qualifications within further education have increasingly become coordinated within a single national framework, and control of colleges has been transferred to a national funding body established by the government.

Higher education at universities has a long history, with those at Oxford and Cambridge dating back to medieval times. In the twentieth century government support for the development of universities in all major cities was extended but undergraduate education remained largely a middle-class pursuit for children leaving grammar schools with good A level qualifications. The introduction of maintenance grants after the war to provide a guaranteed income for all students made it possible for the chidren of poorer parents to undertake higher education, but places at university were still severely restricted. In 1963, however, the Robbins Report on access to higher education set out the aim of a higher education place for anyone capable of undertaking undergraduate education, and in the 1970s provision was extended to a wider range of people and a wider age group. This was achieved in particular by the development of new institutions for higher education – the polytechnics, which were under local authority control and offered work placements and professional qualifications as part of new undergraduate degrees.

Despite this expansion, the proportion of people entering higher education in Britain has been lower than that of many of our European and North American neighbours. In the 1990s the conversion of the polytechnics to universities, under central government control, was accompanied by another period of rapid expansion of provision, with the aim of offering higher education places to a third of school-leavers and to a range of older people 'returning' to university as mature entrants. Support for individual students, however, has been reduced and undergraduates are now expected to borrow money for living costs using state-supported student loans.

Notwithstanding pressures on funding, which it has increasingly experienced in recent years, education provision is Britain is greater in the 1990s, than it has ever been in the past. There are more children taking GCSE and A level examinations, and more people entering further and higher education. However, inequalities in participation and achievement, by class, race and gender, continue to be of importance. Furthermore, the balance between central and local control, and between public and private provision, remains a controversial issue within policy debate.

Personal social services

Despite the existence of a range of general provisions for welfare, there are nevertheless some groups of the population who have special needs resulting from their individual or social circumstances. Since the nineteenth century a range of specific personal services has been developed by state, private and voluntary providers to meet some of these needs; the development and operation of these has now become an important feature of the study of social policy.

The main groups covered by such personal social services are the elderly, people with disabilities or physical handicaps, people with learning disabilities (previously called mentally handicapped), mentally ill people and children. Many people in these groups may, for various reasons, not be able to provide fully for themselves and may seek help from others – or, in the case of children, they may be subject to scrutiny to ensure that they are being cared for adequately by those, usually parents, who are responsible for them.

As we shall discuss in more detail in Chapter 6, much of the help that such vulnerable groups receive is provided on an informal basis by families, friends or local communities. However, the development of more formal provision has been an important feature of the growth of welfare services in Britain and other welfare capitalist countries. In the nineteenth and early twentieth centuries much of this provision was developed by the voluntary sector, in particular under the coordination of the Charity Organisation Society (COS). COS provision was sometimes referred to as *social work*, and this term is still used to refer generically to those employed in the provision of personal social services, although technically speaking it should only be used to refer to those workers who have a specific professional qualification in social work. These workers are concentrated mainly in activities governed by statutory legislation concerning children, the mentally ill and criminal offenders, and they constitute only a minority of those employed in the wide range of personal social services provision.

Although social workers were originally based primarily in voluntary sector agencies, at the time of the major development of state welfare services in the 1940s most were transferred to public social service agencies located in local authorities. In the 1940s these local authority services were divided between children, the mentally ill and other client groups; but, following the Seebohm

Report (1968), they were reorganised in 1970 into generic Social Service Departments (SSDs) with a general responsibility for assessing the needs of, and providing services to, all client groups. Social workers with generic responsibility for all client groups are often referred to as 'field workers' to distinguish them from those working in the specific settings, such as residential homes, which we shall discuss below.

The development of state social services in the 1940s did not, however, curtail voluntary sector or private service provision. For instance, despite the development of local authority children's departments, the National Society for the Prevention of Cruelty to Children (NSPCC) – which had been established in the nineteenth century – continued its work, employing social workers on the same basis as local authorities and frequently collaborating with SSDs in the investigation and protection of children in need. In recent years the number of voluntary and charitable agencies active in the field of child protection has grown significantly, although concern over childcare more generally has also become more acute and child protection remains the major feature of the work of most local authority social workers (Clarke, 1993).

Voluntary agencies have also been active in providing a range of institutional supports for other clients in need such as those with disabilities or the mentally ill. These include 'meals on wheels', luncheon clubs, leisure activity groups and day centres. Such activities sometimes employ social workers but they also employ those without formal social work qualifications, and of course they rely on volunteers. Day centres and other activities are also provided by SSDs, and sometimes these too rely on voluntary support. However, such state-based provision has never displaced the wide range of voluntary initiatives that has been established in this field and, in the 1990s, local authority departments are being required to move away from their role primarily as the providers of services for their clients.

Today, through the use of social workers, SSDs are required to act on behalf of those clients who need some element of care within the community, to help them assess their need for services and gain access to these within the voluntary, the private, or the informal sectors. The legislation bringing about this change refers to authorities acting in an *enabling* role to ensure the provision of appropriate *community care* for clients from whatever is the most appropriate source (Means and Smith, 1994).

For those clients who need more intensive help, however, care has traditionally been provided in residential settings employing workers to look after clients on a 24-hour basis. Residential care has been provided by state agencies, including local authorities and, where medical care is also needed, the NHS. However, it has also been provided by voluntary agencies and by private residential establishments. In recent years the extent of private provision here, too, has expanded, with government support through social security payments for clients too poor to pay for such care themselves and, in the 1990s, with local authorities providing direct support under community care packages for clients. What is more, the expectation is that it will continue to play a major role in the provision of community care into the future – although, as we have already mentioned, the major providers of community care have always been, and will continue to be, the informal carers within families and neighbourhoods.

Housing

The provision of shelter is a basic human need; and the building, maintenance and sale (or rental) of houses a major economic activity. Despite this, the position of housing policy within social policy has always been a rather controversial one, perhaps in part because housing is an area of welfare where the state has played a relatively minor role as provider as compared to those we have discussed above. The majority of housing in Britain has always been provided by the private sector and, although there has been state intervention to regulate (and to stimulate) the private market, there are major debates within social policy about how desirable, and how extensive, such state regulation should be.

The changing focus of state intervention and regulation in housing, and the important role of the private market, can be seen in simple terms by looking at the changing balance between different forms of provision or ownership – or housing *tenures*, as these are usually called. At the turn of the century, around 90 per cent of housing in Britain was provided on a rental basis by private landlords, with most of the rest being owned by the occupants themselves. By the 1970s the private rented sector had declined to around 15 per cent, with almost a half of houses being owner-occupied and a third being rented from the state through local authorities. In the 1990s the private rented sector has declined further, to less than ten per cent; over two thirds of houses are owner-occupied and less than a quarter are rented from local authorities. Thus private provision has shifted from a rental to an ownership basis, and state housing has first expanded and then later declined.

The decline in the private rented sector has been blamed by some on the indirect effect of state regulation. During the First World War the government became concerned that the private landlords, who had built and developed the majority of housing (especially in urban industrial areas), were exploiting their tenants by charging high rents, and they introduced legislation to control the level of rent charges and to give tenants some protection against eviction by their landlord. Although intended initially as a temporary measure this statutory protection for tenants has remained in force in some form ever since. Landlords have frequently argued against such rent control, claiming that it reduces their ability to make a commercial gain from renting and has resulted in many rented houses being demolished or sold. In practice, however, the declining role of private renting seems to have continued inexorably despite periods when rent control was very much reduced. Indeed, in the 1990s the private rented sector is at its lowest ebb at a time when rent protection is less restrictive than it has been at almost any time since 1915.

One reason for the decline in the private rented sector, however, is the fact that many of the rented houses built in the nineteenth century were of poor quality and have been demolished in this century, as part of slum clearance programmes. In inner urban areas these have largely been replaced with public rented local authority dwellings; private investment in housing has shifted to the construction of houses for sale. Both local authorities and private sale builders have been provided with incentives to build houses by government, yet there have been no direct incentives or subsidies to private landlords. The decline of private rented housing is thus the result of the popularity of owner-occupation – and of government support for this and for public renting – rather than simply the impact of rent control.

Indeed, the popularity of owner-occupation has arguably been the most significant feature of housing development in the twentieth century. For those who can afford it, the attraction of having a capital investment in a home that is exclusively your own is a fairly obvious one – especially when set against the past exploitation of private tenants, and the strict regulation under which much public sector housing has been rented. The opportunity to borrow the money to buy the house through a mortgage, which can be repaid gradually over twenty or twenty-five years, and is guaranteed against the value of the house if sold, has also made owner-occupation open to a much wider section of the population. The availability of mortgages to potential owners has also encouraged private builders to speculate in building houses for sale; by the 1960s this was even encouraging private landlords to sell the houses that they currently rented. Since the 1950s owner-occupation has also been directly supported by all governments as a major feature of housing policy, with indirect subsidies being provided to buyers by exempting them from income tax on the money that they used to repay the interest on their mortgage debts. By the end of the 1980s this indirect subsidy amounted to a total of over £7 billion a year.

Up until the 1980s, however, government housing policy had also sought to support the development of a public rented sector of housing, provided through local authorities. This began to be developed after the First World War when local authorities were given subsidies by central government to build houses for rent in order to meet the needs of the returning soldiers and their families; and, although the subsidies were later brought to an end, many local authorities undertook major programmes of house building during the interwar period. Following the Second World War, the commitment to develop state welfare again extended to the greater provision of public rented housing, and local authorities were once more given large subsidies and encouraged to become the major providers of new homes. In the 1940s there was a massive house building programme, and over 80 per cent of the houses built were in the public sector.

In the 1950s the shift to support for owner-occupation led to a relative decline in the importance of local authorities as providers, and by the 1960s new local authority building was largely restricted to the replacement of the inner city slums which were being demolished as unfit for habitation. The replacements for the slums were often flats (in large 'tower blocks') rather than conventional houses, however, and these quickly became unpopular themselves both with policy analysts – and with residents. The tower blocks were instrumental in the development of a negative image for public rented housing in the last quarter of the century; many were so unpopular that by the 1980s they were being demolished – less than twenty years after they had been built.

The unpopularity of public rented housing was accentuated in the 1980s by government policies designed to increase the rents of rented houses and to encourage existing tenants to buy their homes by using a mortgage. By the end of the decade over a million local authority houses had been sold to their tenants. At the same time public subsidies for building for rent were largely transferred to housing associations (non-profit-making private bodies established solely to provide rented housing under statutory powers); these became significant new suppliers of public/private housing. The reduction in direct subsidies for rented housing has, however, been replaced with indirect support through the Housing Benefit which is paid to tenants who are too poor to afford their full rent. As direct subsidies have been removed and rents have risen, so dependency upon Housing Benefit has increased, with the result that most council tenants are also now benefit claimants.

As a consequence of these changes the public rented sector is now in decline. By and large, those who are able to afford to have bought their rented houses, except where the houses (or flats) themselves are unattractive. Thus the tenants remaining in the sector are those unemployed or low-paid workers who cannot afford to buy or even pay their full rent; in effect, therefore, local authority housing has become a residual provision for the less well-off who are excluded from the private market (Cole and Furbey, 1994).

Housing policy in Britain has thus largely been concerned with tenure preferences, in particular the rise and fall of council housing and the growth of owner-occupation. However, there have also been attempts to control and to improve the quality of housing, and to provide for those without housing – the homeless. Slum clearance is obviously the most dramatic form of improvement policy, but improvement of existing dwellings has also been pursued – for instance through the introduction of legislation to set minimum standards of facilities within houses and through the use of government subsidies to provide grants for existing owners to bring their houses up to these standards.

Homelessness was not addressed as an issue within housing policy until the 1970s but, since 1977, homeless people have had a right to apply to local authorities for housing, providing that they fall into those groups defined as being in priority need (primarily parents with children and pregnant women). However, the provision of rights for homeless people in the 1970s coincided with the rundown of local authority housing provision, and many authorities, especially in big cities such as London, were unable to provide proper houses for the homeless and had to place them in hotel rooms or hostels. In the 1990s the legislation covering homelessness was subject to review by government and the rights of even priority groups to permanent housing provision was reduced.

Finally it is worth noting that the primary concern of housing policy in Britain with tenure divisions, and the domination, in recent years in particular, of home ownership over all other forms of housing provision, both contrast sharply with housing policy in other welfare capitalist countries – especially in Europe. In most other European countries the provision and use of rented housing is much more extensive, with more of a mix of public, private and public/private (housing association) rented dwellings. In other countries, too, housing policy appears to be subject to fewer political conflicts and policy changes than has been the case in Britain, where housing policy has sometimes been described as a kind of 'policy football' – first kicked one way and then another.

Employment

Within a capitalist market economy it is perhaps debatable whether employment should be a concern for policy intervention. However, since the Second World War at least, concern over the levels of employment in the country has been a central feature of economic planning in Britain, a point to which we shall return in Chapter 8. The reasons for this are easy to identify – employees contribute to production, and through the wages that they earn they also provide the main basis for consumption. In a wage labour economy, therefore, employment is the primary means through which resources are created and distributed – and from which social status (for men at least) is derived. Employment, income distribution and social class have thus been major concerns of both sociology and economics.

However, because of the concern within policy planning on levels of employment – and because of the recognition by politicians and policy-makers of the central role employment plays in maintaining social structures – it has also become of increasing concern in social policy too. Most notably, once the economic growth associated with the postwar boom in the British (and the international) economy began to come to an end in the 1970s, and the problem of *unemployment* began to expand and to effect a significant proportion of the working population, social policy measures to respond to this began to be developed, aimed in particular at reducing levels of unemployment. As a result, a range of policy interventions seeking to influence patterns of employment now exist.

Social security support of the unemployed through benefits is, of course, in itself a form of employment policy, in particular because of the attempt to keep social security benefits for the unemployed at a low level in order to encourage people to enter even low-paid employment. In recent years the encouragement of the unemployed to enter employment has also extended to more stringent requirements on them to demonstrate that they are seeking jobs, to attend interviews for compulsory advice and assistance after certain periods on benefit, and to use government facilities and support for identifying vacancies and contacting employers. This indirect support and encouragement for the unemployed to find jobs has, of course, always been a feature of social security provision. In particular, registering as unemployed ('signing-on') is well established as a condition for receipt of Unemployment Benefit or Income Support; and the Job Centres run by the Department of Employment have been the major means of matching the demand for labour against the supply of potential workers. With the massive growth in unemployment in the 1970s and 80s, however, this relationship between support for the unemployed and the promotion of employment began to become more significant – and more far-reaching.

The main vehicle for bringing about this changing relationship was the establishment by the Department of Employment in the 1970s of a big new QUANGO (a Quasi-Autonomous Non-Government Organisation) – the Manpower Service Commission (MSC). Although it was set up by government, the MSC was run by an independent board containing industrialists and trades unionists. Its aim was to provide training opportunities and job creation schemes for unemployed people who were experiencing difficulties in returning to the labour market. Two particular groups were the major targets of these new social policies for employment, the young unemployed school-leavers with no work experience, and the long-term adult unemployed with no recent experience of regular employment.

The various schemes for these groups changed on a number of occasions throughout the 1970s and 80s. For 16- to 18-year-olds they developed into a two-year work experience programme, the Youth Training Scheme (YTS), which was more or less compulsory for youngsters leaving school at 16 who were not entering paid employment. For the long-term unemployed they became Employment Training (ET), a period of job readjustment paid at slightly higher than social security benefit level.

Such temporary employment schemes for the unemployed were also developed in other industrialised countries experiencing high levels of employment in the latter quarter of the twentieth century and, as we shall discuss in Chapter 9, there is also EU support for some schemes in Britain. Despite some individual successes, however, these new schemes did not do much to reduce overall levels of unemployment. This was because the primary cause of unemployment was not an inadequate *supply* of appropriately trained workers but rather a declining *demand* for workers during periods of recession – accentuated by the increasing automation of manufacturing. Although the MSC schemes did in one way reduce temporarily the level of recorded unemployment – by removing those on the training schemes from the register of the jobless.

In the late 1980s the MSC was closed down and management of the policies for the training and work experience for the unemployed were passed to local Training and Enterprise Councils (TECs) run by private businesses. Policies to promote the supply of labour have, however, now become a permanent aspect of government strategies for employment, and a significant feature of the social policy agenda.

Family policy

Like employment, family policy has not traditionally been a part of many social policy courses; and this largely reflects a predominant view in government circles that Britain does not have an explicit family policy. This is in contrast to many other advanced industrial countries, however – especially our EU neighbours, such as France – which do place a concern to support, and to structure, family relationships openly onto the policy agenda. If Britain does not have an explicit family policy, however, it is nevertheless true to say that implicitly, and indirectly, most social policies do have a significant – and frequently planned – impact upon family life and family structure.

The lack of comprehensive nursery education, for example, is based upon the assumption that care and education for young children will be carried out largely by their families; and even after the age of five, the organisation of the school day and the school year are predicated upon a continuing provision for children being made by families at home. Indeed, as we shall discuss in more detail in Chapter 6, the role of the informal sector of family-based care is a central assumption of much policy planning, and not only for children.

However, policy planning has not just assumed a particular role for the family, it has also reinforced and recreated this. Reinforcing, and *enf*orcing, family responsibilities, especially those of mothers towards their children, has always been a major concern of social workers in the personal social services. Reinforcing financial responsibilities and dependencies within families is also an essential feature of social security provision where liability to maintain close family members is enshrined in legislation – for instance through the assumption that a woman who is living with a man should be provided for by him and therefore should have no separate, individual entitlement to some types of social security support. The implementation of this has meant, in effect, that social security officers can refuse benefit entitlement to those women who are deemed to be living with a man – a practice that has become known as the *cohabitation rule.*

Social policies reinforce, as well as assume, family values and family structures therefore; but not of course *any* family values that might be held by policy users – rather a relatively specific model of a nuclear family of two parents and their young children. Lone parents or reconstituted (step) families are not really included in the model, nor are homosexual couples; and within the heterosexual family, despite the increasing entry of married women into the labour force, there are clearly delineated roles for men and women. Family policy in Britain is not a policy for families in general, but rather a set of policies for 'the family' in particular – a model family which in practice few families may subscribe to, and even fewer may achieve. And, although this family policy has been implicit in most policy development in Britain, in recent years government concern to shape and to enforce family values and responsibilities has become ever more explicit.

In the 1980s all political parties, both government and opposition, were concerned to present themselves and their policies as supportive of the family in Britain, and the family values implicit in other social policy developments became subject to more open discussion and debate. In the early 1990s the Conservative government made a general appeal for a 'return' to what they regarded as traditional family values in a policy campaign called 'Back to Basics', although unfortunately this coincided with a series of embarrassing revelations about the unconventional family lives of a number of senior government figures and ran into disrepute.

More specifically, however, new social policy measures have developed to reinforce certain family values and responsibilities. For instance, in 1993 the Government established the Child Support Agency (CSA) as an off-shoot of the Department of Social Security with a specific remit for ensuring that estranged parents (usually fathers) provided financial support for their young children. Although part of the Government's motivation for this was the hope that the CSA would reduce the cost of providing social security support for unmarried, divorced and separated single parents, who were growing in number, it was not restricted only to such cases. It clearly had the more general aim of providing a new means for enforcing continuing family responsibilities in an era of widespread breakdown and divorce, as was the case with similar provision in Australia, on which the British agency was partly modelled. What is more, because of the primary focus of its attention on fathers who were not paying adequate maintenance for their estranged children, the CSA also became a controversial policy development in its early years (Garnham and Knights, 1994).

Nevertheless, the use of specific policy measures to pursue family policy aims is now strongly supported by government, and largely accepted by the opposition. In the 1990s, therefore, family policy, together with employment policy, has begun to become an important explicit, as well as an implicit, aspect of government attention and policy development in Britain – and thus a major part of the content of social policy.

Much of the discussion and debate about family and employment policy, as with the more traditional areas of social policy, has, however, tended to focus on the role of government and the state.

While government provision through the state is a major part of social policy in Britain, in this country, as elsewhere, state welfare is only one aspect of the various forms of provision operating in all service areas, as we shall discuss in more detail in the next section.

SECTION TWO

Structure

3

The State

The welfare state

The main focus of study and debate in social policy has been the welfare state. As we discussed in Chapter 1, the Fabian pioneers of the discipline in the early twentieth century were concerned first and foremost with developing academic research and political argument that would put pressure on the British government to use the power of the state to introduce welfare reforms to respond to the social problems which they had identified. Their expectation was that if evidence was produced to demonstrate that the capitalist economy was operating in ways which were leading to hardship or deprivation, it would be the duty of the state to intervene to alleviate or prevent this hardship. Their intention was that this intervention should take the form of services provided directly by the state, using resources collected from citizens in the form of taxation.

Quite how far the state should go in providing such services, of course, has always been a matter of debate and disagreement, both within social policy and beyond. However, after the introduction of reforms such as extended compulsory education and social security protection for pensioners and the unemployed in the early decades of the century, the debate about state welfare has become very much one about *how much* state provision there should be, as opposed to *whether* there should be any. As the textbooks on the history of the welfare state explain (Thane, 1982; Midwinter, 1994), throughout the first half of the century state welfare provision began gradually to expand.

The growth of state welfare provision in Britain was not a product only of the persuasive moral and academic arguments of the Fabian policy reformers – academic and moral argument does not necessarily bring about political change. Nevertheless, the hardship about which the Fabians argued was real enough and, for those who were its victims, it created a source of active social and economic conflict. Britain's capitalist economy thus produced conflict between the poor working class and the rich and powerful – and this was a conflict that produced social movements, not just the theories and statistics of the academics.

The early part of the twentieth century saw the rapid development of such movements – in particular the Trades Union movement, designed to protect the interests of workers against their capitalist employers, and the Labour Party, supported by the unions to pursue the collective demands of workers through the winning of political power within the electoral system. In the 1920s and 30s the trades unions engaged in conflict with capital over hardship and deprivation, organising a general strike in 1926; and the Labour Party achieved political power – for periods at least – in central and local government. In these ways the deprivation produced by capitalism created conditions of conflict and struggle from which intervention by the state became an achievable political goal; with Labour governments, in particular, the Fabian policy reformers had a base within the British political system at which to direct their arguments on the need for welfare reform.

However, the causes of the growth in state intervention for welfare in Britain do not lie only in the successful struggle of the working class and its Fabian middle-class allies. In practice the development of welfare reforms has always had a double-edged impact within capitalist economies. Improved state education, for example, provides employers with a better trained and more able workforce; and, as the development of machinery and automation have made the process of production ever more complex, this has permitted industry to operate more efficiently. Improved housing and health conditions for workers have also improved their overall efficiency, and so have helped the development of the economy. Even social security benefits, although financed in part by contributions from employers, have helped to maintain the unemployed as a labour force in waiting who can be rejected or re-employed as economic forces dictate.

The development of the welfare state, therefore, is not only the product of the attempt to remedy the failings of a capitalist economy but also of the recognition of new ways in which this economy might be maintained and developed. Thus, as social policy theorists now widely recognise, state welfare does not only challenge capitalism – it also functions for it (Gough, 1979).

In the period immediately following the Second World War these pressures for welfare reform, both from within capital and within the working class, appeared all to come together in Britain.

- A Labour government was elected, after a landslide victory, with manifesto commitments to reform capitalism through state intervention.
- Fabian academics and their allies occupied influential positions within the state – notably Beveridge, author of the report on social security reform, and Keynes, a senior economic adviser to the wartime government.
- British capitalism had experienced significant government intervention as part of the war effort, and it needed rapidly to adjust to the changing demands of peacetime production within a restructured world economy.

It is for these reasons that commentators argued that during this postwar period there was a *consensus* in Britain over the desirability of welfare reform between capital and labour, and between their 'representatives' within the major political parties – and that this consensus created a unique opportunity for the rapid development of the welfare state (Addison, 1975).

The Labour government reforms of the 1940s are widely credited as providing the basis for the establishment of the welfare state in Britain, informed by the social policy prescriptions of Beveridge and the economic policy plans of Keynes. For this reason it is sometimes referred to as the *Keynes/Beveridge Welfare State*. The postwar reforms encompassed a wide range of social and economic changes; but three features in particular established a new role for the state within the British capitalist economy:

- the development of public social services
- the nationalisation of major industries
- the commitment to full employment.

The development of *public social services* included the NHS, state education and the National Insurance scheme. These were financed out of taxes and contributions from citizens and they recruited employees into state-run organisations to provide services to all who needed them, generally on a universal basis with free access. These state welfare services could be seen as almost 'socialist' in their aims and structures; and there were some on the left (and the right) who hoped (or feared) that they would be a first step towards a more far-reaching socialist restructuring of Britain's capitalist economy. As we shall see, however, Britain's welfare state, even in this immediate postwar period of expansion, was never socialist either in aim or in achievement; as in the earlier part of the century, state provision for health, education and social security operated as much to support the broader capitalist economy as to challenge it.

The *nationalisation* programme of the postwar Labour government also established a new role for the state within British society. Major industries such as coal and steel were taken into public ownership; they were run by state-appointed managers; and their workers became state employees. The same happened to the main infrastructural services such as gas, electricity and public transport.

Again, these nationalisation measures could appear to be elements of a strategy for the 'socialisation' of the entire capitalist economy. Certainly they significantly restructured British capitalism by introducing a large state sector no longer under the control of private ownership and the profit motive, and this led some commentators to argue that Britain had therefore been transformed from a capitalist economy into a *mixed economy* (Crosland, 1956). However, even the nationalisation of major industries left the vast majority of British capital in private hands, and there was never any intention of carrying through a state take-over of all private firms. Furthermore, the nationalised industries had to trade and contract with private capitalist enterprises and, although they were supported and sometimes subsidised by the state, they were required to operate in the marketplace with profit and loss accounts like private companies. Indeed, the guaranteed operation of such major state industries and services after the 1940s provided both a stable physical and economic environment for private industry and a secure market for many private products. In the welfare field, for instance, the National Health Service provided a major boost to the development of private drug companies.

The commitment to full employment was in part based on a reaction to the high levels of unemployment experienced in Britain during the economic depression of the 1930s. At times of recession exclusion from the labour market is bound to lead to hardship and depression. The commitment to challenge this hardship after the war therefore inevitably focused not only on the provision of social security and other services for the unemployed but also on attempts to use broader state intervention in the economy in order to minimise the risk of unemployment.

This also fitted well, however, with the wider role for state intervention in postwar economic development that had been recommended by Keynes. It was Keynes' belief that governments could, and should, use their role as employers and investors to encourage growth within market economies, as we shall discuss in Chapter 8; and one of the major triggers for such intervention was the commitment to maintain unemployment below an agreed minimum level. Thus, after the war, the state became involved in the orchestration of economic development in order to maintain full (or near full) employment and, as we have seen, policies on employment have since been incorporated into social policy planning across the postwar period.

Therefore, although the postwar welfare state transformed the capitalist economy in Britain, it did not replace it. The political consensus in favour of welfare reform through the state was as much a matter of compromise as a meeting of minds; it was predicated upon the assumption that state welfare reforms would support, and not prejudice, wider economic growth. What is more, as we saw in Chapter 2, the development of state welfare did not entirely displace private provision for health and education; the voluntary and informal sectors of welfare provision continued to operate despite the 1940s reforms. In welfare – as in manufacturing – postwar Britain became a mixed economy in which state provision was only a part of the overall picture.

This was a picture, nonetheless, in which it seemed that state welfare provision was able to grow ever more rapidly to meet more and more social needs as British society became generally more and more affluent in the years following the war – expanding welfare could even be seen as part of an inevitable process of development within a capitalist economy. This can be seen most clearly in the growing size of the state welfare sector as a proportion of economic activity in the country, and in the achievements of state welfare services. Welfare expenditure has grown dramatically from around 2.5

per cent of Gross Domestic Product (GDP) in 1900, to around 15 per cent in 1945, and to over 25 per cent in 1980 (Hills, 1990, p. 21). As a result of this, significant social improvements have been achieved – for example educational standards have risen, mortality and morbidity rates have declined, housing problems have been reduced, and basic living standards have been increased. However, as we shall discuss in more detail in Chapter 8, such growth was far from inevitable – it was the product of international economic trends and national government policies, both of which could change. And when these did change, particularly in the 1970s, the future of an ever-expanding welfare state began to come into question, and the role of public provision became subject to a much more critical scrutiny.

What is the state?

We probably all have some idea to what we are referring when we talk about the state and state involvement in welfare provision in a country such as Britain; but in fact the various institutions and individuals which make up the state in an advanced capitalist country together make up quite a complex constitutional picture. Furthermore, the various parts of the state are subject to rules and political conventions that sometimes define fairly closely the powers and responsibilities that they are able to exercise. We do not have room here to examine the complex constitutional processes of the British state; but a brief overview of the main constituent parts, and the different functions that each fulfils in the implementation of economic and social policy, will provide us with some background understanding to both its scale and scope.

Many people perhaps assume that the state is the same thing as the government; and it is obviously the case that the government has overall power over, and responsibility for, the activities of the state, through its electoral mandate which it secures from the population. However, technically speaking, the government is merely the collective views of the majority of Members of Parliament (MPs) in the House of Commons; and Parliament also includes the House of Lords, which can, and sometimes does, disagree with the views of MPs in the Commons. All laws enacted by Parliament must be agreed by both Houses, and subsequently must be ratified by the Queen as the constitutional monarch – although in practice this is a formality as the monarch is a figurehead and plays no active part in the legislative process.

However, because of the system of political parties which contest elections in Britain, the government is in practice made up of the senior MPs from the majority party. These meet regularly as a *cabinet* under the leadership of the Prime Minister to plan future policies and the legislation required to implement them. Most policy decisions are thus made in the cabinet, and later approved by the majority of MPs in Parliament at Westminster. Policies are then implemented by state employees (civil servants) based in the different departments of the state, with each department being under the overall control of a Secretary of State, who is a member of the cabinet.

In theory then, policy is decided by the cabinet in *Westminster,* and is implemented by the civil servants in the Departments based (mainly) in *Whitehall.* This Westminster–Whitehall division symbolises the split between the democratic (policy making) aspect of the state, and the bureaucratic (policy implementation) aspect of it. Although, as books that concentrate in more detail on the policy-making and policy-implementation process reveal, this division is far from a watertight one in practice – many MPs play little part in policy making and some civil servants have much power and influence over it (Ham and Hill, 1993).

Political scientists also often attach importance to the distinction that is made between the policy-making, or legislative, process, and the enforcement of the rights granted by this through the courts under the control of the *judiciary.* Where there is a dispute over the implementation of policies in particular cases, or even over the powers of government to make policy, everyone has the right to go to court for a judicial ruling – although, given the cost of using the law, this is a right that in practice may only be open to those with signif-icant financial resources or to those poor enough to qualify for state support through legal aid. The judges in court are bound to follow the rules laid down by Parliament and by previous legal rulings, through precedent. In exercising judgement under these rules they are quite independent of the government, and of the civil service – and they sometimes make decisions that government ministers or civil servants do not like. Despite this, however, the members of the judiciary are public employees and they are an integral part of the state; their role in interpreting the law, and enforcing rights developed through the policy-making process, is thus an important part of state activity in the provision of welfare.

Like Westminster and Whitehall, however, the judiciary are a part of a centralised state power within Britain. The policies that are developed and the rules that are enforced here are produced on behalf of, and are provided for, the whole of British society. However, these central state institutions are not the only features of state power involved in the provision of welfare services in the country. State welfare is also developed at a local and at a subnational level in Britain, and also at a supranational level within the EU. In practice, these aspects are as important in determining the shape of the welfare state in Britain as are the main arms of central government in London.

The role of *local government* has been of critical importance in the development of welfare in Britain, as we shall discuss in more detail in Chapter 10. Local authorities (or local councils) became subject to democratic election towards the end of the nineteenth century, and since then have played a major role in promoting state provision for education, health, housing and other social services. Indeed, in many ways the creation of the welfare state in the 1940s was really a period of the centralisation and standardisation within Whitehall of the welfare services developed, albeit unevenly, by local government in the first half of the century. It was not, however, a complete centralisation; as we shall see later, local authorities have remained the major providers of state education and social services, of public housing and of a range of other services.

The *subnational* context of state policy making in Britain is a peculiar product of the constitution of the country as a 'United Kingdom' of formerly separate nations. Britain thus comprises in effect the subnations England, Scotland, Wales and Northern Ireland. As a result of this, for Scotland and Northern Ireland in particular, there are separate government departments responsible for the development and delivery of distinct national policies in these areas; this is also true to a lesser extent for Wales.

Public policy making at a *supranational* level operates in Britain as a result of the country's membership since 1973 of the European Union (EU). As we shall discuss in Chapter 9, the EU now provides a more and more influential international context for policy development and, more immediately, policies and rules determined by the Commission and other EU bodies in Brussels now have a direct impact in all member states – including Britain. In fact this country has in recent years been a rather reluctant partner in the development of European-wide policy initiatives but, in the 1990s, EU commitments to the further development of supranational policy making are likely to provide pressures that future British governments will find it more and more difficult to resist.

The functions of the state

Most discussion of state welfare is focused upon social services which are provided for people by the institutions or agencies of the state – in other words, where the function of the state is as the *provider* of services. State provision in Britain includes, for example, the National Health Service, the state education system and the social security benefits schemes. In all of these the state employs workers (doctors, nurses and teachers) based in publicly owned and operated institutions (hospitals and schools) to provide services to all citizens who are in need of, or are entitled to, them. To do this the state uses public money collected by government, largely in the form of taxes, to purchase buildings and equipment and to pay workers; and the plans for spending this money have to be justified and agreed through the political process either nationally or locally. These spending plans are therefore a central – and in recent years a controversial – feature of government policy development.

Clearly such comprehensive provision of services is the most obvious, and arguably the most extensive, function of the state in welfare provision – but it is far from the only one. In addition to being a provider of welfare the state also fulfils other functions that have an equally direct and important impact on the development and implementation of welfare policy within the country.

First, as well as using public money to provide welfare through public agencies, the state also provides public money to subsidise welfare services which are provided on a private, voluntary or informal basis. The role of state *subsidies* has always been important in the development of non-state welfare, including both direct subsidies – for example state support for voluntary agencies such as the Women's Royal Voluntary Service (WRVS) or the Citizens Advice Bureaux (CABs); and indirect subsidies – for example exemption from taxation for voluntary agencies or for income spent on purchasing private services.

Indirect subsidies have been of particular importance in the development of both private and voluntary welfare services in Britain. The tax reliefs on private welfare, such as pension plans or mortgages for the purchase of owner-occupied housing, and subsidies channelled through employers for occupational benefits, such as sick pay protection or company pensions, have constituted an ever growing feature of state expenditure since the Second World War. Such tax reliefs are also not always recognised or discussed as a form of expenditure, although, as Titmuss recognised as early as 1956, these aspects of the welfare state in Britain have benefited primarily the middle classes and those in secure well-paid employment.

Second, although public subsidies can shape and direct the development of private and voluntary welfare provision, this provision can also be controlled more directly by legal regulation through the state. The state also functions therefore as a *regulator* of welfare, through the law – indeed this is perhaps the oldest aspect of state policy intervention. Legal rules set the limits within which private markets have developed and voluntary organisations have operated and, of course, regulation also determines the structure of state provided welfare. As we discussed above, the courts and the judiciary are an important aspect of the use of state power. Through the enactment and enforcement of rules and procedures the state can control a wide range of welfare provision, even though it is not owned or funded by any public body. Thus private pensions and private health insurance, for instance, are closely regulated through statute law; and voluntary bodies are subject to a range of legal controls including the long-standing, and sometimes obscure, rulings on the definition and extent of charitable purposes.

Finally, in its role in the provision of services, and in its roles in subsidising and regulating these, the state is also acting as an *employer* of those working in state institutions such as the courts or government departments. Indeed, the state, through both central and local government, is now the largest single employer in Britain – by quite some way. And, of course, for those working for the state their welfare as employees – and any broader occupational protections, such as sick pay or pensions, which they enjoy – are determined by the role of the state as an employer and the policies that it adopts towards its workforce.

As an employer, the state in fact has a rather inconsistent record in Britain. Some state employees, for instance senior civil servants, enjoy some of the best working conditions and most extensive occupational benefits of any employees in the country at large. However, there are others, for instance cleaners or porters in schools or hospitals, who are on part-time contracts and levels of pay that leave them needing to claim social security benefits to top up their weekly incomes in order to meet their families' needs. It might seem a little odd that the state as employer is paying wages so low that this in effect requires its employees to become also social security claimants – although, of course, what this really reveals is the lack of overall planning across the different functions of the state in welfare provision.

The role of the state as employer is not one that is usually directly addressed in policy planning by government or by civil servants; this is also true to some extent of the relationship between this function and that of the state as a regulator or subsidiser. Social policy commentators might argue that it ought to be the case that these various aspects of state welfare should be seen as complementary and therefore should receive greater coordination; but they must also recognise that this is not consistently understood by those responsible for these different functions. Thus analysis of the role of the state in the provision of welfare involves analysis of the separate development of these different functions and of the sometimes contradictory relationship between them – as well as assessment of the overall extent, and the limitations, of the state's welfare role.

The limits of the state

During the period of the gradual, and incremental, growth of state welfare provision in Britain, in particular in the decades following the Second World War, it seemed to most commentators – and certainly to those acting as protagonists for the growth of state welfare – that there were no limits beyond which state welfare might not extend. There seemed to exist a widely shared assumption that the greater identification of social needs would create the case for improved state services and that the continuing growth of economic production would provide the resources that could be harnessed, through taxation, to pay for these. Thus, although there might be questions about the speed or emphasis of the development of state provision, there could be no doubt about its overall desirability – or viability.

In the last quarter of the twentieth century, however, this assumption about the limitless role for the state has come into question in Britain – and indeed in all other welfare capitalist countries. Questions about the limits of the welfare state have arisen primarily as a result of two developments that may appear to be contradictory but, in practice, are inextricably interrelated.

First, despite the successes of state welfare in meeting welfare needs and reducing social problems, social policy research has continued to provide evidence of further needs and problems that could, or should, be the focus of additional state provision. Some of these problems might be argued to be the result of the failure of state welfare services to meet existing targets – for instance Abel-Smith and Townsend's (1965) 'rediscovery of poverty' which identified over a million people, mainly pensioners, living below state assistance benefit levels in the early 1960s. Others, however, are the product of more general social and technological progress that has gradually overtaken past provision – for instance expanding demand for higher education in universities, or for heart transplants or chemotherapy treatment in the NHS. Whatever the reasons, however, there is no shortage of evidence of the continued existence, and continuing growth, of needs which current state welfare provision does not meet.

Second, alongside the evidence of growing needs, there has been acceptance in the last quarter of the twentieth century, by both Labour and Conservative governments, that state expenditure on welfare cannot simply be expanded indefinitely to meet increased demand. The economic recession of the 1970s and early 1980s forced first Labour and then the Conservatives to restrict, and in places to cut, state welfare expenditure. In fact, despite the cuts, welfare expenditure continued to grow during this period – much to the annoyance of some members of the Thatcherite Conservative government, who were outspoken in their criticisms of 'too much' costly welfare expenditure. Nevertheless, controls on state expenditure were introduced, and did have an effect in restricting expansion at least; and, by the 1990s both the government and opposition parties were agreed that it was not possible, or desirable, to continue to raise taxation levels significantly in order to finance further expansion of the welfare state.

The incremental growth of state welfare is thus clearly no longer regarded as inevitable. The political consensus, or the political compromise, of the 1990s has focused attention rather on the question of how to balance the desire to meet growing welfare needs against the desire to control growing public expenditure – a dilemma presented graphically in the mid 1990s, for example, in a government paper outlining fears about the growth of social security (Department of

Social Security, 1993). Of course the political parties do not agree on the nature or the extent of the balance to be struck; and, as academic research has revealed, the evidence on which some of the arguments for further restrictions in expenditure are based can be questioned by looking more closely at both demographic trends and economic projections (Hills, 1993). Nevertheless, there is acceptance of the need to strike a balance, and thus of the recognition that the ability of state welfare to respond to all social needs will be limited by the constraints of cost.

However, it is not only cost which sets limits to the extent of state welfare. In particular as the provider of welfare services, there are limits on the ability of the state to recognise and to meet all social needs; and these limits apply also, if less obviously, to the state's subsidising and regulatory roles too. State provision of welfare requires the departments of central or local government to identify social needs and then to provide services that meet them. However, this is neither a non-controversial nor a one-way process.

Critics have argued that state welfare often fails to identify the welfare needs of many people – for instance it is often, rightly, accused of failing to address the needs of many of Britain's ethnic minority communities. Even where needs are identified, state welfare also sometimes provides services that do not adequately satisfy those needs – for instance the tower blocks of council flats have often created as many housing problems as they have solved. Although such failings sometimes mean that needs go unmet, they may also lead, indirectly at least, to the development by people of alternative, non-state, forms of welfare service to fill the gaps left by inadequate state services – for instance through the establishment of community-based, self-help groups in black community areas, or through the development of housing cooperatives to build, or to renovate, houses for rent. However, although such alternative provision may complement state welfare, it may also create pressure for state provision to be expanded to meet these additional or new needs; and so in some cases non-state activity can led to an extension of the limits of public provision.

Even where they are successfully meeting a range of social needs, however, state welfare services can also acquire complex, and remote, bureaucratic structures that can alienate or exclude some potential service users – an issue to which we will return in more general terms in Chapter 13. In an influential book published in 1981, Hadley and Hatch argued that there was in fact an inevitable contradiction here between the development of state bureaucracies and their ability to meet real social need; and that alternative forms of provision should therefore actually be welcomed and supported by policy analysts – and by citizens. Of course, as we know, alternative forms of welfare provision, through the informal, voluntary and private sectors, have in any case continued to co-exist, and to grow, alongside state welfare – recognition of their role in welfare was not a new discovery in 1981. However, recognition that there must be limits to the ability of state provision to identify and meet all needs, or to anticipate and support or regulate the development of all community or private alternatives to state services, is significant in pointing to the limitations in the role of the state that arise from organisational and cultural factors, as well as simply from economic ones.

Therefore the state cannot provide, or regulate, all welfare services because it cannot know of all needs nor control all actions. As a result, the other sectors of welfare provision – the informal, the voluntary and the private – will continue to constitute an important feature of social policy analysis, as we will explore in more detail in the next few chapters. However, although there are limits to the *maximum* role of the state, there are limits to its *minimum* role too.

In any complex society a state structure will be needed to organise, to support and to regulate the activities of citizens; and this applies to the provision of welfare as much as it does, for instance, to the control of crime. Although voluntary agencies or private companies may develop services for groups of people, only the state has the legitimacy and the power, politically and legally, to act on behalf of *all* citizens. Where regulation of the activities of non-state providers is required, for instance to guarantee minimum standards in private education or health care, only the state has the power to provide this. Where financial support is sought, as it often is, to help the development or maintenance of private or voluntary social provision, only the state can call on public resources to provide this. Where private, voluntary or informal providers cannot, or will not, operate to provide for social needs, only the state can be required to step in.

Despite the beliefs, or the hopes, of some right-wing theorists who would like to see a return to a society in which all citizens are able to provide for themselves (for instance, Murray, 1984), no advanced society has been able to remove or to replace entirely state welfare provision. Even where state provision is restricted to the role of a 'safety net', to catch those who slip between the gaps in private and voluntary provision, it is still there to prevent citizens falling through – and perhaps starving or freezing to death. Of course, in practice the safety net may not always work but that has not been used as an argument for removing it. Indeed it is more likely to be used to argue for strengthening it – or, to put it another way, the failure of minimal state welfare may suggest that such limited protection is inadequate and should be extended, not abandoned.

As we discussed at the beginning of this chapter, therefore, the debate about the role of the state in welfare services in Britain, and indeed in other advanced industrial societies, is a debate about the *extent* of state welfare – not about the overall *need* for it. Welfare provision in modern capitalist societies requires the state to play a range of roles in the provision and control of social services. Of course, such state provision and control of welfare have their limits, both minimum and maximum limits; but the extent of those limits is the result of political processes – not some iron laws of market freedom or socialist development. The role of the state thus varies in different countries, and it changes over time, but in some form or other it is always there – and so, too, are the market and the other sectors of welfare provision, as we shall see next.

4

The Market

The commercial sector

The provision of social services through the welfare state is often discussed by commentators as *public* provision of welfare – and this is contrasted with *private* provision arranged by individuals, families or organisations outside the state. This distinction between public and private welfare is a bit misleading, however, because much private provision is public in the sense that it is in the public domain and available to any would-be purchaser. Private health care, for instance, is publicly available, and indeed is advertised as such on television. The public–private distinction might, therefore, better be used to distinguish between individual and family-provided services and those provided collectively to a range of people either through the state or by other agencies. We will return in Chapter 6 to examine this 'private' dimension in more detail; but such a distinction is not one widely used in social policy literature.

More commonly, social policy analysis makes a distinction between state and non-state services. This too can be misleading, however, if non-state is taken to mean exclusively profit-based, private market provision – for, as we shall see in Chapter 5, not all non-state welfare provision is profit based. There is in fact a vast range of non-profit organisations engaged in all kinds of welfare activity, and operating according to quite different aims and principles from both the state and the market sectors. We need to distinguish in addition, therefore, between these non-profit (voluntary) organisations and those operating for profit on a commercial basis. It is perhaps this commercial aspect that does serve best to distinguish these organisations from both the state and the voluntary sector – and from the private, informal, sector too.

Commercial organisations operate with budgets and balance sheets. They levy charges for services and use these charges to employ workers and invest in equipment to provide future services. They also generally seek to make a profit out of the difference between their charges and the cost of providing the services. For most commercial organisations it is the expectation of profit that is the motivating factor for the establishment and development of them by their owners or shareholders, who will benefit from the profit – although on some occasions charges may not exceed costs and no profit, in practice, is made. In fact there are many small (and not-so-small) commercial organisations who do not set out to make a profit. These include small residential homes, whose owners merely wish to recover their operating costs, and some major institutions, such as building societies, which do not traditionally declare profits from their activities.

Nevertheless, even where they are not profit-seeking, commercial organisations such as these can still be distinguished from both state and voluntary sector agencies by their financial structure – in particular by the charges they make for services, and the location of their operations within a competitive market. We might, therefore, most accurately call these organisations the *commercial* sector but, in practice, social policy commentators commonly refer to them as the *market* – in particular when the market is being contrasted with the *state*.

Market-based activity of course extends much beyond welfare services. Most goods and services in Britain are exchanged through markets, and the labour market provides the main means of employment and subsistence for the majority of the population, either directly or indirectly. It was the development of a market basis for production and distribution in the seventeenth and eighteenth centuries that established the basis for the development of capitalism in Britain, and for the creation of modern society in the nineteenth and twentieth centuries. And it is into this capitalist market economy that state welfare has been developed in the twentieth century, as we discussed in Chapter 3. Despite the development of state welfare, we all of us rely heavily on markets for a large part of our daily individual and social needs; and, as we shall see in Chapter 8, the economic development of markets, and the ability of states to control or manipulate them, are crucial factors in structuring the broader context in which social policy planning takes place.

Welfare state provision has thus influenced, and in some cases has altered, markets; but it has not displaced them. It is for this reason that commentators refer to all modern economies with developed state welfare provision as *welfare capitalism* – a compromise, or collaboration, between the state and the market. Of course, the nature of this compromise – the relationship between state and market – varies significantly between different welfare capitalist countries. In social democratic countries, such as Sweden, much welfare support is provided by the state and the state takes an active role in controlling and regulating many aspects of commercial markets. By contrast, in the liberal USA many welfare services, such as health care, are provided on a private market basis and the state plays a much more residual role. In Japan occupational and private services are the 'front line' of welfare provision, and it is through the labour market that most social protection is delivered.

Furthermore, the relationship, or the balance, between state and market in any one country is not fixed, and it can change over time. In Britain in the 1980s, for example, the role of commercial market provision was expanded significantly at the expense of state provision as a direct result of government policy, in some cases by requiring state services to be put out to private tender by commercial providers. In the former socialist countries of Eastern Europe rapid changes have been taking place in recent years to replace previous state monopoly provision with private markets for a wide range of goods and services. Indeed, the changes in the balance between state and market are an intrinsic feature of the development of welfare provision in all countries, and are a major focus of the study of social policy.

The case for markets

Proponents of market-based welfare have often claimed that the operation of markets to provide services is preferable to the use of state power. Indeed, some have argued that state intervention is not compatible with the successful operation of markets and that, where it is pursued, it results in *perverse incentives* (to rely on state support rather than entering the market) which disrupt the natural flow of market development. These arguments received particular prominence in social policy debate in Britain in the 1980s, associated with the rise of the New Right (Barry, 1987; King, 1987); but they are not new arguments. In fact they are based on long-standing liberal theories of the workings of markets, which go back to the work of Adam Smith in the eighteenth century.

In his book, *An Enquiry into the Nature and Causes of the Wealth of Nations*, Smith (1776) argued that in theory markets created a natural equilibrium within the social order, because individuals exercising free choice over the purchase of goods and services would create a demand for those services which they wanted. This demand would be expressed in terms of the price that they would be prepared to pay for the service, and the price would then attract suppliers to provide such a service in order to profit from the price charged. The profit motive would not lead prices to rise unduly, however, because a high price would attract many suppliers, who would then be in competition and would thus be required to reduce the price to reflect more closely the costs of production and the demand for the product. Therefore, in a situation of perfect equilibrium, all needs would be met by suppliers and all prices would reflect the legitimate costs of production.

Because the exchange of goods and services (buying and selling through the market) arises naturally in any social order, supporters of markets claim that they constitute a 'natural' social order – and also that they are self-regulating, with new demands leading to new supply and inefficient providers being weeded out by their unacceptably high prices. Smith referred to this as the 'invisible hand' of the market mechanism; and its cause has been taken up in twentieth-century welfare capitalist countries such as Britain by new neo-liberals, such as Hayek (1944) and Friedman (1962).

As a result of this, therefore, pro-market theorists also argue that attempts by governments to intervene in, or control, markets will be doomed to failure. Government support for inefficient producers will distort the price mechanism; state provision of services will create potential monopoly producers not subject to the influence of purchasers' choices; and state regulation of providers or purchasers will prevent their free choice of the most optimal forms of service provision. Hayek argued in the 1940s (Hayek, 1944), at the height of political support for state intervention in the capitalist economy in Britain, that such intervention would be ineffective and self-defeating. In the 1960s, as Keynesian interventions in the economy began to come under question, the same theme was taken up by the American economist Milton Friedman (1962).

Hayek, Friedman and others argue that the fundamental weakness of state intervention is the problem that no agents of the state, such as government ministers or senior civil servants, could have sufficient knowledge of the needs, wants and circumstances of the individuals living in a complex modern society to be able to judge when, or where, to intervene in the market, or what sort of goods or services to provide. The result is that interventions distort, rather than support, markets, and that state services become paternalistic and bureaucratic monopolies. This, they argue, is the cause of the economic crises experienced by welfare capitalist countries in the 1970s and 80s, and also of the hostility found in these countries towards many features of state welfare provision, such as oppressive local authority landlords and long hospital waiting lists. The solution to these problems, they argue, is a return to free market provision through the removal of state intervention and the breaking up of state monopoly services. However, in theory there are problems in relying on markets to deliver welfare provision in modern societies, as we shall discuss shortly; and in practice the operation of market provision relies heavily on the support of the state.

The market and the state

Indeed, even the most ardent supporters of the free-market provision of goods and services recognise that the state does have some role to play in supporting markets. In order for markets to function freely there must be laws concerning property ownership and contract rights, and these need to be enforced independently through the state. There must also be a policing function provided by the state, to detect and prevent abuses of the law. And there must be provision for defence of society against the threat to the markets of one country imposed by the imperialistic designs of external enemies. The liberals thus concede the need for state law, a police force, and national defence.

It is clear, however, that other state functions are also recognised to be necessary in any modern economy – for instance the provision of air traffic control and the development of motorways and trunk roads. Obviously for such functions it is quite possible for government agents to have a full understanding of peoples' needs, and of the importance of a centrally planned response to these. Furthermore, as we suggested in Chapter 3, there are many other state activities and services which operate in effect to *support*, rather than to *undermine*, the operation of a modern market economy.

- State provision, for instance of education and health care, meets the long-term strategic demands for an adequately equipped labour force that individual employers alone could not efficiently replicate.
- State regulation ensures maintenance of minimum standards that private individuals could not be expected to monitor, for instance in housing or pension provision, and ensures that competition takes place according to criteria of efficiency and price rather than basic quality.
- State protection, for instance for the unemployed or chronically sick, ensures that individuals do not suffer unduly where the market fails or is unable to reach all.

Furthermore, the limitations and contradictions of market provision in complex modern welfare capitalist countries mean that state interventions are needed to prevent potential social problems and to protect all citizens.

- There is the ever-present danger of monopolies or cartels developing that would subvert the natural self-regulation of the market operation, for instance in the supply of gas and water or in the production of specialist drugs.
- In many areas where markets do operate consumers are clearly unable to make informed choices about how best their needs might be met, for instance consumer ignorance of medical needs and practices or of higher education standards mean that real free choice cannot in practice mean the freedom to choose anything on offer.
- Most importantly of all in our unequal society, free choice in the market will be constrained by consumer immobility and consumer poverty, so, for instance, for most children the state will have to ensure provision of a local school, and for certain categories of people free or subsidised access to essential services will have to be guaranteed.

Perhaps the best example, however, of a case where state provision, organised according to altruistic rather than profit-oriented principles, is superior in social and economic terms to market-based provision is Titmuss's comparative study of blood donation – *The Gift Relationship* (Titmuss, 1970). In this he argues that the state-organised system of blood donation in Britain, which relies upon free donation of blood, is both safer and more effective than the market-based systems of countries such as the USA and Japan, which pay donors for their blood. This is because the financial incentive provides an inappropriate inducement where the primary concern, as here, is with the quality and consistency of the supply of blood across a range of blood groups, some of which are in scarcer supply than others. Thus Titmuss found that the blood banks in countries where donors were paid were much more likely to obtain and to distribute contaminated blood, and to experience problems in securing donors in some areas.

It seems clear, therefore, that the free, and unregulated, market to which Hayek and Friedman aspire does not exist in practice in modern capitalist states, and what is more could not effectively be 'revitalised' within them. Nevertheless, market provision of many goods and services continues to be of major importance in these societies. There are of course two sides to this coin; just as markets in practice need the state – so in many ways does the state need markets.

From the purchase of clothing to provision of housing there is no doubt that individuals expect to have a large measure of choice over their lifestyle, and are prepared to 'shop around' in the market to secure this. In many welfare services the retention, or introduction, of elements of commercially based provision in the market has enhanced both consumer choice and consumer responsiveness – for example in the marketisation of optical services in the 1980s. Market provision also provides an attractive supplement to basic state protection for many people in certain areas of welfare – for instance private and occupational pension protection, or private rooms and additional 'hotel' benefits during hospital stays.

In these more general terms therefore, the case for regulated market provision alongside state welfare is now widely accepted within welfare capitalist societies – and markets are indeed also rapidly being developed in the former state socialist regimes of Eastern Europe. However, the pure markets espoused by the neo-liberals do not exist – and never have; market freedom has always in practice needed to be balanced by state regulation, and state subsidy and protection, in order to guarantee effective policy development and delivery.

Forms of commercial welfare

Within a complex welfare mix, such as that in modern Britain, the commercial development of welfare takes a variety of forms, some of which in practice overlap, in part at least, with aspects of state provision or with provision in the voluntary or informal sectors. At the time of the creation of the modern welfare state in Britain in the 1940s, however, commercial provision was consciously retained alongside public services, even in the areas of major universal provision, such as education and health.

- In education private schools (misleadingly called public schools) which charge pupils for attendance have continued to operate on a fee-paying basis, and have continued to attract pupils, despite the existence of free state education.
- In the health service doctors have been permitted to retain fee-paying patients who pay for special treatment in NHS hospitals (the so-called *pay beds*) following a much publicised compromise between the government minister (Bevan) charged with introducing the NHS and the British Medical Association (BMA) representing the doctors, who feared that state provision would remove their ability to secure an income through charging for health care.

What is more, in the 1950s, after the establishment of state welfare, commercial provision – as an alternative, or a supplement, to state provision – actually began to grow. During this decade private house building rapidly began to outstrip public building, with large numbers of people choosing to buy their homes privately, rather than to rent them publicly. At the same time occupational pensions providing additional pension protection for workers (referred to as *superannuation*) also began to grow; by the mid 1960s over 12 million workers were members of such private schemes.

In the 1980s this growth went much further as the Thatcher governments of the time adopted a policy of openly encouraging commercial provision as a substitute for state provision – sometimes described as a policy of *privatisation* (Johnson, 1990). The largest privatisation measures of the 1980s were the, highly publicised, break-up and sale of the major utilities (gas, electrictiy and water) that had initially been developed by local, not central, government, as we discuss in Chapter 10. State industries, such as British Steel, were also sold to private shareholders although here what really occurred was a *re*privatisation – as these had first been set up by state take-over of old private companies. In the welfare field privatisation in the 1980s took a number of forms, including the replacement of state provision, the removal of state subsidies, and the withdrawal of state regulation.

- The sale of *council houses* to tenants, and later the wholesale transfer of estates to private landlords, was a significant, and high profile, example of the transfer of provision from the state to the market sectors – although many estate transfers in practice went to housing associations in the voluntary sector.
- Private provision in health was directly encouraged, and began to grow. Between 1979 and 1989 the proportion of the population covered by private *health insurance* grew from 5 per cent to 9 per cent, and over 50 new private hospitals were opened.
- Similar changes occurred in education; between 1979 and 1991 the number of children in *private education* increased from 5.8 per cent to 7.4 per cent.
- The introduction of sick pay and maternity pay transferred *social security* protection from the Department of Social Security to private employers.
- The use of charges increased, in particular *prescription charges* for drugs purchased as part of medical treatment under the NHS, which increased from 20p in 1979 to over £3 in 1990.
- The public regulation of services, such as *public transport*, was largely withdrawn, with these being thrown open to competition between various commercial providers.

Important and far-reaching though these provisions were, however, they did not amount to anything like a full-scale privatisation of welfare services – and, although this had been called for by some commentators from the New Right, it is not at all certain that the government considered it either feasible or desirable. For instance, although private education and health care grew, they remained very much a minority provision alongside the comprehensive state provision in these fields. By the 1990s it was clear that what had happened in practice in Britain in the 1980s had been not so much a replacement of the state with the market but rather a change in the welfare mix, in which state welfare was retained and market provision was more widely, and more variously, developed.

Thus in the 1990s a range of private welfare services co-exist alongside state welfare provision.

- Direct purchase of services is available, for example in the provision of houses or spectacles.
- Insurance-based protection operates in the fields of pension protection and health care.
- Occupationally based provision is also widespread, with many workers getting additional benefits, such as sickness pay, superannuation and private health care, from their employers on top of their cash wage.
- Charges have been introduced to cover the costs of much provision previously provided free within the state sector, for example charges for personal social services such as home care.

Of course not all of these forms of provision are profit making – indeed, occupational pensions and home care charges are not motivated at all by the goal of profit maximisation. In fact, many features of market-based provision cannot even exist on a break-even basis and effectively only continue to operate with the support of major subsidies from the state. In the case of statutory sick pay, for instance, the employers providing the service have been subsidised by rebates from the National Insurance scheme. In the case of mortgage interest payments and private pensions an indirect subsidy is provided to purchasers through a rebate on their taxation or National Insurance contributions. In the case of assisted places in private schools a direct cash subsidy to users is available. There is also a range of means-tested subsidies provided to poor users who cannot pay the full cost of commercial prices or charges, for instance for Housing Benefit or free NHS prescriptions.

The commercial provision of welfare is, consequently, not always intended to be profitable; and in fact is supported by the state. Nevertheless, the market basis for provision is now widely and securely established alongside the state, and voluntary, sectors in

Britain – as it is in all other welfare capitalist countries. Further than this, however, in some countries market principles have begun to invade what had previously been seen as exclusively state-based provision. In Britain in the 1990s this has taken the form of the widespread use of *quasi-markets* into the state welfare sector.

Quasi-markets

The extension of quasi-markets within welfare provision in Britain is a relatively recent phenomenon dating largely from the late 1980s but the idea behind them is really quite an old one and is based on an attempt to combine in one form the advantages of both market and state provision of welfare.

- The advantages of markets are that they gear the allocation of resources towards consumer needs and consumer preferences and that, in operating on a cash basis, they maximise cost effectiveness through price sensitivity. Compared to this state provision is paternalistic, consumers' needs cannot all be accurately identified and accommodated and so decisions are taken by professional providers; state provision is potentially expensive because, since services are provided free of charge, neither providers nor consumers have any incentive to reduce costs.
- The disadvantages of markets, as we have just discussed, are that they cannot afford to meet all needs and that they require consumers to have knowledge and power to be able to exercise realistic choices between competing service providers. By contrast, state provision can guarantee that no-one will be excluded from access to provision and that minimum service standards will be provided even where consumers are unable themselves to monitor these.

Quasi-markets are based in state services and funding is guaranteed by the state, with access to services generally being free – thus no-one is excluded on grounds of poverty. However, a division is introduced between the purchaser (or consumer) and the provider, so that purchasers can choose from which provider they will select a service, and providers are forced to gear their service provision to meet these consumer preferences. One example of this, although it has not been widely utilised in Britain, is the education *voucher,* which provides a pupil (or their parents) with a voucher equivalent to the cost of schooling that can then be 'cashed in' at any school of their choosing.

In higher education the student grant (plus fees), which permits suitably qualified applicants to choose a university place, operates something like a voucher scheme for adults. Furthermore, since the Education Reform Act 1988, local management of schools has meant that these now can accept any pupils that they choose to (Bartlett, 1993). This gives children and their parents some freedom of choice between schools. This choice has been facilitated, in theory at least, by the requirement for schools to publish regularly information about their achievements – for example the GCSE and A level grades secured by their pupils. However, it is not a fully fledged voucher scheme as schools can also refuse pupils and local authorities are still required to secure local places for all children.

As well as the education reforms of the late 1980s, quasi-markets were also introduced at this time into health and social services and here the purchaser–provider split can be more clearly seen. Prior to the reforms, health care provision, for instance, had largely been determined by doctors; GPs assessed patients' health needs and then referred them to the appropriate local hospital (or clinic) where consultants determined the appropriate treatment. Hospitals were then required to provide this treatment, although in some cases it was much in demand – hence the growth of massive waiting lists with allegations that some referred patients were waiting several years to receive minor operations. In practice, with different levels of demand in different areas, waiting lists often varied widely from one health authority to the next and, although health authorities were supposed to gear local services to meet health care needs in their area, it was not always easy to adapt existing services quickly to meet changes in these. What is more, after the 1970s in particular, services were also constrained by overall expenditure restrictions.

The 1980s reforms aimed to respond to these problems by introducing market principles into the state health service. They permitted hospitals and other major service providers, such as ambulance services, to become organisationally and financially independent of the health authority and to be run as independent *trusts,* whose income would depend upon the services they provided to purchasers. At the same time larger general practice (GP) surgeries also became independent and were allocated notional cash budgets, based on the size of their list of registered patients, by the local family services health authority and became 'fund-holding' practices. Thus, rather than simply referring patients to the local hospital, these GPs could now use their budgets to purchase the health care their patients needed from whichever hospital trust was offering the best service at the best price. GPs are thus constrained to seek cost effective care, in order not to exhaust their budgets; and hospitals can compete to offer this, in order to secure an income to continue their work.

This *purchaser–provider* split thus introduced the advantages of consumer preference and price sensitivity into the NHS but, at the same time, the safeguards of a state service were maintained. Inequality or poverty does not prevent consumers securing a service, because the cost is still met by the state through the budget allocation to GPs; and consumer ignorance of complex medical practices is no bar to appropriate care, because treatment decisions are still made on the consumer's behalf by professionals.

Much the same mixture of benefits is now also intended to operate in the provision of social services for adult clients, referred to as *community care*. Here the providers, for instance residential homes, are again treated as separate agencies – and in this case are indeed likely to be privately run either for profit or by a voluntary organisation. The purchasers are social workers (referred to as 'care managers'), who act on behalf of their clients to secure the most appropriate care setting. These social workers are still employed by the state in local authorities; but now they operate within limited budgets, and are expected to act as enablers for their clients rather than as providers of care services.

The NHS and community care reforms of the 1980s provide probably the clearest example of the introduction of quasi-markets in British social policy, although Le Grand and Bartlett (1993, p. 10) argue that similar trends can be identified in education, housing and social security provision. They identify three features of these quasi-markets as

> non-profit organisations competing for public contracts, sometimes in competition with for-profit organisations; consumer purchasing power either centralised in a single purchasing agency or allocated to users in the form of vouchers rather than cash; and, in some cases, the consumers represented in the market by agents instead of operating by themselves.

The interaction with the market and voluntary sectors is thus an important feature of such quasi-market provision. As in community care, this may be an integral feature of the provision or, as in the case of health care, it may be a significant further development – for instance if GPs became able to purchase services for patients on the private market, or if patients were permitted to supplement GP budgets in order to secure better private care. If developments such as these are pursued, quasi-markets may turn out to be only a half-way stage on the route to a full-scale marketisation (or privatisation) of health care or other state services. This may indeed happen in Britain; although it is perhaps more likely that quasi-markets (albeit in an ever-changing form) will remain because of the safeguards that they provide against some of the worst problems of market-based welfare provision.

We shall return to discuss some of these problems in a little more detail in Chapter 12 when we look at the some of the controversial issues and potential difficulties involved in paying for welfare services in this way. The danger is that such mechanisms can operate to introduce the distorted incentives of the private profit principle into public service delivery. However, quasi-markets also introduce some more pragmatic problems into state services because of the commercial procedures that they inevitably require.

Managing budgets, for instance, requires a fair portion of accountancy, and perhaps these days computing, skills. Doctors, social workers and other welfare professionals often do not have these skills and might understandably be reluctant to develop them. Good doctors do not necessarily make good accountants – and yet, if they do not, they may find that they are no longer able to be good doctors, because their budgets do not balance. Furthermore, such budgeting exercises take time, and – as all accountants (at least) know – time costs money. When doctors are engaged in accountancy, they are not engaged in medical work; and in this way the operation of quasi-markets has introduced significant extra administrative costs into the health care system, many of which may be unknowingly disguised in unplanned and even unidentified service cuts. Quasi-markets thus require additional resources and additional skills that state welfare services have not been used to providing. It may be that efficiency savings can generate the scope for these within existing service provision; but, where they do not, quasi-markets could prove to be an expensive means of importing price sensitivity into state services.

Problems with markets

The neo-liberal claim that a free market economy will provide for efficiency and consumer sovereignty through self-regulation, even if it were attractive in theory, cannot realistically be applied to the welfare provision of modern welfare capitalist countries. Markets in such countries are too complex for individual consumers to negotiate and they are intertwined with state, and voluntary sector, provision. So, although neo-liberal theorists have pleaded for a return to a pure market economy, no government has in practice sought to pursue such a radical path.

Thus markets exist in welfare, as in the economy generally, alongside state and voluntary provision. In this context they frequently provide advantages in service development and delivery that could perhaps not be achieved in any other manner. Where consumers have resources and knowledge, their ability to choose – and the incentive on providers to improve services in order to secure that choice – provides a powerful motor for innovation and improvement. In the case of housing provision, for instance, it is this consumer sovereignty that has made owner-occupation so much more attractive to people than public renting.

In a mixed economy of welfare, therefore, markets have their advantages. However, they also have their problems. Even where they do not actually make a profit, the commercial operators within markets are inevitably driven primarily by financial considerations rather than service priorities since, through the charges that they make for services, they must ensure that they continue to retain the viability to operate. This means that all commercial operators are forced to levy charges that, at least, meet their costs. However, in the unequal social order in which these charges operate, some consumers will be better able to meet them than others. Wealthy people are able to purchase a wide range of services through the market that arguably they do not need, such as colour televisions and mobile telephones in private hospital rooms. More importantly from the point of view of social policy, poor people faced with charges are therefore unable to pay for services that they desperately need.

In an unequal society a pure market system will inevitably fail to meet the service demands of poor people in need. Indeed, it is just such market failure that motivated the Fabian reformers, and the trades union and political representatives of the poor working classes, to press for state welfare services to be introduced in the early part of the twentieth century. Unlike the drive for profit, which distributes market-based provision to those most able to pay, state services or state support can be allocated according to need. Thus state provision can ensure that poor people are not excluded from protection – either through direct non-market provision to them or through the subsidisation of poor purchasers within markets. Even where they do operate to provide welfare, therefore, markets have to be supplemented by state provision.

However, markets do not only fail individual poor people; they also fail to meet certain welfare needs which may often be associated with poverty more generally. Because commercial operators must seek to ensure financial profitability, or at least viability, there are likely to be certain services areas that they will not be willing to enter at all.

This is largely true, for instance, of protection for unemployment. Unemployed people are outside the labour market and they, and their dependants, need financial support. Commercial provision of this support would only be likely if charges could be levied on employed people, on an insurance basis, to cover the costs of their potential unemployment. However, many employed people may be unwilling to pay charges to meet the support needs of the unemployed – especially if they themselves are unlikely to be threatened with unemployment. A scheme collecting charges only from those who did fear unemployment may not be sufficiently buoyant to meet the needs of all those unemployed – especially in periods of economic recession. For example, in the early 1990s the government sought to encourage private protection for the repayment of mortgage debts for those becoming unemployed by removing some of the state protection for this. However, few private insurance providers were willing to develop insurance protection for those most at risk of unemployment and such schemes as were developed offered only very limited and short-term financial protection. Commercial provision for protection for the unemployed has thus not developed in Britain or in other welfare capitalist countries; and, although a variety of different schemes providing support for unemployment exist, they are all organised (and partly financed) by the state, on behalf of society as a whole.

Whatever the extravagant claims of its protagonists, therefore, the fact remanins that market provision cannot meet all the needs of all the people – all of the time. It is for this reason that voluntary organisations and state welfare services have developed in all modern market economies, even though their development has to some extent operated to supplement, rather than to displace, market-based services. Successful policy development in the future will be likely to ensure that markets are continued permission to operate where they can genuinely provide a responsiveness and sensitivity which monopolistic state services could not do – and that they are replaced, or supplemented, where they threaten to exclude necessary services or needy consumers.

5

The Voluntary Sector

The scope of the sector

The focus of debate and policy development on the relative roles of
the state and the market in the provision of welfare services has
meant that the size and the scope of the voluntary organisation of
welfare has often not been fully appreciated and that the role and
importance of the voluntary sector has not been clearly analysed or
understood. These are significant omissions, for the voluntary sector
in Britain, and in other welfare capitalist countries, is vast in size and
generally is effective in its role in reaching the needs that the state
and the market sectors cannot meet. In their influential report on the
future of voluntary organisations in 1977, the Wolfenden
Committee estimated that voluntary activity in Britain was equivalent to the work of 400 000 full-time workers; and, in his study of
voluntary sector activity in three English towns, Hatch (1980)
discovered 294 organisations operating in one West Midlands
metropolitan borough. This is a major slice of organised welfare
activity taking place outside both the state and the market.

In historical terms, too, the role of the voluntary sector is of
central importance in the development of welfare provision. In
practice the collective provision of both self-protection and altruistic
service to others preceded both the state and the market; and, as we
shall discuss below, both state and market forms of welfare have built
on structures and practices developed by voluntary organisation and
activity. Indeed, although the development of state welfare provision,
in particular the 'comprehensive' provisions of the postwar welfare

state, did aim to take over many of the structures and functions of previous voluntary sector provision, voluntary organisations have continued to operate alongside the new statutory services of the welfare state. In the last quarter of the twentieth century, as state welfare services have come under increasing pressure and criticism, voluntary sector activity, and the range and scope of voluntary organisations, have begun once again to grow (Finlayson, 1994; Davis Smith *et al.*, 1995). In fact the voluntary sector has even been represented by some social policy analysts as a preferable alternative to the state for the provision of many welfare services (Hadley and Hatch, 1981).

The voluntary sector thus plays an important role in the development and delivery of welfare services but it is a complex and diverse role. Voluntary sector organisations vary in size and shape, from neighbourhood parent and toddler groups to international aid organisations like Oxfam. It is almost impossible to generalise about their structure or their activities and, as we shall see shortly, there are problems even in defining what we mean by the term *voluntary organisations*. However, problems of definition should not detract from recognition, if perhaps belated, of the centrality of an understanding of the voluntary sector for social policy. In general terms we can provide some definitional parameters to shape our study of the sector – even if only negatively by specifying what is not encompassed within it.

Voluntary sector organisations are *not* part of the state provision of services, either at central or local level. They are *not* constituted by statutory legislation, although their activities are of course affected by legislation. They are *not* directly accountable to elected state representatives either nationally or locally; their employees, where they exist, are *not* officers of government or local authority departments. Voluntary organisations are thus in one sense *private* bodies but they are *not* part of the private market or commercial provision of welfare, primarily because they do not operate with profit and loss accounts. Commercial organisations seek to make a profit out of their activities, or at a minimum to cover their costs, and thus have to charge for the provision of services – at least in most cases. Voluntary organisations are *not* motivated by the pursuit of profit and in most cases will seek to avoid charging for services.

However, voluntary organisations are *organisations*. Even the neighbourhood parent and toddler group requires organisation.

There have to be meetings, which require notification and premises. There has to be a membership list, to know who to invite to the meetings. This will require a secretary and perhaps a chair and other officers. All this requires organisation – and results in an organisation, which is something much more than the informal support and services that are provided, without any organisational structure, by families and neighbours. To put it another way, although they differ from the state and market sectors, voluntary organisations are nevertheless a form of *collective* welfare activity, which is distinct from the individual or family protection provided informally and without collective structure, to which we shall return in Chapter 6.

Of course these boundaries between the state, market, voluntary and informal sectors are not always clear-cut – and they are not watertight. Considerable development in the social policy analysis of voluntary organisations in recent years has taken place at the Centre for Voluntary Organisation at the LSE. Billis, the director of the centre, has examined the relationship between voluntary organisations and the other 'worlds' of government bureaucracy, business bureaucracy and the personal sphere. He has presented these relationships as a series of circles, which intersect in various places, demonstrating the overlap between the different sectors (see Figure 5.1 [Billis, 1989, p. 20]).

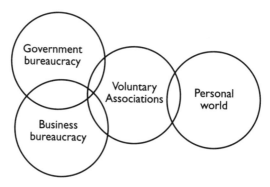

Figure 5.1 The overlapping boundaries of the voluntary sector

What Billis's circles represent are the overlapping boundaries between the different sectors and, as he points out, these boundaries provide challenges to the organisation and development of those voluntary sector bodies which are, or might be, situated within these boundary areas – for instance those on the boundary with business will be under pressure to operate according to commercial criteria, and those on the boundary with government will be likely to be restricted by public policy and statutory control. Thus, although the voluntary sector is distinct from the statutory, commercial and personal sectors, it is not entirely separate from, or independent of, them. Furthermore, both for individual voluntary organisations, and for the sector as a whole, these boundaries are neither fixed nor immutable. Individual organisations may change their relationship with the state sector, perhaps by securing grant funding from the state; and the general relationship between the state and the voluntary sector may change as a result of national, or international, policy shifts which, as we shall see, has been happening to some extent recently in Britain and in other welfare capitalist countries.

The problem of definition

Because of the wide variety of organisations operating within the voluntary sector, it is not easy to specify exactly what we mean when we talk about a voluntary organisation. In particular the term *voluntary* can be misleading – and it is misleadingly used to describe organisations that in practice have public funding and employ paid workers – sometimes well-paid ones. As a result of these misconceptions the use of the generic term voluntary sector to refer to such a varied range of organisations and activities has sometimes been questioned. However, despite the development of some of the alternative definitions discussed below, the use of the term voluntary sector is at present still well entrenched. It is the most widely used term – even if it is somewhat inaccurate.

It is in the role of volunteers (and volunteering) itself where many of the misconceptions about the voluntary sector begin. The unpaid time, freely given, of volunteers is in a sense the essence of voluntary activity. It is virtually the sole resource of many, in particular local community-based, organisations; and, if it could be costed in financial terms, or in comparison with full-time paid employment, as suggested above by the Wolfenden Report, it would undoubtedly be seen to be the main resource of the sector as a whole. However, not all volunteering takes place *within* the voluntary sector – for example statutory welfare agencies such as social services departments and probation services make quite extensive use of volunteers to supplement the statutory services that they provide through the use of public money. More importantly perhaps, voluntary organisations often do not rely *only* on volunteers.

Any organisation operating at more than a neighbourhood level is going to find it difficult to survive as an organisation by relying solely on volunteers. Volunteers, no matter how well meaning, can only give up so much of their time – they are also likely to have jobs or family commitments. What is more, volunteers, no matter how capable, are likely to have limited skills; but large organisations require secretaries and accountants – and managers. Where these organisations are providing complicated services, specialist skills or training for staff may be required. If some specialist tasks can be carried out by paid workers, on a full-time or a part-time basis, the organisation may be better able to meet its service goals – and may be able to make better use of its volunteer labour.

Large international or national voluntary organisations, like Oxfam or the National Society for the Prevention of Cruelty to Children (NSPCC), employ a wide range of paid staff both to run the organisation itself and to provide services to users. They have a salary structure and career structure, and provide training and development for their workers. However, many smaller local organisations also employ paid workers. For example, most Citizens Advice Bureaux (CABs) have at least one paid, and trained, manager and advice worker, as well as relying heavily on the commitment of volunteer advisors. Many of these paid workers have made a career out of their work in the voluntary sector, and many have an ideological or political commitment to working in organisations that are not part of the state and also do not seek to make a profit. Some workers have also moved from, or between, the statutory, commercial and voluntary sectors in pursuit of a career; they are able to bring knowledge and experience of the strengths and weaknesses of each sector to their work in the others.

Of course the employment of paid workers means that organisations need to have the financial resources at their disposal to pay workers. To do this voluntary organisations require more than just the efforts of volunteers. Those organisations with paid workers may be distinguished from those without because of their need to secure regular funding to support their work; but in fact even organisations relying entirely on voluntary effort usually require some financial resources to pay for equipment and materials, which these days may mean a telephone, a home computer or a photocopier, and to pay for premises in which to work or to meet. Rather than distinguishing organisations on the basis of their need for funding, therefore, it may be more logical to distinguish them on the basis of their *use* of funds (paid workers or volunteers only) or on their *sources* of such funding.

One source of funding for voluntary organisations is *charitable giving*. Just as some people may be willing to give their time to a particular local or national group, others may be willing, and able, to give money. Charitable giving has been the financial mainstay of most major voluntary organisations in Britain and elsewhere. Nineteenth-century social service agencies relied on such charitable sources, coordinated by the Charity Organisation Society (COS) (Humphries, 1995; Lewis, 1995); and in the late twentieth century the Thatcher government of the 1980s openly extolled the virtues of charity as a basis for improved welfare services.

The status of *charities,* however, is a particular – and a particularly important – one within British social policy because recognised charities enjoy significant tax concessions, which act as a form of indirect public subsidy to them. For instance, some donations to charities from earned income are exempt from income tax and charities using premises do not have to pay local property taxes. However, determination of charitable status depends upon an obscure legal statute of 1601 that limits charitable status to organisations performing specific services for specific groups of beneficiaries (Brenton, 1985, pp. 96–100, 248–9). There has been pressure in recent times to update such an archaic law but thus far nothing has been done about this. In addition to the obscurity of the rules themselves, the process of applying for, and securing, charitable status is a complex and costly one. Thus many smaller voluntary organisations do not bother going through with it, although they do rely heavily (or entirely) on charitable funding and might well have turned out to be legal charities if they could have gone through with the process.

Distinguishing organisations on the basis of charitable funding is not therefore a straightforward solution. However, charitable giving for altruistic purposes to provide services for others can be distinguished from making payments into voluntary organisations that are intended rather as a form of *self-protection.* Collective self-protection through pooled donations was also a form of voluntary organisation that developed significantly in Britain in the nineteenth century – for instance in order to provide income protection for workers in times of sickness or temporary unemployment. Unlike insurance protection on the private market, this protection involved a joint commitment to collective self-protection for specific groups of workers and their families, into which contributions would be made in the expectation of future support at times of need. The *friendly societies*, as these organisations came to be known, were an important feature of the early development of social security protection outside the state. Their model of mutual self-protection was later copied and incorporated into state protection through national insurance, with the result that, following the introduction in the 1940s of the Beveridge insurance scheme, they largely disappeared from the scene.

In other countries, for example in the Netherlands, such organisations moved into partnership with the state, rather than being taken over by it, and became major providers of welfare for the communities that they represented. In Britain, despite the development of both state and market provision in the twentieth century, the role and scope of self-protection organisations has continued to expand. At the end of the century new community-based organisations for the exchange of goods and services between unemployed people have begun to develop. These are referred to as *local exchange and trading schemes* (LETS) and they provide an alternative form of mutual economic support for those unable to buy what they need on the private market. There has also been a rapid growth of new credit agencies focusing upon groups of people within local areas. These are called *credit unions*; they are membership organisations into which contributers make regular payments and from which they can then borrow lump sums at low rates of interest (Thomas and Balloch, 1994).

Thus funding for voluntary organisations may be provided by private individuals either for charitable purposes or out of self-interest; and the funding will be likely to be used, in part at least, to employ paid workers to run the organisation and provide the services. Such organisations are nevertheless voluntary in the sense that the provision of funding is the result of voluntary decisions by individual contributors. However, many 'voluntary organisations' receive finances not only from private individuals but also from public funds from the central or the local state.

The *state* may fund voluntary sector organisations in a number of different ways and for a number of different reasons. Exemption from payment of taxes is a form of state support for charities; however, money is also given directly to organisations to help them provide services or employ workers. For instance, CABs are supported by national government grants through their umbrella organisation, the National Association of Citizens Advice Bureaux (NACAB) and by direct provision of resources by local government. National funding is also provided to other established charities, such as the Women's Royal Voluntary Service (WRVS). Local authorities also provide public financial support for many other voluntary organisations operating within their area, such as play schemes or tenants' associations. Local authority funding has, in the past, generally been provided in the form of grants to voluntary groups but, as we shall discuss shortly, it may also take the form of a more formal contract for services; this source of funding has become more common in the 1990s. However, public support, from local government in particular, does not always take the form of cash payments. Assistance may also be provided in kind, for instance through free use for local groups of council premises, such as schools, or free access to council equipment or mailing facilities – or through the provision of paid workers to support voluntary groups, for instance community social workers who may help to set up and to manage community-based activities.

National funding has also been provided for *local* groups, sometimes in partnership with local authority funding. This, too, has become more common in the late twentieth century through the establishment of government programmes to support community-based voluntary sector activity, in particular in deprived urban areas. An example of this is the *Urban Programme* which provided national funding, alongside local authority support, for neighbourhood-based projects in deprived urban areas. This was a major stimulus to the growth of community-based voluntary organisations in the 1970s and 80s, until the programme was cut as a result of public expenditure constraints in the early 1990s.

The curtailment of the Urban Programme in Britain in the 1990s in fact resulted in a number of voluntary organisations being themselves forced to close, as a result of the loss of the government funding on which they had been dependent. Despite their 'voluntary' nature this dependency on state funding is in practice quite common among organisations operating to provide services outside the state and the market in Britain – and in most other welfare capitalist countries too. As one well-known analyst of the voluntary sector, Kramer (1990, p. 3), concluded:

> In fact, there is no country today where there is a substantial voluntary sector, that is not dependent on governmental support to a greater or lesser degree.

State funding is thus a crucial feature of the resource base and organisational structure of many voluntary organisations; and this is widely understood by voluntary agencies and by other funding agencies. For instance, one of the main aims of some voluntary organisations, including both local neighbourhood groups and major national charities, is to campaign to secure state support for their activities or for activities or services that their members want. Voluntary organisations thus actively seek state support. Furthermore, charitable funding for voluntary organisations, for example from major charitable trusts such as Rowntree or Nuffield, is often provided on a temporary or pilot basis, on the assumption that, once operating, the organisation will be able to secure more permanent funding from the state.

It is perhaps unfortunate, therefore, that the cuts and restrictions on state expenditure at both central and local level in the 1980s and 90s, for instance through the closure of the Urban Programme, has resulted in reductions in the sources of state support that can be sought by voluntary organisations to support their activities. As we said, this has sometimes even resulted in the collapse or closure of some voluntary activity. State support has not disappeared entirely, however, and indeed the curtailment or withdrawal of state support has been seen by some, including politicians in the government, as a form of indirect stimulus to voluntary activity. Voluntary organisations have thus been encouraged to seek financial support from other sources, for example from the commercial sector in the form of corporate donations or sponsorships, although the overall value of these should not be exaggerated – private sponsorship is still only a minor source of support for voluntary activity in Britain.

Thus, although the source of funding may be one way of distinguishing between different types of voluntary organisation, the picture here is a rather complex one. What is more, in practice many organisations receive funding from more than one source and the balance of these sources may well change over time. As we shall discuss below, therefore, source of funding alone is not a very helpful definitional starting point. Funding would need to be set against other characteristics such as basic organisational structure to provide us with a general outline of the sector in which different organisations could be placed.

Furthermore, debate over definition of the voluntary sector still turns primarily on what the sector is *not* rather than what it *is*. Because they are not part of the state, voluntary organisations are sometimes referred to as the *non-government sector*. Because they are not generally established by state legislation, they are sometimes referred to as the *non-statutory sector*. In the USA, in particular, their distinction from commercial organisations has led to them being referred to as the *non-profit sector*. It was also in the USA that the more neutral, but nevertheless still essentially negative, definition of the *third sector* developed – after the first (state) and second (market) sectors. This now has international currency in the title of a major international research society aiming to promote the sector, the International Society for Third-Sector Research (ISTR).

This intermediary role between the public, market and family sectors of provision, and between the formal–informal, public–private, and profit–non-profit features of provision can be presented in diagrammatic form – in a more sophisticated model than Billis's circles – to reveal how this notion of the 'third sector' distinguishes it from other aspects of welfare provision. In this model third sector organisations can be seen to be formal, non-profit, private agencies existing inbetween the state, the market and the family (see Figure 5.2).

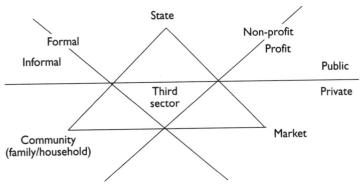

Figure 5.2 The intermediary role of the voluntary sector

However, this non-state, non-market nature of the sector can be more positively stressed by referring to this as the *independent sector*. The focus on independence emphasises the value of operating outside the constraints of public accountability or the profit motive; it is a term that has become more widely used in recent years – in particular by some voluntary organisations to refer to themselves. Unfortunately this term, too, has not yet attracted widespread usage, perhaps because of its continued association with private sector provision, for instance in the term 'independent schools' – used to describe private education. Thus the problem of definition remains, in general, a muddy one in which no consistent approach is adopted by all and this is compounded as the structure of the sector itself becomes ever more complex – a point to which we shall return shortly. However, to most people, both analysts and activists, the term most commonly employed is still the *voluntary sector* – and so, despite the inaccuracies and misleading images that it portrays, we will stick with this.

The structure of the sector

The voluntary sector is a vast and varied collection of organisations composed of different groups of people pursuing different aims at different levels of society. Indeed, the variety is so great that it is almost as difficult to identify any structure within the sector as it is to arrive at a consistent definition of it. As we have seen, funding for the sector, although it may not have helped to define groups, does provide one structural dimension to it; funding may be provided for altruistic reasons or with the expectation that the providers of funding will receive some service in return. This provides a basis for distinction, based on structural goals and procedures, between protective, representative, campaigning and service organisations.

- *Protective* organisations have been set up by their members for mutual self-protection or benefit – for example, the nineteenth-century friendly societies and the twentieth-century credit unions. The organisation of these *protective* associations is focused internally on maintaining their effective operation; the motivation for participation is self-interest.
- *Representative* organisations promote or represent the self-interest of members but do this through external activity, in

particular promoting their needs and campaigning for improved services from other sources. These include small lone parent groups like Gingerbread; but they would also include the largest, and most successful, voluntary sector organisations, the trades unions.

- *Campaigning* organisations do not act specifically on behalf of their members but campaign more generally on issues that effect large numbers of people throughout society. These organisations are motivated primarily by altruism rather than representation, although in some cases it may be an altruism with a clear political message. They include the Child Poverty Action Group (CPAG), campaigning for poor children in Britain, and Greenpeace or Friends of the Earth, campaigning for world-wide environmental change.

- *Service* organisations are also generally motivated by altruism, in particular the charitable motive of giving in order to help others. Many of the largest and most successful voluntary sector groups continue to be those whose aim is to provide services to others in need. These include international agencies such as Oxfam and national organisations like the WRVS and the NSPCC, as well as others that may also have a religious dimension, such as Christian Aid or the Salvation Army. They also include the many small and diverse neighbourhood activities designed to help local people in need.

As with funding differences, of course, these structural features do not constitute watertight boundaries between organisations. Some campaigning organisations may include a mixture of representative and altruistic activities, and they may also provide services to members or to others. This is true, for instance, of the CPAG, which has branches representing local poor people but campaigns primarily at national government level and also provides advice and advocacy services both to its own members, and to non-members who use its handbooks and its Citizens' Rights Office.

Nevertheless, the boundaries do provide us with something of a guide to the different structures of voluntary organisations, and these differences can be supplemented by comparing the levels at which different organisations operate. As we have seen, some voluntary sector organisations work at a major international level; others operate at a national level, although they may have separate 'branches' in different countries, and in the UK they may have separate organisations for England, Scotland, Wales or Northern Ireland.

National and international organisations are by definition large in size; but many, indeed most, voluntary organisations are not. As Hatch (1980) found in one study, local areas have large numbers of voluntary organisations operating within them. Hatch's study focused on three English towns; and if we take the town, city or other local authority area as an empirical base point many local organisations can be found operating in each area, including tenants' associations, luncheon clubs or associations of people with disabilities. However, we might want to distinguish between such *local* organisations, perhaps comprising a range of people throughout a town or city district, and *neighbourhood-* or *community*-based groups operating only in a small area with a relatively homogeneous social group.

Much has been written about communities and the community base for voluntary activity (Frankenburg, 1966; Willmott, 1984; Mayo, 1994). Communities have always been a central feature of life; but community structures also change as broader social structures change. Thus, as recent research at the European level has demonstrated, community-based voluntary activity takes a wide variety of forms in different community settings at different times (Chanan, 1992). We can distinguish in particular here between organisations based on traditional and modern notions of the community base.

- *Traditional* communities are generally seen as being determined geographically, for example by the local village or neighbourhood. Here local organisations may represent many aspects of the lives of local people.
- *Modern* communities are a product of the declining importance of geographical boundaries, as mobility and communication increase, and of the growing diversity of modern life. Thus modern community-based organisations represent only one aspect of our lives, such as the lone parents or disabled persons group, and even may be based on cultural or political ties, such as the music collective or the wildlife protection group.

Overall therefore, we can distinguish between community-based groups and larger organisations, and between these and national and international agencies. We could perhaps put all these distinctions together to produce a simple diagram outlining the various classifications of voluntary organisations (see Figure 5.3).

	Level			
Structure	**Community**	**Local**	**National**	**International**
Protective	LETS	Credit union	Friendly society	World Health Organisation
Representative	Music Collective	Gingerbread	Trades union	International Labour Office
Campaigning	New bypass opposition	Local transport campaign	CPAG	Greenpeace
Service	Lone parent group	CABs	WRVS	Oxfam

Figure 5.3 The classification of voluntary organisations

Thus far we have been discussing individual voluntary organisations. However, organisations frequently do not exist or operate in isolation, rather they may be part of a broader group or collection of agencies. For instance, all CABs are members of the National Association (NACAB); and other organisations have local groups which are members of a national coordinating structure, such as Age Concern. National federations of voluntary organisations are in fact quite common; but there may also be local federations to which several organisations belong – for example many cities have local federations of tenants' associations representing all the associations from estates across the city. In Sheffield in the 1980s and 90s there was a similar federation representing rights and advice agencies within the city, the Sheffield Advice Centres Group (SACG).

Local federations may not only be based on particular types of organisation. Most local areas also have more general umbrella organisations representing voluntary groups, sometimes known as the local Council for Voluntary Services (CVS). Such umbrella federations also operate on a national basis – for example the National Council for Voluntary Organisations (NCVO) and the Community Development Federation (CDF), representing voluntary and community organisations in Britain. Umbrella federations exist on an international basis too – for example the European Anti-

Poverty Network (EAPN) representing various locally based organisations campaigning against poverty within the EU.

The history of voluntary activity

Voluntary sector organisations representing people and delivering services preceded the development of both state and market provision of welfare in Britain and in other welfare capitalist countries. Yet they have also survived the development of these newer sectors and have continued to accommodate and adapt their activities alongside them. Thus even the major protagonists of state welfare have recognised the significant and continuing role played by the voluntary sector. In the early part of the twentieth century, for instance, the Webbs talked about the continued importance of a voluntary sector operating alongside state welfare provision. They contrasted two ways in which such a partnership might operate, although they made it clear that they preferred the second model:

- the 'parallel bars' approach – where the state and the voluntary sector each provided separately for different social needs
- the 'extension ladder' approach – where voluntary activity was developed as a supplement to the basic state services that were guaranteed for all.

Beveridge, too, became an advocate for the voluntary sector, when he wrote in 1948 pointing out that state provision should not stifle the initiative and enterprise of citizens for voluntary action (Beveridge, 1948).

As we have seen, the state welfare services that developed in the first half of the twentieth century drew heavily on voluntary sector models and voluntary sector organisations, for instance on the friendly societies for social insurance and on the COS for social work. The establishment of the 'welfare state' following the Second World War in the 1940s saw the replacement of the friendly societies and the COS with state welfare agencies for major social needs, including social security and social work. However, comprehensive state welfare provision in the 1940s did not signify the end of voluntary sector activity. Although the Wolfenden Report (1977, p. 20) later commented that voluntary organisations seemed to be 'marking time' during the first fifteen years or so of the welfare state, in fact new local organisations, such as the CABs established earlier in 1939, continued to flourish and some important new national organisations, such as the Marriage Guidance Council and the Samaritans, were set up.

Indeed, once state welfare had been established in the latter half of the twentieth century, this in fact operated to provide a new and different impetus for voluntary organisation, based upon the aim of extending state provision through voluntary campaigning or upon securing state support for voluntary action itself. In the late 1960s and early 1970s this interrelationship between the state and the voluntary sectors received further encouragement from the new state programmes aimed at tackling the persistence of poverty and deprivation, especially in urban areas – for example the Urban Programme, mentioned earlier, which provided state support for community-based voluntary organisations seeking to develop neighbourhood-based activities involving local poor people.

By the 1970s, therefore, rather than state welfare displacing the voluntary sector, state support was being used extensively to foster its expansion and further development. It was in this context that an independent committee was set up by the Rowntree Memorial Trust, headed by Lord Wolfenden, to review the future role and function of the sector in the UK (Brenton, 1985, pp. 48–53). The main conclusions of the committee were that the voluntary sector would have an important role to play in the future development of welfare services and, consequently, that this role should be the subject of strategic planning by government and would require the support of public funds. Although some tacit support for the conclusions of the Wolfenden Committee was received from the government, there was no commitment to a long-term strategy for the sector, and all that followed immediately was the extension of programme funding for pilot projects.

In the 1980s, however, the commitment of the Thatcher governments to reduce public expenditure and to 'roll back' the boundaries of state welfare provided a further, if in one sense indirect, incentive for the expansion of voluntary sector activity. However, central government rhetoric was also translated into more tangible reality by an increase in support for voluntary organisations from local authorities in many areas, especially Labour-controlled authorities that wished to utilise voluntary organisations as a means of working with local people to protect and develop welfare services that might be under threat from government cuts.

An example of this happened in London under the influence of the Greater London Council (GLC). In the early 1980s the GLC provided funding and other support for a wide range of new (and established) voluntary organisations in the capital; in large part this support was motivated by a desire to encourage the non-state sector in active service provision. For the GLC, however, support for the voluntary sector was also in part a political challenge to the central government over restrictions on welfare expenditure, and it resulted ultimately in the abolition of the council – a point to which we shall return in Chapter 10.

More generally, restrictions on local authority, as well as national government, welfare expenditure in the 1980s and early 1990s also began to threaten the grant funding on which many new, particularly community-based, organisations had grown to depend during the previous two decades. However, despite this, the government's rhetorical support for the voluntary sector continued and by the 1990s began to take a new form with the development of policies for *community care* and the move towards a *contractual* basis for relations between the state and voluntary sectors.

The aim of recent community care policy is to shift the role of the state, in particular the local authorities, from being the providers of care for social service clients towards a different role as *enablers*. As enablers they are expected to work in partnership with providers in the private and voluntary sectors and are able to channel public resources to organisations in these sectors through the clients who are placed with them. These resources are provided on a contractual basis, however, in return for clearly agreed service delivery targets. Following the community care approach it is likely that state funding for voluntary organisations will move more widely on to a contractual basis in the later 1990s, with the support grants and 'pump priming' funding being replaced by contractual payments tied to the delivery of an agreed level of service provision over an agreed time scale, for which voluntary organisations will be expected to compete by submitting tenders for the provision of services.

This new 'contract culture' may be welcomed by many voluntary organisations who feel it will recognise more directly the services that they are being expected to provide and will give them a right to consistent and relatively secure funding for them. However, as Kramer (1990, p. 9) observed in a review of voluntary organisations and the welfare state in the 1990s, it is not a model that will be appropriate for all and many small or community-based organisations, '...may be unable or unwilling to compete for contracts because they cannot meet the requirements for greater specificity, accountability and compliance with regulations'. Such a competition for state contracts is likely to be one of the many dilemmas facing voluntary organisations as they look forward to new roles in welfare policy at the end of the twentieth century; and, as we shall see, the resolution of these dilemmas could take the voluntary sector down a number of different roads over the coming decades.

The dilemmas of voluntary organisation

As we said, it is perhaps more accurate, and more positive, to describe voluntary organisations as comprising an independent sector – independent of both the state and the market. However, recognition of the importance of independence also reveals quite clearly many of the dilemmas facing the sector. For in practice this independence is in many cases only partial. Many agencies rely on state support and state funding either in terms of cash or kind; for many agencies it is the state, either locally or nationally, that is the main focus for their activity – either as a target for campaigns to secure changes in state policy, or as a source of potential support for further work. Voluntary activity is thus in practice often conducted 'in and against the state' – not outside it.

To some extent this is true of relations with the market too. Many organisations rely on the private market for support, either directly in the form of sponsorship or, more commonly, indirectly through selling goods or services on the market. Although sponsorship does not provide a major source of funding for the sector as a whole, it is of increasing importance, especially for larger national or international organisations. For example, many such organisations now have an employed fund raiser, who aims to secure sponsorship support. Shops for selling (often secondhand) goods to raise funds for charitable organisations, both national and local, are also now quite common; marketing activity such as this needs to be properly and effectively organised. This requires organisations to acquire market skills and to develop market niches for their products, in much the same way as commercial operators need to do. Independent organisations, though they may not declare profits, thus frequently operate within the market too.

The dilemmas for the independent sector, therefore, are not so much how to maintain their independence but rather how to negotiate their relations with the other sectors. There are a number of different forms which such relationships could take.

- *Alternative.* Voluntary organisations could aim to be an alternative to the state and the market. This is what some purists might argue that they ought to be. Such a role can be an important one, especially in some areas where both the state and the market have failed to meet social needs. This has arguably been an important factor in the growth of many of the voluntary organisations based in ethnic minority communities in Britain. These communities have frequently experienced discrimination in, or exclusion from, state and market services, as we shall discuss in Chapter 11, and have developed independent, ethnically based, organisations to provide some of the services that otherwise they would lack.
- *Complementary.* Voluntary activities may also be complementary to other service provision, as in the 'extension ladder' model championed by the Webbs. Voluntary organisations thus complement the basic services provided, in particular, through the state. For example, play schemes catering for children outside school hours or in the holidays complement collective education and childcare provision for working parents.
- *Partnership.* Rather than complementing state provision, voluntary activity may work in partnership with the state. The NSPCC has worked in partnership with social services departments in providing for children at risk, with NSPCC officers sometimes working alongside state social workers in particular cases. Some housing associations have worked in partnerhsip with local authority housing departments to allocate new tenancies to people on the authority's waiting list.
- *Contractual.* Partnership activity is intended to develop further, especially in the health and social services area, as a result of policies for community care. The enabling role of the local authority will require it to enter into agreements with external agencies for the provision of identified services for particular

clients. As we have mentioned, these agreements are likely to take a contractual form; and contractual working is likely to be a more widespread feature of the operation of a wide range of voluntary organisations in the future as they enter into specific agreements in order to secure continued support.

- *Advocacy.* Finally there are some organisations that will not wish to be seen as partners with the state, because they wish to adopt a campaigning, or an advocacy, role towards it. Challenging the state, or the market, either collectively or on behalf of individuals pursuing their rights is an activity where independent organisations have a crucial function to perform, as the national Consumers' Association or the local rights and advice centre testify.

Of course, some organisations may have different relations with the state and the market at different times, or in different circumstances. For example, advocacy organisations may also be seeking contractual funding for their work and in cases like this the dilemmas inherent in these different relations can readily come to the fore. For instance, should funding agencies be able to specify what sort of individual cases a rights and advice agency can take on?

As well as dilemmas concerning relations with other bodies, many voluntary organisations also face dilemmas concerning their internal structure and forms of operation. Voluntary activity is frequently perceived as altruistic, outward looking, and generally a good thing. However, as we know, not all organisations are altruistic. Some operate specifically to provide protection for their members. The terms on which this protection is provided may be unacceptable to some who need it – for instance credit unions usually require members to make regular contributions and abide by strict rules; some people with major debt problems may not be able to meet these requirements. Protective organisations may also exclude certain categories of people (indeed most do) and many are focused only on specific groups, for example employees of a particular enterprise. This exclusion can mean that others have no means of securing such protection; and exclusion can be sharply discriminatory – for instance, where it is exercised on the grounds of race or gender.

Exclusion and discrimination can also be a problem in organisations providing representation or providing services; and here, arguably, it is an even more serious dilemma. Not all voluntary organisations are outward looking. Some can be quite narrowly focused and dominated by a few powerful individuals and their individual interests. Because voluntary activity relies, in essence, on voluntary participation this can often mean that many are excluded either passively (because they do not take part) or actively (because they are told that they are not wanted). And this exclusion, too, can be structured by race, gender, class or other social divisions. Indeed, it may be argued that most voluntary organisations exclude some potential activists, or potential beneficiaries, through social divisions of one kind or another.

Most significant, perhaps, is the assumption that voluntary organisations are intrinsically a good thing. Not surprisingly much that has been written about the voluntary sector has been written by those who wish to promote its role in social policy development – for instance Hadley and Hatch's (1981) championing of the sector as alternative to 'the failure of the state'. Apart from the exclusive nature of many organisations, however, it is not always the case that they have a positive role to offer. Indeed, some organisations may be directly pursuing anti-welfare goals, such as a campaign to prevent the opening of a hostel for the mentally ill in a particular neighbourhood; others may pursue goals that might benefit their members at the expense of others, which is certainly what the trades unions have done on many occasions.

At a more general level, too, the activities of voluntary organisations may to some extent be counterproductive from a broader policy perspective. For instance, the existence of some voluntary activity in an area may be used as a reason for the state not providing services which it otherwise would (and perhaps should) do, and where state provision would probably be more comprehensive and effective than the voluntary sector could ever hope to achieve. Taking this further, in the 1980s the (potential) role of the voluntary sector was presented by some in government as a reason for the withdrawal of state welfare services. Indeed, the community care policy for health and social services was largely based upon the assumption that other sectors could take over this area of provision from the state.

Voluntary organisations, however, cannot act merely as substitutes for the state, for, as we have discussed, these organisations themselves frequently rely upon the state for support, both directly and indirectly. Thus where state support is withdrawn, this can have the effect of undermining voluntary activity rather than stimulating it. Evidence of this can be found in the consequences of the closure in 1988 of the Community Programme (a job creation scheme for the unemployed that supported temporary employees in a wide range of voluntary sector organisations) and of the Urban Programme in 1993. Loss of funding from these sources meant that many organisations, especially small neighbourhood groups in urban areas, either closed or had to restrict dramatically their level of activity. Although some protagonists have suggested that market-based funding might be used to replace state support here, this was not a feasible option for large numbers of these organisations; and many have also found that the secondhand charity shop may not match the funding levels that state programmes had been able to provide.

Even more importantly, however, it must be emphasised that the great strengths of the voluntary sector – its variety and spontaneity – are also its greatest weaknesses. Voluntary sector organisations have largely developed on an *ad hoc* basis, as activists and innovators have turned their ideas into collective action. The distribution of such activists, however, is both uneven and unplanned. There may be an excellent community play scheme or independent advice centre in a local area; but it is equally likely that there may not be. The NSPCC provides an important additional service to protect children in need; but there are other needy groups for whom no such charitable body exists. Furthermore, some organisations receive much more popular support, and charitable donations, than others – for example the national association for the blind has always been more popular than similar organisations for those with hearing disabilities. Voluntary sector activity is thus not comprehensive, or even equitable; against the good initiatives must be contrasted the major gaps. Protagonists who see an expanded future role for the voluntary sector in social policy development must come to terms with the enormous holes which riddle its structure.

The future of voluntary action

That there will be a future role, or roles, for voluntary action within welfare provision can hardly be doubted by students of social policy. The voluntary sector preceded state and market provision, and it has survived and prospered alongside the development of these. Also, as state and market provision is subject to ever more criticism, it has increasingly been presented as an alternative to the limitations of both – most notably by Hadley and Hatch (1981).

International comparisons further underline the importance of this third arm of welfare delivery. In countries like the USA, with more limited state welfare provision, the non-profit sector, as it is often called there, is large both in scale and scope. By contrast, in many European countries with well-developed welfare states, the sector nevertheless has crucial roles to play. In the Netherlands, for instance, although welfare services, such as education and health are largely funded by the state, they were developed and initially administered by independent bodies based around the 'pillars' of religious affiliation and membership of organisations linked to the Catholic or Protestant Churches. Religious organisations, especially those based in the Catholic Church, are also important in providing services in the Mediterranean countries such as Italy and Spain. In social democatic regimes in the EU, such as Sweden and Denmark, voluntary sector activity is weaker but even here voluntary activity has been of significant importance – and in Denmark, in particular, it has been expanding rapidly, with government support, in the 1980s and 90s.

In liberal, corporatist and social democratic welfare regimes therefore, voluntary sector activity is of central importance in social policy. Despite their differences all, like Britain, have mixed economies of welfare, in which the different sectors interrelate and overlap. The balance of provision varies between different countries, and will vary in individual countries over time. In Britain the last two decades have seen an expansion in voluntary sector activity, especially at the community level, in part because of disillusion with (and restrictions in) state support; and this is likely to continue in the near future – despite cutbacks in funding for some groups.

The voluntary sector is varied, flexible, innovative, non-bureacratic, accessible – and, perhaps most significantly, cheap. But it is also unpredictable, unstable, incomplete and sometimes oppressive and exclusionary. With the exception of some of the state programmes designed to support community development in the late twentieth century, it has also developed largely on an unplanned basis. Social policy planning must recognise this, and also recognise the limitations inherent in it. In the future, greater recognition of the role and structure of the sector will perhaps be incorporated more closely into social and economic planning; this may act to minimise some of the problems of inconsistency and non-comprehensiveness. At the same time, however, planners must recognise that complete control over voluntary activity never could – or should – be achieved. Voluntary sector organisations will always seek out, and challenge, the gaps and contradictions in state and market welfare provision; this capacity for innovation cannot be suppressed.

6

The Informal Sector

The importance of informal provision

It is probably now true to say that the previous concentration in social policy analysis upon state provision of welfare service has begun to give way in recent years to a focus on the plurality of forms of welfare provision and, as a result of this, more recognition has been given to the other sectors of welfare provision. However, despite this broadening concern, it remains the case that debate about the different sectors of welfare still pays relatively little attention to what is, in volume terms at least, the major provider of social services – the informal sector. Although, as Means and Smith (1994, p. 204) comment, 'It is now recognised that, in all welfare regimes, the informal sector has played the dominant, albeit often invisible, role'.

The unorganised and unrecorded activities of family, friends and neighbours in caring for and supporting each other has always been the underlying social fabric upon which all other welfare activity is based. That such care and support will be provided is something that we take for granted as academics and policy makers and, more importantly perhaps, that we take for granted as members of society too. It is of course understandable that we should take such support for granted; in practice it is desirable – indeed even essential – that we should be able to do so. There is an implied reciprocity and mutual interdependence in all interpersonal relationships that could never fully be planned, predicted or neatly pigeon-holed. However, taking such support for granted should not prevent us from recognising its importance in broader social policy terms, nor from analysing, and acting upon, its interrelations with other forms of support in other sectors.

It is precisely because informal support has always been there in the past and, we trust, will always be in the future, that we must seek to understand its scope and its problems – and to make sure that what we take for granted, we do not also ignore or exploit. In practice the state welfare services that have been developed throughout the twentieth century in Britain have taken for granted, or more positively have been predicated upon, the support and care provided informally by families and communities. In other words, certain responsibilities have been assumed to exist within particular restricted groups – for example education policy assumes that parents will be available to support children outside the school day and school year; health policy assumes that both minor acute conditions and chronic sickness or disability can be provided for informally at home; and social security assumes that some family members will pool resources and support one another.

Without the informal services provided at home and in the neighbourhood, state services, and private or voluntary services, would not be able to operate in the way that they do – or indeed in many cases would not be able to operate at all. Informal provision is thus crucially important. It is also massive. Because it is not organised or recorded, it would be impossible to measure the size of the informal sector, although, as we shall see later, some attempts have been made to count the numbers involved in giving and receiving some aspects of informal care. However, the fact that we cannot measure informal welfare activity does not mean that it does not have any costs. As Wright (1987) pointed out in a study of the economics of informal care for the elderly, in broader economic terms informal care is in fact very costly. It is costly immediately in terms of the time provided by carers and supporters; and it is costly indirectly to these people in terms of the lost earnings and opportunities that this caring work imposes on them – sometimes referred to as *opportunity costs* (Joshi, 1988).

Recognition of the costs involved in the informal provision of services is an important part of social policy analysis of them. It also suggests important policy responses. In some cases these costs could, and perhaps should, be covered, or at least subsidised. For instance, this could be done through the provision of income in the form of social security benefits for informal carers and this does, to some extent, take place. Informal service providers could also be supported and assisted in their tasks by a range of other means and measures, and we shall return to discuss these shortly.

Where such support is provided, however, informal provision is clearly going to overlap with support from the state, or from the private sector where these means are purchased on the market. As we discussed in the case of the voluntary sector, the informal sector, too, overlaps with the others and, where this overlap exists, the distinction between informal provision and organised services in the state, private or voluntary sectors becomes blurred. The relationship with the voluntary sector, in particular, can be a complex one – for instance, when does a baby-sitting circle cease to be neighbourly support and become a voluntary organisation? There are problems, therefore, in defining precisely what we mean by the informal sector; and, even if these definitional problems cannot be entirely resolved, they must be addressed.

The problem of definition

In fact it is the question of overlap that is perhaps the most important difficulty faced in seeking to define what we mean by the informal sector. As we discussed in Chapter 4, public provision is often contrasted with private provision within social policy debate. Although private provision is sometimes taken to mean commercially provided welfare in the market, it can also include informal services provided privately at home. Private provision thus includes the informal sector, although is not conterminous with it.

However, there is a danger in perceiving informal provision simply as private welfare. The public–private dichotomy can be a misleading one, especially where it is used to suggest that somehow private provision is not a matter of public concern or that it cannot, or should not, be the subject of public policy. Feminist critics, for example, have pointed to attempts to reduce family relations to such a private (or personal) sphere and have argued strongly that such relationships are not in reality separate from broader socioeconomic structures. As they often put it – 'the personal is also political'. And, as Ungerson (1987) signified in the title of her book on informal care, *Policy is Personal* too. Just as it is unhelpful to define commercial services as private, so it is inaccurate to perceive the informal sector as a separate private sphere too.

A more significant feature of the informal sector, for definitional purposes at least, is its unorganised – or more accurately *non-organised* – nature. State bureaucracies and business companies organise the services they offer to their clients, or customers. Indeed, it is just this organisation, and the bureaucracy which accompanies it, that has often been a feature of the criticisms that have sometimes been levelled at these sectors. Voluntary organisations aim to avoid these structural constraints; but, even where they are controlled and managed by their own users, these bodies are nevertheless organisations. In contrast, the provision of care and support on an informal basis, other than for children by parents, is not organised, either by an external agency or by those providing the service themselves. There are no rules or regulations governing what is done or how it is done. There is no enforceable contract or even a formal goodwill agreement. There is only the willingness to care and the expectation to benefit.

This is not to say, however, that services provided informally are not both reliable and predictable. Indeed they are usually both – and often more so than those supposedly provided under strict legal rules and statutory obligations. The willingness to care and the expectation of support are the two sides of the reciprocal nature of most informal services; in practice this reciprocity ensures that we do care for others because we know that others will care for us – even if this may be a different 'other' at a relatively distant time. Reciprocity is thus at the heart of informal care and support; and reciprocal relations between individuals are not generally amenable to formal organisation or control, for then the obligation moves from the individual to the structural level. Of course, as with all definitions in this area, the distinction is a blurred one – support provided by a neighbour may, for example, be incorporated into a package of care by a social worker, thus including it within a form of state service. However, insofar as the commitment to provide the support moves from an individual offer to a structural obligation, the service moves from the informal to the state, or perhaps the voluntary, sector.

The non-organised provision of informal care and support is usually based within families or communities. Thus the informal sector might be identified with the relationships within families and communities; as a definitional base, however, this too provides us with some difficulties. For a start the definition and structure of family relations is constantly changing. Despite appeals in some quarters at some times for a return to 'traditional' family values, family relations have always been in a state of flux. Relationships change – people marry earlier (or now later, or not at all), have fewer children, or separate and divorce; and definitions change – those whom we might have included within our (extended) family in the past may now be regarded rather differently as distant relatives, from whom support would not be expected. If the informal sector is based on families, then what exactly does this mean?

Much the same problems arise with the notion of community. As we saw in Chapter 5, types of community differ significantly. Although commentators and policy makers often refer to 'the community' and talk – usually in complimentary terms – about things like community schools or community policing, quite different things are often meant, and understood, by these references to community structure.

As we shall discuss in a little more detail shortly, recent policies to encourage the 'community care' of people with mental or physical health problems are based, at least in theory, on the assumption that there are community structures existing in modern British society that will automatically provide a supportive and caring environment to cater for the needs of such people. However, in fact it is doubtful whether such close knit and caring communities have ever been widespread within British society; certainly they do not exist in this simple form now. There are community activities and organisations in which people may, or may not, be involved or to which they may feel allegiance; but these are constantly changing structures from which allegiances may be withdrawn or transferred. Furthermore, as we have seen, modern communities are political and cultural, as well as geographical and social; and many community structures are quite ill-equipped – and indeed unwilling – to be a base for informal social services.

Where community-based social services are provided it is generally in practice the individual family, friends and neighbours of those in need who provide the service rather than any broader community group. Family, friends and neighbours can sometimes constitute what American commentators have called 'helping networks' (Johnson, 1987, p. 64). The point about such networks is that they may in practice provide a range of support and care services, without the formal organisation of the state or even a voluntary group.

Families do, of course, provide care and support, at least for those within the close family group – whether that is a lone parent or a three-generation household. Friends we choose, and presumably they choose us. They may expect to give, and receive, support – as the old saying goes, 'a friend in need is a friend indeed'. Neighbours we, probably, do not choose; but they are likely to know us and to know of our needs for care and support. Friends and neighbours can undertake a wide range of informal services, including shopping, cooking, gardening, providing transport or even just keeping a watchful eye (surveillance), albeit only in a minority of cases – for instance Rossiter and Wicks (1982) calculated that around eight per cent of elderly people received regular support of this kind from neighbours.

Drawing on evidence from research into informal care, Johnson (1987, p. 90) lists five categories of social service regularly provided on an informal basis:

- Personal care – washing, dressing, feeding, etc
- Domestic care – cooking and cleaning
- Auxiliary care – gardening and odd jobs
- Social support – visiting and companionship
- Surveillance – keeping an eye on vulnerable people.

Family members may provide services in all these categories, but friends or neighbours are more likely to provide those in the latter two or three only. Thus, here we have a classification of the types of activity involved in informal social services and some idea of who might be involved in providing these. As far as a definition of the informal sector goes, this may be as good as we can get: it is family, friends and neighbours providing a range of individual services through unorganised helping networks.

The development of informal care

The informal provision of care and support preceded the development of modern social policy planning, and to some extent it has since then remained outside the formal service planning process. The point about the informal sector is that it is not planned or organised like the other sectors. However, informal activity is affected by the changes and developments within the formal welfare sectors, indeed such developments have been crucially important in changing the context within which voluntary activity takes place – and the expectations that both service providers and recipients have of it.

Many voluntary sector organisations have grown out of informal activity. These include the neighbours' baby-sitting circle that becomes the local mother and toddler group or the squatters' group that becomes a campaign against homelessness. The boundaries between the voluntary and informal sectors remain constantly blurred and, in particular, changes in the size and scope of voluntary sector activity are likely to relieve, or to accentuate, pressure on informal service providers to take on caring or supporting roles. Furthermore, these changes occur both over time, and across different places.

The development of commercial welfare services has also affected the informal sector. The wider range of services available commercially can displace informal care. Those with resources have always been able to buy the personal care that they need, for example through the employment of nannies and nurses; and with growing affluence this commercial replacement of informal care is utilised by a broader range of the population – albeit still largely by a better-off minority. Commercial services can also, however, support informal activity. Adaptations to homes, such as a stair lift, and personal aids, such as an electric wheelchair, can make the provision of informal care much less onerous. Commercial care plans or health insurance policies can provide financial support if, or when, a need for informal care arises. Again, these services are likely to be more widely used by the better off; nevertheless, their impact on the size, and shape, of the informal sector is extensive.

Most importantly of all, however, the development of state welfare services has affected the informal sector in a wide manner of ways; and changes within state welfare services have continued to alter the relationship between the two. To a large extent much of the early development of the welfare state was predicated upon an attempt to remove the burden of informal care and support for all welfare needs from the individual and replace this with collectively organised services provided by all – and for the benefit of all. The state health and education services have taken responsibility for much of the provision of these services away from the family who, perforce, would have provided more of them before. The development of state social work services has resulted in the provision of more and better quality public residential care for children and adults in need of extensive support, of day care and drop-in services for those with more limited needs, and of counselling and advice for those uncertain of how to secure the assistance they need.

During the postwar period the establishment of the welfare state in Britain saw a major extension of state welfare services, which were intended, in part at least, to ensure that collective provision should replace the informal demands made on family, friends and neighbours in the past. However, since then the pendulum of policy planning has to some extent swung away from state provision and back towards an explicit expectation of, and reliance upon, informal sector care. Within two decades of the establishment of postwar state services, criticisms began to emerge of the discomfort, insensitivity and even brutality of state institutional care – for example Townsend's (1962) study of homes for older people. These criticisms of the undesirability of 'total institutions' have now become widespread (Jones and Fowles, 1984); children's homes or older persons' homes are still sometimes viewed negatively with a mixture of fear and pity.

Perhaps the most negative images of state collective care, however, have been reserved for mental hospitals. Here a state service is seen in popular culture primarily as a threatening place, to be avoided almost at all costs. Such negative imagery has resulted in a shift away from such residential care in social policy planning. In Italy, in the 1970s, this shift was a stark one; all large mental hospitals were closed down and their patients transferred to community-based care schemes. Policy change has not moved so rapidly in Britain; but it has moved in the same direction.

In the last two decades, in particular, there has been a more and more explicit emphasis on 'community care' as a more desirable substitute for state residential provision. After 1990 this was enshrined in legislation requiring health authorities and local authority social service departments to work in partnership to assess the needs of people requiring extensive care and support and to seek, where possible, to ensure that this was provided in a community context. Such community care can avoid the insensitivity, and the stigma, of state residential provision; it can also be more flexible and adaptable to the particular needs of different people – although it can also still require the support of organised services within the home.

However, the shift towards community care is not just a product of political and policy rejection of the value of public residential provision, it is also the result of financial pressure on state services provision and a narrower economic assessment of the (apparent) costs of these different models and sectors of care. Public residential care is expensive to provide and large amounts of public money are needed to purchase and maintain institutions and pay workers within them. Community-based care provided informally by family, friends and neighbours has much less of an impact on the public purse, especially where, as has often been the case in Britain, the state services to support such care have themselves been restricted by lack of resources. Of course, as we have already pointed out, informal care in the community is also costly in other ways – in particular it imposes costs on those individuals who do the caring work. However, this does not register in the economic or political calculations of the resourcing of community care; and thus the shift back to the informal sector has been assumed to create much needed savings in state welfare provision. These savings have been experienced as an increased pressure on the informal sector, resulting directly from developments within the state sector.

Informal care

Although the welfare services provided informally vary widely in form and scope, the most significant feature of the sector, especially from a social policy perspective, is the role played by the informal provision of individual care in the home. Caring services can encompass a range of activities; in particular they include the personal and domestic tasks outlined above. These forms of care are provided by adults (usually parents, and especially mothers) for their young children; but they are also provided by adults (and occasionally by children) for other adults – in particular those who through illness or disability are unable to care adequately for themselves.

Care for children is not often discussed in social policy debates, largely because it is taken for granted that parents can, and do, provide such care. In practice, however, it is generally mothers, rather than fathers, who provide the majority of the care for young children and who, in particular, forgo paid employment in order to do this. As we have pointed out, the long-term consequences of this can be significant for mothers in terms of their lost opportunities for receipt of wages and for career experience and enhancement. When children are older and can go to school this relieves to some extent the burden of care at home but the limitations of the school day and school year mean that it is still extremely difficult for mothers to combine childcare with full-time employment.

Because of these pressures on the family-based care for children, the provision of collective childcare has become a significant, if rather narrowly debated, issue for social policy. Although local authorities do provide some nursery places for very young children, these are generally in very limited supply and are frequently allocated primarily to children deemed to be in special need because of a troubled home environment. Private collective childcare is also available but obviously only for those able to afford what can be quite high fees. Such care may also be provided by employers for the young children of their employees, either free or for a charge but, despite more widespread debate about the need for such workplace childcare provision, relatively little of it actually exists.

Private childcare can also be purchased on an individual basis, however, and here provision is much more common. From the full-time, live-in nanny to the neighbour who is paid to look after the children for a few mornings a week, private childcare provision supplements the informal provision of care through families – and overlaps with it, as many private arrangements are extremely informal. Of course, such private childcare arrangements are not new; they have always been a central feature of the family-based informal care of children. However, they have often been overlooked in discussion of both childcare and family structure. Policy planning for childcare could in the future pay closer attention to the complex interaction of the informal and market sectors of welfare provision here – and to the consequences this has for women, in particular, both as mothers and as employees.

Unfortunately, perhaps, policy planning for childcare in the informal sector has concentrated largely, not on the complex working arrangements that many families *do* successfully make for the care of their children, but rather on the *failure* of some families to provide care adequately and the consequent need for state intervention through social work to ensure that the harm done to children in such cases in minimised. Social workers operate, in practice, in the role of a state monitor over the informal sector, and within this the prevention of harm and abuse to children in families has become the most important policy priority. Such 'childcare' work, as it is usually called, dominates the workloads of the social workers employed by local authorities and by major voluntary sector bodies such as the NSPCC (Clarke, 1993).

While the majority of informal care is provided for young children, a significant, and growing, proportion of informal sector activity concerns care for vulnerable adults. In practice, the informal care of those suffering from chronic sickness or disability has generally been a somewhat overlooked aspect of welfare provision in Britain – although its role is now more widely debated within social policy and is the subject of specific policy planning, most notably in the 1990s provisions for 'community care'. Such care is largely provided by close family members, especially spouses and adult children (Rossiter and Wicks, 1982), and usually this is done without any formal support from either the state or the other sectors of welfare. Like most informal services, the provision of such care is often taken for granted by policy planners – and by the family members themselves; although in practice, as we have said, it frequently creates many problems for those involved in it.

It is feminist commentators, in particular, who have elevated the issue, and the problems, of informal care for adults onto the policy agenda. As they have pointed out, it is mainly women who provide such care and experience many of the problems related to it (Finch and Groves, 1983; Ungerson, 1987). Parker (1990, p. 93) makes the point that there is a significant, yet hidden, burden being carried disproportionately by women here, 'Generally, female carers have been shown to be more likely to give up their jobs, lose more money and to experience more stress than are male carers'. However, it would be wrong to assume that all informal care in the home is carried out by women; men do provide care, indeed research has suggested that over a third of informal carers are men (Green, H, 1988).

The contradictions that underlie this burden are brought out sharply in the title of Finch and Groves' (1983) edited collection in informal care – *A Labour of Love*. For women especially, the fusion of labour and love is manifest in the double meaning of the word *care*. Care can mean caring *about* someone and it can also mean caring *for* them. The provision of much informal care is predicated on the assumption that, because we care about someone, we can also therefore be expected to care for them in times of need. This is an assumption that may be strongly held – most significantly by those in need of care, and those who feel obliged to care for them. Here the presumed, and yet unplanned, reciprocity of the informal sector can begin to take on a coercive, and even an oppressive, form.

The costs of caring for a vulnerable or dependent adult can be great, both immediately and indirectly over the longer term (Joshi, 1992). It can also, unlike childcare, frequently be a long, and ultimately depressing, ordeal ending only with the death of the recipient of the care. Yet the provision of such care is widespread and is vitally important at both an individual and a broader social level. It is also an area of provision that is growing rapidly, and is likely to grow further in the future.

Summarising research from a number of surveys of dependent adults and their carers, Parker (1990, p. 24) concluded that there were around 6 million people providing informal care for a sick, handicapped or elderly person, with around 1.3 million acting as the 'main carers' for disabled adults and children. This means that around 14 per cent of all adults are providing care. This is a significant proportion, and yet it is likely to grow further as the numbers of older people and disabled people are projected to increase in the future – at the same time as institutional provision for them is pared back. Greater levels of poverty among the elderly and disabled than within the rest of the population also mean that relatively fewer are likely to be able to buy care services, either individually or collectively, on the commercial market.

However, while the demand for informal care is growing, the 'helping networks', in particular the families, that provide it are changing in ways that seem likely to reduce their capacity to continue to do so in the future. There has been a continuing decline in the number of younger single people to provide informal care, in particular the single daughters of older parents; and at the same time there has been a reduction in the size of families with the result that there are fewer children to provide a future pool of potential carers. Changes in family stability have also further reduced the potential source of carers here, with increased numbers of divorces meaning that previously experienced family obligations are now frequently severed. However, perhaps most significant is the continuing growth of women's (especially married women's) participation in the labour market. Of course, some married women do give up paid employment in order to provide informal care; but this is a hard financial, as well as emotional, decision which more are having to face – and which more may decide to refuse to make. These refusals may, of course, lead to a growth in the market provision of such care – perhaps even in organisations employing women as paid carers – but such a shift away from the informal towards the market sector is both uncertain and fraught with difficulties, especially for those too poor to purchase such services.

A shift from informal to market-based caring services may not, of course, necessarily be a bad thing for those requiring such care. The moves towards 'community care' in the latter part of the twentieth century seem to have been informed by an almost unquestionable belief in the desirability of informal, individual, care as against collectively provided services, founded largely on the criticisms of the worst of state residential provision. These criticisms focused almost exclusively upon the disadvantages of collective care from the point of view of the recipients of it, the *cared for*, and ignored the problems experienced by *carers* in the informal sector – a point to which we shall return shortly. They were also rarely based on any evidence of the realities of informal caring services.

As more recent research has demonstrated, although informal care can be very good, it can also be highly problematic (Qureshi and Walker, 1989). Very much depends upon the dedication and commitment of the carer, and upon the support services available to supplement their informal provision. Both the former and latter can vary dramatically. Support services, in particular, remain very patchy and have not been expanded significantly to meet the growing needs created by the move towards community care.

It is the absence of attention to the role of carers, however, that has been the most glaring omission in much social policy debate about the informal sector. Policy planning for the informal sector, or the lack of it, makes assumptions about both the ability and availability of carers which in practice conceal a range of important issues. As Twigg (1989) points out, policy planning for informal care has been constructed around the needs of the cared for, not the carers; carers' needs have generally been quite inadequately conceptualised. For instance, carers may be perceived as *resources* for service provision, or they may be perceived as *co-workers* with those in other sectors, or they may be perceived as *co-clients* with the person they are caring for. These different perceptions lead to different ways of supporting carers, all of which have been variously pursued – sometimes simultaneously.

One of the most important problems facing carers is the source (and the adequacy) of their income, especially where they are excluded from paid employment as result of their caring work. Since 1975 there has been a social security benefit specifically designed to provide an income for carers, Invalid Care Allowance (ICA). However, the value of this benefit is very low, so those without any other source of income are still left depending upon Income Support; nor does it extend to those caring for elderly people. Yet even this low level of benefit was not provided for married and cohabiting female carers prior to 1986, because of the assumption that they could be provided for by their male partners. The discriminatory perspective that informed this assumption reveals much about past (and perhaps still present) policy assumptions about the structure and workings of the informal sector. Such discrimination was, however, in breach of an EU equal treatment directive, which meant that the British government was eventually forced to extend entitlement – resulting in a massive increase in the numbers claiming the benefit.

Caring work is thus frequently associated with financial dependency upon inadequate social security benefits, with all the long-term costs of lack of saving and investment associated with this added to the immediate pressures of caring work on a low income. As Glendinning (1992) points out, however, such work is also associated with *interdependency* between carer and cared for. This is true at the formal level as entitlement to ICA is predicated upon receipt of Disability Living Allowance by the recipient of care – a problem that significantly reduces take-up levels of both benefits because of the complexities involved in claiming them. It is also, and more significantly perhaps, true at the informal level. Where care is provided within family relationships, this may well involve a pooling of resources within the household; thus all sources of income, however inadequate, are likely to be used to support all family members. As a result of this the caring relationship can come to dominate the financial arrangements of the whole household – and, of course, their financial prospects for the future too.

The dependency links between caring work and social security entitlement revealed here are, however, only one aspect of the interrelationship between the informal and formal sectors of welfare that can have significant implications for carers. The support for the other needs of carers which is – or is not – provided, in particular by the state welfare services, can make a considerable difference to their lives and the lives of those for whom they care. Such support services include things like help at home with cleaning and catering, 'meals on wheels', aids and adaptations to the house, and day centres and respite care to provide relief for carers. It has sometimes been suggested by critics of state welfare that the provision of services by the state discourages individuals and families from providing these for themselves; yet in practice it is the expansion of services such as these that could make a policy of community-based informal care both more tolerable and more successful. Unfortunately economic pressure on local authority social service departments, the main providers of such services, has meant that frequently this is not realised.

While support services can make a major difference to the circumstances of all carers and recipients of care, the receipt of such services varies significantly between different sorts of carer, in particular by gender, age and household composition – with single male carers generally receiving considerably more in the way of support services than other carers, especially women (Arber *et al.*, 1988). Thus, not only is it the case that women are more frequently providing informal care than are men, but also that where women do care the burden of this work is likely to be more demanding.

The recent shift in policy planning towards more open and direct support for community care is a recognition of the important role played here by the informal sector – indeed, it is something of a return to informal welfare, after the rapid expansion of state-based services in the immediate postwar period. Seen positively, community care is an example of partnership between the sectors, of the mixed economy of welfare in action. However, early examinations of the operation of community care policies in practice have suggested that this mixed economy is not providing the kind of partnership working that some carers and recipients need (Baldock and Ungerson, 1994); and without the support for informal carers, which the notion of partnership implies, the result is likely to be an increased pressure to care on a diminishing pool of carers.

The policy prospects

The informal sector of welfare, although it dominates provision in terms of current volume and past history, has always operated in something of a policy vacuum within welfare provision in Britain. In part it is in the very nature of informal provision to defy policy prescription – that, some might argue, is its great strength. However, the relative absence in Britain of explicit policies for family structure and community structure is not directly replicated in all other welfare capitalist countries. Although they are very different, both France and Sweden, for example, have much more explicit family policies with a high political profile; and in Germany the 'subsidiarity' principle that operates in general as an encouragment for the development of voluntary sector activity, also acts to promote the role of the informal sector there, by requiring support for welfare provision to be provided at the level which is closest to the circumstances of the recipients of that support.

As we have seen, recent moves towards community care, for all their limitations, have elevated the informal sector more firmly onto the policy agenda in Britain today. It is perhaps significant that the responsibility for the implementation of the community care policy has been placed largely upon the shoulders of the local authority social service departments, for it is through social work most specifically that the interrelationships between the informal and formal sectors of welfare have been managed and developed. Social workers, in their concern for the care of children in families and the provision of support for mentally ill or disabled adults in the community, operate on this formal–informal interface, monitoring from within the state the provision of informal care. In Sheffield, for instance, the social services department is called 'Family and Community Services'; and more generally, social workers have sometimes been referred to as the 'soft cops', who are *policing* families and communities.

In the 1990s, however, the aim of policy development for adult social services has been to change the role of social workers from one of policing to one of *enabling* – helping and facilitating the informal sector rather than checking and controlling it. Although, as we mentioned in Chapter 2, child protection work within social services has remained a central focus of concern, the shift in the role of social workers in their relations with adult service users has created pressure to change the working practices of social services and their connections with the informal sector – whether this will change the informal sector itself is far from clear. Such a change would certainly require a much more proactive response to relationships with the informal sector from the major statutory and voluntary organisations than has been the case in the past.

One important role that social workers have always played in their relations with their clients, however, is that of intervention or representation on behalf of clients with other agencies. Social workers take up issues on behalf of clients with local authority housing department or housing associations, with social security or benefits agency offices, and with health authorities or hospital trusts. Frequently they are able to negotiate for clients with these agencies, or even to challenge directly their practices or their decisions. This is a role that focuses on the *rights* (welfare rights) of clients rather than their *needs*; and it is one that is likely to become more important as the shift to an enabling culture within social services develops. However, it is also a role which will inevitably lead, if successful, to changed relationships between such agencies and the families and communities which they serve – and which rely on them.

The shift from a policing to an enabling role within social services is thus a symbolic representation of – as well as a potential catalyst for – a changing relationship between the informal activities of families and communities and the formal organisations of state, commercial and voluntary welfare. It is a change that is predicated upon a more open and explicit recognition of the active part played by the informal sector in welfare provision and a more positive desire to see this operate in partnership with formal welfare provision – rather than, as sometimes in the past, largely outside it.

Such a positive partnership suggests a greater recognition, at last, of the importance of the informal sector in welfare policy – and this will result in changes in the way the other sectors interact with it. The immediate prospects for such a policy of partnership rest heavily on changes in social work practice, where the emphasis of policy development in community care, for example, is based. In the longer term, however, partnership working must extend to other agencies and organisations too. This heralds an important new future for the once marginalised informal sector – and consequently for the formal sectors of welfare too.

SECTION THREE

Context

7

Ideologies of Welfare

Ideology

The concept of ideology is one of the most important in social
science. However, it is also one of the most contested – and one of
the most misused and misunderstood. For instance, ideology is
sometimes taken to mean the adoption of a false or inaccurate
perception of the real world; this is then contrasted with the correct
perspective which is supposedly provided by scientific inquiry. This
is not the sense in which ideology is normally understood in social
policy debate; and it is not the sense in which it is used in this book.
We use ideology more broadly as a concept that refers to the systems
of beliefs within which *all* individuals perceive *all* social phenomena.
In this usage no one system of beliefs is more correct, or more
privileged, than any other.

In this sense, therefore, all of us have ideologies – our own systems
of beliefs that shape and structure the way we see the world, and
make judgements about it. And, of course, each individual's ideological perspective is different and unique. We do not all agree with one
another about everything. Indeed, it our disagreements and differences that make debate and development both desirable and
possible. If we were all the same it would not only be a dull world –
in terms of social development, it would be a dead one. Thus
individual ideologies differ, and they are a source of debate – and
conflict. Individual ideologies are also both *critical* and *prescriptive* –
we know what is wrong with what we see, and we know what should
be done about it. As a result of this they are therefore *partial* and
value laden – we do not know or understand everything but we do
know what we like and do not like.

Ideological perspectives therefore condition the way in which all of us perceive the world in which we live, and they do so in a way that leaves all of us with a more or less restricted and biased perspective on it. If this seems to be a rather depressing starting point, it should not be judged so. No-one can know everything or be right about everything; but that does not mean that we do not know anything or that our views are always only a product of our own personal values. Our individual ideological perspectives are limited and biased, and they are unique; but they are not isolated. As individuals we are also part of broader social structures from which we receive the support we need to survive – and through which we give support to others. Our individual systems of belief are also part of broader ideological perspectives from which we draw the ideas and values which we use to form judgements – and to which we may contribute ideas and values of our own.

Individual ideologies are constructed within wider ideological perspectives in which views are shared and debated, and within which shared views are held and disseminated. Such broader ideological perspectives may be held by relatively small social groups and may focus specifically upon particular issues, for example the neighbourhood campaign group who all wish to preserve the character of their area and oppose new development plans. However, they may also be much wider in both scale and scope, enlisting adherence or support from the majority of people throughout the country (or even across countries) and addressing a range of social issues from a particular perspective. Such broader ideological perspectives influence the way individual ideological views are formed and developed, and through this influence on those individuals, or groups, who are in positions of power they are able to shape the world in which we live. Indeed it is *because* ideologies shape the social world that we debate so passionately about them – and within them. The power of ideology cannot be overestimated in social science; and, as we shall see, in social policy ideologies of welfare have shaped and structured all perceptions of welfare policy and the development of all policy planning.

It is important to recognise here, however, that ideological perspectives not only determine which policies we propose to develop or support but also influence how we view, and judge, policy developments that have already taken place. Take, for example, the introduction of the right of all tenants to buy their council houses by the

Conservative government in 1980. For many commentators with a right-wing political perspective, including some members of the government, this was seen as a victory for the rights of individual freedom and self-determination over the paternalistic control of state welfare bureaucrats. For some other Conservative politicians, and for some social policy commentators, it was seen as a necessary development within housing policy to accommodate more rationally the 'mixed economy' of welfare and the overlap, or partnership, between state and private sector provision. For some on the political left, however, the sale of council houses was a dissipation of public assets and a betrayal of one of the major planks of the welfare state.

No one of these ideological judgements is any more right or wrong than any of the others, although they are all perspectives on the same policy development. They are merely different ideological judgements, from different ideological standpoints; and, of course, they do not exhaust the different ideological views that might be held. However, they are not just the product of idiosyncratic individual attitudes, they are quite widely shared ideological views and are based within broader perspectives on welfare policy from within which similar judgements would be likely to be made about other policy initiatives. In other words, they are part of broader ideologies of welfare.

At this broader social level, however, the size and scope of ideological perspectives will vary dramatically. A perspective shared by the majority of people in a country will be rather more important than one shared by a small group of friends and neighbours. In their discussion of ideologies of welfare, George and Wilding (1994) discuss this point and argue that *major* ideological perspectives must possess certain characteristics in order to be regarded as of particular social importance. They outline four such characteristics:

- *coherence* – ideological perspectives must have an internal logic and theoretical consistency
- *pervasiveness* – ideological perspectives must be current and relevant, old perspectives may have lost their social base
- *extensiveness* – ideological perspectives must be widely shared within, or across, societies
- *intensiveness* – ideological perspectives must command the support, and commitment, of those who share them; they must really be believed.

Therefore an ideological perspective is a shared view, or set of views, with a clear social impact. Of course not all ideological perspectives focus on, or even address, social policy issues – indeed most do not. We are not concerned here, however, with all ideologies; only with those that do address welfare issues and focus on description, and judgement, of policy development, and prescription for future policy reform. These we can call *ideologies of welfare.*

Ideology and theory

If ideologies of welfare are widely shared and coherent perspectives on policy and reform, this raises the question of what, if any, is the distinction between such ideological perspectives and theoretical analysis and debate of welfare issues. What about *theories of welfare?* In practice (and in theory!) the distinction between ideology and theory is not a clear or watertight one – nor is it uncontested. Sometimes the two concepts are used more or less interchangeably – one person's theory is another person's ideology. However, it is probably fair to say that some broad differences in usage and understanding do exist, even though these would not be universally accepted.

A theoretical perspective may exist within a broader, and looser, ideological perspective. However, theoretical discourse is likely to be less partial and less value laden than ideology, and to be more comprehensive and logical. A theoretical perspective has more than an individual coherence, it has a systematic logical structure that is allied to a descriptive, rather than a prescriptive, approach to policy issues; it is generally presented in academic terms, for a largely academic audience. Theorists are not generally seeking to popularise or to persuade, but rather to describe and to convince; and they aim to convince only those who share their academic interests – and can follow their academic arguments.

Theories of welfare are therefore produced by, and for, a relatively narrow group of academics and their students. In contrast, although ideologies of welfare are more partial, political and prescriptive, they are also more popular. While few people would claim any knowledge of, or support for, a theoretical approach to welfare, many would no doubt hold, and debate, ideological perspectives on welfare – or at least on welfare issues. Thus, although we are not all academics (or theorists), we do all have, and share, ideologies of welfare. Or to put it another way – we may not know about, or even understand, the welfare pluralist case against unaccountable state monopoly providers but we do know that we want independent advice about the refusal of our claim for a social security payment.

Theories of welfare are therefore narrower and more academic than ideological perspectives; it is for this reason that we focus here on the broader category of ideology. Both theory and ideology, however, are also linked to *politics*. As we discussed in Chapter 1, social policy is a prescriptive discipline – it focuses on the development and implementation of political changes. Inevitably, and in most cases avowedly, therefore, it seeks to intervene in, and influence, political debate. Ideologies of welfare are linked to the politics of welfare and different political allegiances and practices are based in different ideological perspectives.

Commentators have frequently attempted to compare ideologies of welfare according to their location within a continuum of political preferences. George and Wilding did this in 1976 in their first book on ideology and social welfare and it was taken up again by Lee and Raban in 1983. In their more recent text, George and Wilding (1994, p. 9) produce a table summarising a total of ten separate analyses of ideologies of welfare. These various analyses identify a range of different numbers of perspectives and also sometimes give these perspectives different names. In practice, however, many analysts place the different perspectives that they identify at different points within a continuum moving from the political left to the political right – in particular in terms of their support for, or opposition to, the role of the state in welfare provision.

Thus on the *left* are socialists or Marxists, who believe that the state should play a major, or exclusive, role in the provision of social policy; on the *right* are anti-collectivists or liberals, who believe that individuals should be free to provide (or not) for whatever needs they wish. In between are the Fabians, the social democrats, the reluctant collectivists and others. Of course, not all ideologies of welfare can be so readily classified along such a left to right political continuum, as we shall see later. Nevertheless, the link between ideology and politics in social policy, and the central role played in both of debate about the relative roles of the state and the market, means that political differences here are also likely to represent ideological differences – and vice versa.

Ideology and politics

Ideology and politics may be linked but they are not the same thing. Ideology is concerned with ideas, ideals and principles – politics is concerned with pragmatism and results. Thus debate and study of the politics of welfare focuses not primarily upon differing perspectives and approaches, still less on the differing explanations that are the concern of theory, but rather upon events and achievements. Thus both Deakin's (1994) book, *The Politics of Welfare,* and Sullivan's (1992) book, *The Politics of Social Policy,* examine the changes in British welfare policy since the Second World War, pointing out how the changes in policy are the result of changes in the power and influence of different political perspectives. In other words, the differences in view are contrasted in terms of their impact on the development and implementation of policy.

During the first two decades following the war, however, the appearance of political consensus over the future direction of policy development, characterised by the notion of *Butskellism,* suggested that such political differences had been superseded. Commentators argued that this also implied that ideological differences had effectively disappeared – in particular the differences between left and right over the role of the state – and therefore suggested that future political conflict would be 'a fight without ideologies' (Lipset, 1963, p. 408). This *end of ideology* thesis proved to be a little premature, or oversimplistic, however, for ideological disagreements did remain and, in particular after the early 1970s, they were represented again in political debate and conflict over the future direction of reform.

In more recent times another version of an end of ideology thesis has emerged in discussion of the, alleged, onset of *postmodernism* – in both theory and society. This is a complex, and much overused, concept. In part, it is used to suggest that, as societies have become ever larger – and thus more complex, diverse and fragmented – the broad political movements (for example representing capital and labour) and wide-ranging ideological perspectives, which had previously dominated policy development, have been replaced by a much more extensive range of more diffuse perspectives representing smaller social groups and narrower social interests. The result of this is that neither politics nor ideology are focused any more primarily upon the left–right debate about the role of the state but rather that there are a plethora of different political organisations pursuing their own interests and a range of new ideological perspectives emerging that do not fit into the simplistic left–right continuum.

Postmodernist commentators argue that this is a reflection of changes in economic and social structure that have moved societies away from the mass production of modern capitalism, with its 'capitalist versus working class' conflict, towards a *post*modernist society with flexible production and flexible employment (part-time work for small employers) and with conflicts focusing not only on class but also on differences of gender, race, age and other issues. This means that the problems on which policy might focus are also more complex and cannot be resolved, or relieved, simply by moves to expand, or contract, state welfare. Postmodernism therefore implies not so much an end to ideology itself, as an end to all-encompassing ideological perspectives.

Certainly there is evidence of the emergence of new, and different, ideological perspectives on welfare, not based on the 'old' divisions between capital and labour. George and Wilding (1994) include *feminism* and *greenism* in their new typology of ideologies of welfare. Williams (1989), in her critical introduction to social policy, argues that differences, and conflicts, of gender and race have been overlooked in traditional studies of the discipline. There are also now clear political groupings that cut across the traditional left–right divide, for example the feminist movement, the anti-nuclear campaigns, or the ecological parties. These are sometimes referred to as the *new social movements*; although, as we shall return to discuss shortly, they are not in fact necessarily all that new.

Keane (1988) and others have argued that these changes mark a turning point in political and social structure of modern (or postmodern) societies. They are evidence that *class* politics have been replaced by *plural* politics and that the central role of the state has been displaced by the growing importance of *civil society*, with its variety of organisations, agencies and allegiances. As a result of this, Keane argues, constitutional change is required in countries like Britain to shift the policy process onto a more plural democratic basis – leading to a restructuring of central political institutions and a devolution and decentralisation of power throughout society.

These are interesting, and perhaps even desirable, proposals; and, in so far as they reflect the growing influence of new social movement politics, they do presage the development of new perspectives on welfare reform. However, the presentation of this diversity of politics and ideology as a phenomenon, or a product, only of industrial societies in the late twentieth century is based upon rather dubious presumptions about what preceded it, and it reveals that something of an ahistorical myth has been created at the heart of the postmodernist thesis.

Social divisions of gender, race and age are not only a product of the late twentieth century and class politics have not always dominated political conflict – even if they have dominated the thinking of political commentators. Similarly, ideologies of welfare have always included a wider range of perspectives than the traditional left–right disagreement over the state – again even if some of these have been relatively ignored by social policy analysts. For instance, in 1943 Abbot and Bompas provided a feminist critique of the recommendations of the Beveridge Report, although this was not taken up by either of the main political parties at the time.

The postmodernist myth also suggests that the supposedly traditional ideologies of welfare have not themselves changed alongside the changes to social and economic structures. This is not true. The rise of the New Right in the 1970s and 80s, which we shall discuss shortly, was not simply a continuation, or resurrection, of nineteenth-century liberalism; it was very much a product of changed socioeconomic forces. Similarly, the pro-state Fabianism of the early twentieth century has been replaced in Fabianist thinking in the 1990s by discussion of, and support for, devolution of power and for a mixed economy of welfare provision.

Ideologies of welfare have, in reality, always been in a state of flux. Existing ideological perspectives change and new ones develop. They cannot all be classified simply in terms of support for, or opposition to, state welfare provision. Their influence on the political process does not only depend upon their alliance with major political parties. Politics is more complex than this, and it always has been; and ideological debate is more wide-ranging. Postmodernism may therefore be a useful term for characterising the changes in economic and social forces that are taking place at the end of the twentieth century; but it should not be taken to imply that such structural changes are a new phenomenon (changes in economic and social structure have always been taking place) – nor that these have led to a fundamental shift, or decline, in ideological debate.

Despite this recognition of the permanence – and yet fluidity – of diversity, we do nevertheless need to be able to delineate *major* ideological forces from more *minor* ones, to compare significant differences in approaches towards social policy and welfare reform and to assess the likely influence of competing perspectives on academic debate and policy development. Bearing in mind the caveats discussed above therefore, we can still identify a number of important and influential ideologies of welfare that continue to dominate social policy in the 1990s.

New Right

The New Right is the term used to refer to the pro-market, anti-state ideological perspective that developed more widespread support in Britain (and in some other countries such as the USA) in the 1970s and 80s, and also became associated with the Thatcherite Conservative governments of the 1980s. It was this new-found political influence, together with the rapid growth in the numbers of commentators contributing their ideas to this, that made the New Right *new*. In practice, their ideas, and the broader perspective from within which they are drawn, are not all that new and are mainly an attempt to adapt classical nineteenth-century *laissez-faire* liberalism to late twentieth-century circumstances. The New Right are thus also known as *Neo-liberals* or *Market Liberals*.

Many of the recent New Right theorists draw directly, and explicitly, upon the writings of Hayek, who had been consistently developing the case for market liberalism throughout the period of the establishment and growth of the postwar welfare state (Hayek, 1944, 1960, 1982). Hayek's argument was that there was a fundamental contradiction between the operation of markets and the intervention of the state, and that state intervention would inevitably lead to market dysfunction. He also argued that state intervention involved an unwarranted interference with the freedom of individuals to organise their own affairs and, therefore, that intervention was only justified if its aim was to protect individual freedom – for example the use of the criminal law to protect private property.

Hayek's preference for market over state was also shared by the other main source of New Right theory and ideology, the American writer Milton Friedmann (1962). Friedmann too argued that, left to their own devices, markets would naturally protect individuals because consumer sovereignty would ensure that producers adapted their services to meet consumer needs but that, if the state intervened to seek to meet needs directly, this would distort the working of the market and lead to an economic collapse, in which both state and individuals would suffer.

Throughout the postwar period the ideas of Hayek and Friedmann were propounded in Britain by a right-wing 'think tank', the Institute of Economic Affairs (IEA), but theirs was very much a minority voice against the welfare 'consensus' of the time. In the 1970s, however, the onset of inflation and rising unemployment and the collapse in the world economy appeared to demonstrate that the predictions of market distortion and dysfunction through state intervention were correct and the IEA found a new confidence in, and a new audience for, their proposals for rolling back the boundaries of state welfare and restoring the free market. Other voices also then joined with the IEA in the chorus of anti-state criticism. In 1974 the Centre for Policy Studies (CPS), another think tank, was formed by Margaret Thatcher (later Conservative Prime Minister) and Keith Joseph (one of her close political allies); and in 1979 an independent right-wing policy centre, the Adam Smith Institute (ASI), was also formed. Together these new organisations, and their new-found political allies, gave neo-liberal thinking a powerful push towards the centre stage of ideological debate.

The main plank of New Right ideological thinking on welfare is its opposition to extensive state intervention to provide public services, in effect opposition to the very idea of a 'welfare state'. The welfare state is undesirable, New Right theorists argue, on economic, ideological and political grounds – and, because it is undesirable in theory, it is also unworkable in practice.

In *economic* terms they argue that the welfare state is undesirable because it involves interference with the free working of market. This leads to a failure of markets to develop properly, because state monopolies dominate many areas of provision – for example rented housing. More pertinently perhaps, however, it also leads to a crippling drain on private market wealth (and therefore investment) because of the ever-growing fiscal demands of public expenditure to meet the costs of expanding state welfare services. State intervention thus leads to economic recession – as, it was claimed, was realised in Britain and elsewhere in the 1970s; and economic growth is only restored by cutting public expenditure and reducing the role, and scope, of the state – as, it was alleged, was successfully achieved in the 1980s. What is more, it follows from this, therefore, that future economic growth can only continue to be sustained if welfare is further and further contained.

The *ideological* objections of the New Right to state welfare centre around their concern over the supposed problems of *perverse incentives* and the *dependency culture*. By providing welfare services for all through the state, it is argued, individuals are effectively discouraged from providing these for themselves or for their families. Indeed, people are not only discouraged, they are effectively trapped into wholesale reliance upon the support of others – the dependency culture. This is most clearly revealed in the 'problem' of perverse incentives – an idea associated in particular with the work of the American theorist, Charles Murray (1984, 1990, 1994). Murray focuses primarily upon the operation of social security protection, which he argues, by providing everyone with a guaranteed basic standard of living, makes it attractive for some people to opt for this rather than seeking to provide for themselves through paid employment. This is particularly the case with means-tested benefits, where entitlement is related to individual income levels, so that increases in income merely lead to loss of benefits. This has long been recognised in the problem of the *poverty trap* (Deacon and Bradshaw, 1983, Ch. 8). Murray's argument gives it a different ideological slant, focusing on the moral perversity of state dependency and its effect in driving people out of the labour market. The British Conservative MP, Rhodes Boyson (1971, p. 7), put it rather more pejoratively when he argued that the welfare state 'saps the collective moral fibre of our people as a nation'.

The *political* undesirability of the welfare state for the New Right is best exemplified through an examination of what they refer to as *public choice theory*. This too has its roots in US scholarship, especially in the writing of a group of theorists called the 'Virginia School' (Buchanan, 1986). Public choice theory involves the application of microeconomic calculation to party political behaviour (in itself a rather dubious exercise); and in particular it involves the analysis of politics from the assumption that all political actors are motivated only by self-interest. Despite the dubious assumptions, however, the argument is an important and a persuasive one. The main point is that within established welfare states all social groups will inevitably press for state support for their needs to be met and that this pressure is likely to be supported by state welfare bureaucrats for whom expanded welfare services mean an expanded power base – and by politicians who can make themselves electorally popular by promising to legislate to meet more and more welfare needs. Thus no-one in the political process has any interest in controlling the expansionary tendencies of state welfare, with the result that it acquires the momentum of a runaway train – with, it is argued, ultimately much the same disastrous consequences for all on board.

State welfare is thus seen by the New Right to be economically distorting, ideologically perverse and politically uncontrollable. It is also, they claim, in any event hopelessly *impractical*. State provision of welfare services assumes that politicians and bureaucrats within the state machinery can be trusted with the provision of welfare services to all. Even if they could be trusted ideologically and politically – and of course the New Right do not believe that they could be – how could they be trusted in practice to know what sort of welfare services different people want or need? In a large and diverse society, they argue, it is simply not possible to know how to meet all social needs. The result of this is: at *best*, that people act themselves to tailor or extend state services through private adaptations; and, at *worst*, that standardised services are provided which meet the real needs of no-one – for instance the council houses all painted alternately with red and green doors.

Nevertheless, although the New Right argue that state welfare is neither desirable nor practical, they are not necessarily prepared to countenance its complete disappearance. Even Hayek envisaged some role for state welfare, primarily as a selective and residual provision for those unable to provide for themselves on the private market, although Friedmann's position was rather different (George and Page, 1995). Most of the more recent New Right theorists have also argued that such a 'safety net' state welfare sector will in reality still be needed – and therefore, presumably, still be desirable. Despite the anti-state rhetoric, the New Right perspective thus remains within the bounds of the mixed economy of welfare, which is found in practice in all modern welfare capitalist countries. New Right ideology might shift the boundary between the state and the market sectors of welfare; but it would retain both.

During the Thatcherite Conservative governments of the 1980s, this limitation of New Right welfare ideology to a shifting of the boundaries of welfare rather than a revolutionary challenge to the state, was demonstrated in practice by the process of political change. Despite some of the recommendations of right-wing think tanks, such as the IEA and the ASI, for the removal of the NHS or the state education system, the Prime Minister and her closest followers had to wrestle with those within the Conservative Party – as well as those outside – who wanted to retain these universal state services. In the end reform was restricted to the restructuring of the management and operation of welfare services and to the more direct encouragement of separate private provision alongside these.

Of course, in a sense this merely reveals in practice our previous point about the importance of the difference between ideological perspectives and real political practices. However, it also reveals that, even within the government of the 1980s, there were other ideological perspectives at play.

Middle Way

The term 'Middle Way' is taken from the title of a book on social and economic policy written in 1938 by the Conservative politician (and later in the 1950s, Prime Minister) Harold Macmillan. It is used by George and Wilding (1994) to refer to a perspective which to some extent spans the political divide between the Conservative, Liberal and Labour parties, and which they referred to in their earlier analysis of ideologies of welfare as *reluctant collectivism* (George and Wilding, 1976). Other Conservative supporters of the Middle Way include the prominent postwar architect of the reform of state education R A B Butler, and more recently Gilmour (1978). All of them were supporters of the positive role of state welfare within advanced capitalist economies, and this of course distanced them significantly from the Neo-Liberals, and later the New Right.

However, the Middle Way is more than just the ideology of the centrist wing of the Conservative Party. Through the views of Butler, in particular, it is associated with the supposed cross-party consensus on the role of state welfare that dominated politics in the period immediately following the Second World War, and is captured in the term *Butskellism*, as we discussed Chapter 1. It is thus the ideological perspective that informed Beveridge and Keynes in their recommendations for social and economic reform, and that formed the basis of postwar policy development. Both Keynes and Beveridge were

Liberals, and this perspective has also therefore been referred to as *Liberal Collectivism*.

The common theme which unites both left and right adherents to the Middle Way, therefore, is their commitment to the collective provision of social services and the planning of economic development, through use of the power and legitimacy of the state. They do not believe that the free market alone can be relied upon to protect all citizens. However, as the phrase reluctant collectivists implies, Middle Way supporters are concerned about the principles of collectivism espoused by socialist perspectives to the left. In particular, they justify the role of collective provision because of the practical benefits that it provides for a market economy, not because of the alternative to this that it might represent. In other words, reluctant collectivists stress the advantages of partnership between state and market rather than the opposition between them that those to the right and left foresee.

This partnership between state and market is based upon the practical benefits that state intervention can provide for the development and growth of a capitalist economy. Keynes envisaged state intervention as a means of ensuring growth and profitability in a market economy and his commitment was to state intervention, rather than merely state planning, as we shall see in Chapter 8. It is also a partnership that is based, however, upon the obligations that the government in a market economy carries to ensure the social protection of all citizens. Thus, where the market cannot provide, the state must (perhaps reluctantly) be moved in. This is predicated upon a holistic vision of social structure and social obligations, captured in the phrase *One Nation*, which was the title adopted by a backbench group of Conservative Middle Way MPs in the 1950s. However, it is not a vision based on only one model of social protection. Middle Way support for a political partnership between the market and the state was also expected to be replicated within welfare provision; as Beveridge himself envisaged, the presumption was that a mixed economy of welfare agencies would continue to operate in which the state would rarely be a monopoly provider.

The Middle Way is thus an ideological perspective forged out of pragmatism rather than principle. Social needs are recognised and acknowledged to be a public responsibility; but so, too, is private investment and economic growth. Middle Way theorists, such as Keynes, argued that both were inextricably interlinked. Economic growth is needed in order to ensure that social needs can continue to be met; but economic growth will not be achieved in a society where social problems and social divisions are permitted to continue unchecked.

It might be argued, albeit with mixed success, that such a pragmatic perspective has dominated policy development in postwar Britain – although it certainly came under threat from the New Right during the Thatcherite governments of the 1980s. A similar picture can also be found in many other European welfare capitalist countries over the same period. In Germany, France, Belgium, the Netherlands and Italy, for example, welfare state protections have been supported, and introduced, within capitalist market economies and have contributed to the continuing growth of these economies – in recent years more successfully than in Britain. Within Europe, too, there has been support for an explicit partnership between state and market and this has attracted political support across the various party systems, which in many cases has been further encouraged by electoral systems that produce more frequent coalition governments.

Indeed, it is probably true to say that the Middle Way is now more widely established in the countries of continental Western Europe, such as those mentioned above, than in Britain. In many cases it is the perspective openly espoused by the dominant political party, notably the Christian Democrats in Germany. Here the Christian Democratic tradition of support for the state, the market and the family within an electoral democracy and a mixed economy, has produced a range of welfare policies that have proved more robust in the face of economic recession than those recently followed in Britain.

Social Democracy

Social Democracy is the main ideological perspective to the left of the Middle Way; and in Britain it is associated with the Fabian tradition on the left of the Labour Party. In many continental European countries, however, parties going explicitly under the title of Social Democrats have frequently constituted the main political opposition to the Christian Democrats, and also have been in government themselves.

There is some debate about whether the Social Democratic perspective can be separated from *democratic socialism*, the term used by George and Wilding in 1994. One distinction may be that democratic socialism implies a commitment to radical socialist change – albeit achieved by democratic means; whereas Social Democracy implies support for existing democratic structures but the use of these to pursue policies that are more interventionist and socially responsible. However, such a distinction is not consistently born out in practice; and, even if there might be potential theoretical disagreement between the two perspectives over *ends*, there is substantial ideological and political consensus across them over *means*.

The common ground that Social Democrats and democratic socialists share here is the pursuit of social justice through the gradual reform of the predominantly capitalist market economy. As the early Fabians openly claimed, all Social Democrats are gradualists rather than revolutionaries; and, although they frequently identify major social problems within capitalist economies, they are committed to using the existing structures of power to seek a resolution, or amelioration, of these problems within immediate social circumstances. For Social Democrats reform is very much a case of bread today rather than jam tomorrow.

The Social Democrat belief in the pursuit of social justice within a capitalist economy, however, is based both on practical politics and moral principles. The *practical politics* is the use of working-class power, both through the industrial muscle of the trades union movement and through the electoral success of the Labour Party (formed by the trades unions), to force the capitalist holders of wealth and control to concede to a redistribution of these privileges, under the implicit threat of otherwise more revolutionary or disruptive social change. Social Democracy in Britain, therefore, has sought a political home in the Labour Party. The *moral principles* are those of fraternity (and more recently sorority) and solidarity, in other words the desirability of mutual support. These principles have also sometimes been linked to Christian values of care and concern for one's fellow man, or woman. Many leading Social Democrats, such as Tawney, have been Christians – although of course many have not.

Perhaps the earliest theoretical exposition of the major themes of Social Democracy can be found in Tawney's (1931) discussion of the *strategy of equality*, in which he argued that social justice could, and should, be pursued within a capitalist economy through the introduction of state welfare services and redistributive tax and benefit policies. Fifteen years later the postwar welfare state reforms could be seen as an attempt by the left-wing Labour government of the period, under the leadership of Attlee, to engage directly in such a strategy. Subsequent criticisms of the achievements of state welfare, in particular in securing greater inequality through the focusing of welfare services onto the less well-off, have cast doubt upon the viability of such a strategy (Le Grand, 1982). However, during the early postwar years, Fabian politicians and academics such as Crosland (1956) and Titmuss (1958) argued that, despite remaining inequalities, the welfare state had resulted in an irreversible transfer of power and resources to the lower classes and had therefore fundamentally altered the character of the social and economic structure of society.

Despite the later criticisms – and the anti-state reforms of the 1980s – there can be little doubt that Crosland and Titmuss were, in part at least, correct in their assessment of the impact of the welfare state. The introduction of universal state provision for health and education and of a, supposedly, comprehensive scheme for social security through social insurance did effectively displace much private market provision in these areas – and of course this is why the New Right have opposed such measures. The universal welfare state is often claimed by Social Democrats as the embodiment of their ideological support for the pursuit of social justice, and they contrast this with the grudging support for more limited state welfare advanced by the Middle Way.

In Britain it is arguable that Social Democratic ideology only achieved any real political influence during the brief period of Labour Party government from 1945–51, although even then by no means all members of the Labour government could be called Social Democrats. However, in some other European countries, notably in Scandinavia, Social Democratic governments have been in power for the major part of the latter half of the twentieth century, and here the gradual transformation of capitalism and the pursuit of a strategy of equality through universal state welfare have been more consistently attempted – and achieved (Baldwin, 1990).

Scandinavian Social Democrat theorists such as Esping-Andersen (1985) and Korpi (1983) have argued openly for the pursuit of a 'democratic road' to socialism through the transformatory politics of state welfare. In countries such as Sweden and Denmark universal state provision has led to more extensive welfare protection and to greater social equality than in other welfare capitalist countries such as Britain. Electoral support for Social Democracy in Scandinavia suggests that such an ideological perspective can in practice be popular; and, even though more centrist governments were elected to power there during the world recession of the 1980s, both Sweden and Denmark returned to Social Democratic governments in the 1990s.

Another Scandinavian theorist, Therborn (see, for example Therborn and Roebroek, 1986), has argued further that, once achieved, the welfare state becomes an irreversible feature of any modern democratic society, both because it is functional for the economy and because the protection that it provides will guarantee its electoral popularity – or rather the popularity of those parties that claim to protect it. This may suggest that the democratic road to socialism is more than just an ideological vision – it is a social fact. Research in Britain has consistently demonstrated the popular support for state welfare services even during periods of right-wing Conservative government (Taylor-Gooby, 1991, Ch. 5).

However, evidence of support for state welfare is not evidence of the superior status of the Social Democratic perspective. Support for state welfare may be shared by Middle Way supporters and by more left-wing socialists. And support for state welfare is no longer unquestioned at the heart of Social Democratic welfare ideology. Indeed, the statism of the early Fabians, such as the Webbs and Tawney, has been criticised by more recent Fabian commentators (Plant, 1988) because of its belief in the scientific inevitability of collectivism and its failure to recognise the importance of the rights and powers of the consumers of welfare services, and the continued desirability of a mixed economy approach to welfare provision.

In the 1990s, arguably, a 'New Fabianism' has arisen out of these criticisms of the statist assumptions of past Social Democracy. New Fabians recognise the importance of consumer and citizenship rights, and partnership between the state, market and other welfare sectors. Le Grand, one of the critics of the achievements of state welfare in the pursuit of social justice, has recently argued for a move towards a new notion of *market socialism* (Le Grand and Estrin, 1989). In its recommendations for social welfare reform published in 1994, the Borrie Commission on Social Justice, established by the then Labour Party leader John Smith after the 1992 election defeat, made a sharp distinction between those it called the *levellers* – the supporters of old-style Social Democratic justice through redistribution, and those it called the *investors* – whom it preferred – who linked social justice to support for, and investment in, economic growth within a market economy. The report of the Borrie Commission (1994) may be evidence of a shift in Social Democratic ideology, to accommodate a continued role for markets in the gradual transition to a more socially just society – although it may also of course be evidence that some of the Social Democratic members of the Commission have merely moved across to the Middle Way. As we said earlier, the boundaries within, and between, these broad ideological perspectives are continually changing; Social Democracy has moved on as other perspectives have influenced its adherents.

Marxism

Opposition to both the inequities of the market and the ineffectiveness of the welfare state has for some time come from the far left of the political perspective and has been voiced by critics who sometimes trace this opposition back to the theoretical analysis of capitalist economies developed in the nineteenth century by Karl Marx (Marx, 1970). Marx's claim was that capitalism was an inherently oppressive economic structure in which the working class were exploited by the capitalist class through the labour market. The conflict to which this oppression gave rise would lead eventually to the overturning of capitalist power and its replacement with a socialist state in which all the people would own all the means of production, and all social needs could therefore be met. Marxists are thus also usually *socialists*. However, some also make a distinction between socialism and *communism*, which is a situation reached after state socialism when all production is in the hands of the people and the need for central state control has 'withered away'.

Socialism, or communism, is argued by Marxists to be the logical, and desirable, alternative to the failures of both capitalist markets and state welfare. However, their visions of socialist society are generally rather utopian and contain no clear view of the route to be taken to achieve such equilibrium and harmony, except for the claim that revolutionary, rather than gradual, social change would be necessary, involving the overthrow of existing democratic governments (which in effect support capital) and the seizure of power by the representatives of the working class.

This is not a political programme that has ever attracted much effective support in Britain or in any other Western European country; thus its political potential here is pretty limited. However, socialist revolution, inspired by Marx, did take place in Russia at the beginning of the twentieth century. Throughout most of the century state socialism, under Communist Party rule, was practised in the USSR (as it became) and, after the Second World War, was extended to the countries of Eastern Europe too.

Despite some of the advances and achievements of state socialism in these countries, the collapse of the Eastern European and Soviet communist regimes at the end of the 1980s, and the exposure of continuing inequalities and hardships within them, cast a deep shadow over the aspirations of the supporters of Marxism. It seemed to many that in the only countries in which revolutionary socialism had been attempted as a solution to the problems of capitalism it had failed. Some supporters of Marxism have of course pointed to the continuation of communist rule in a few other countries, such as China and Cuba – although here, too, serious problems have recently been revealed. Others have suggested that perhaps state socialism was not proper socialism in any case and that without international change to replace capitalism on a global scale it was bound to fail.

Despite such expressions of continued revolutionary optimism, the collapse of Eastern Bloc socialism has severely undermined the appeal and the influence of Marxist perspectives on welfare, because it has appeared to give a lie to their prescriptions for a revolutionary utopia. In contrast to such prescriptive visions, however, much Marxist debate and scholarship has in fact been directed, not so much at making out the case for socialist revolution, as at pointing out the failings and limitations of capitalism in meeting the needs of all citizens. Marx himself, of course, was primarily known for his critical analysis of capitalism, including analysis of early examples of welfare reform such as the factory legislation of the mid nineteenth century, rather than for his ideas on the future of socialism. Many Marxist critics have continued this tradition into the analysis of welfare capitalism – albeit that ultimately their message is a negative one.

In the 1970s Gough and Ginsburg produced cogent critiques of the British welfare state from within a Marxist perspective. Ginsburg (1979) argued that institutions of welfare operated within British society to control and suppress people as well as to provide for them – for instance, arguing that the social security scheme in practice stigmatised benefit claimants and forced them into low-waged employment. Gough's (1979) more extended analysis took this further, pointing out the *dual* character of the welfare state, which –

although it was in part a product of the success of working-class struggle, as the democratic socialists claimed – was also an adaptation of capitalism to meet changed economic and social circumstances. He argued, for example, that state education and health services operated in practice to prepare workers for skilled employment and to keep them healthy for work.

The strength of the Marxist critique of welfare within capitalism is its ability to demonstrate the contradictory nature of social policy as providing at one and the same time both social *protection* and social *control*. Some commentators, such as O'Connor (1973), have referred to these contradictory goals slightly differently as the *accumulation* and *legitimation* functions of welfare. Through its support for the continued operation of the market, welfare permits capital to continue to accumulate; and yet, through its provision of social protection, it also legitimates capitalist power by providing protection for all its citizens. However, in times of crisis – for example during the recession of the 1970s and 80s – these two functions can come into conflict; continued support for accumulation requires cutbacks in the costs of legitimation. Indeed, cuts in welfare spending were introduced in Britain, and in most other welfare capitalist countries, during this period. The welfare state within capitalism is thus not only contradictory – it is also inherently unstable.

This Marxist critique of the development and operation of welfare within capitalist societies is considerably more plausible, and influential, than the appeal to support for a communist revolution; and, as such an influential critique of capitalist welfare, the Marxist perspective has survived despite the collapse of the socialist regimes to which it might have been seen to have allegiance. However, the continuing changes in production processes, class structures and political activity in modern capitalist countries make the legacy of Marx, on which some commentators have claimed to draw, an ever more distant one.

Many such commentators, who continue to point to the contradictory and unstable nature of social and economic policies in welfare capitalist countries, no longer refer to themselves as Marxists. Some, such as Gough (Alcock *et al.*, 1989), have moved towards Social Democracy. Others have even begun to suggest that the perspective must now be called *post-Marxism*. This, they argue, is because the social and economic changes that have divided the workforce and produced a large group of unemployed and marginal workers have rendered the role of the working class in the transformation of capitalism obsolete; as a result of this, they suggest that revolutionary change will therefore take a different form in the future. In particular, it will no longer involve taking the means of production into the hands of the workers but rather will be based upon a postindustrial economy in which work and production are no longer at the centre of material life (Gorz, 1982).

The development of post-Marxism and the reform of former Marxists demonstrates that, despite its links to the past, this perspective, too, is constantly changing and adapting as new ideas develop and as social circumstances change. Marxism may have lost the concrete appeal of Soviet communism to oppose the inequities of capitalism, and it may have had to adapt to the restructuring of labour markets and class allegiances, but its ability to link a critique of the failings of welfare to the development of the structural forces of the capitalist economy retains a powerful ideological appeal. Thus to the left of the Social Democrats, Marxist critics of welfare can still be found (Novak, 1988).

New radicals

One of the consequences of the declining size and influence of the working class in modern societies has been a growing recognition of the existence, and importance, of other social divisions as bases for conflict and political change in society – and of other political and ideological issues beyond the exploitation of the labour market as a focus for critical comment and action. These include, for instance, gender differences and feminist politics, racial conflict and anti-racism, disability awareness and action, environmentalism and green politics and the anti-nuclear movement. Of course social divisions, such as gender and race, are not new sources of ideological and political conflict, even if widespread recognition of their importance has only relatively recently developed (Williams, 1989). Many radical-left Marxists have moved in recent years to embrace these political struggles as well as the more traditional politics of the labour movement and the working class.

For some of these older radicals the embracement of feminism, anti-racism or greenism may indeed be the product of a shift in ideological, or theoretical, awareness to address the more diverse and complex divisions, disadvantages and struggles that have in the past been ignored by radical politics. However, much of the recent development of a critical concern, and activity, over such structures and issues is the result of the growth and development of new political actors and new ideological arguments. In other words, it is not just that some old radicals have recognised that ideological differences extend beyond the right–left (capitalism–working class) continuum; rather – and more importantly – new social movements have grown up around these issues aiming to influence ideological debate and political action from a new perspective. There are many such new political actors and ideological perspectives – although it is the women's movement that provides perhaps the most wide-ranging and important example.

These more diverse ideological perspectives are sometimes referred to as *new social movements* (Williams, 1989) – although, of course, some are newer than others and many are not new at all, except perhaps in the eyes of some commentators. Nevertheless, their greater impact on the political stage and in ideological debate is new; here they have significantly shifted the focus of debate away from the narrow focus on the advantages and disadvantages of capitalism and markets. In this sense, therefore, the impact of these new perspectives is a collective one and there have been attempts to characterise such movements together as constituting a new political force. In the USA this has been referred to as the *Rainbow Alliance*, suggesting the coming together of different colours (or political perspectives) across the spectrum.

However, there are serious political and ideological problems involved in trying to lump together the very different movements and perspectives of feminism, anti-racism, greenism, and others. Where some of these focus on social divisions, the divisions they focus on are very different – and sometimes mutually conflicting – as the disagreements over the allegiances of black women, for example, have demonstrated. What is more, not all movements focus on social divisions – for example green and anti-nuclear politics are responding to very different social and economic forces. There is thus no real common ground across the new social movements, even though some radicals might wish that there were. All that they have in common is that they are not focusing on the capital–labour divide; negative unity does not provide the basis for an ideological perspective – or for political action.

These new social movements are discussed together here, therefore, not out of a misguided belief in their common features, but because the pressures of time and space do not permit adequate discussion of them all separately. George and Wilding's 1994 text on ideologies of welfare makes something of a compromise in containing extended discussion of feminism and greenism; and Williams's (1989) social policy text focuses on feminist and anti-racist critiques of welfare. These are clearly three of the more influential perspectives, though they are not the only important ones. The problem of the failure of past social policy development to recognise the important social divisions of gender and race is an issue to which we shall return in Chapter 11.

Environmental politics presents – potentially at least – an even more fundamental critique of social welfare, for green ideologists argue that current welfare protection is based upon the continuation of forms of economic growth that are unsustainable in the world in the longer term because of their environmental destructiveness. However, this environmental argument is a complex one. For a start, both commentators – and green activists themselves – often make a distinction between different perspectives within environmental politics. In particular, a distinction is made between the reformists (the *light* greens), who argue for change within existing economic structures, and the revolutionaries (the *dark* greens), who argue that only a fundamental transformation of socioeconomic planning can guarantee a long-term future for welfare. Despite these differences, however, the focus of green politics upon sustainable economic policy in order to support viable social policy is now an influential perspective within the discipline (Cahill, 1994).

As we said above, the supporters of these various new perspectives are only united in the sense that they place themselves outside the traditional debates about welfare that focus on the relative values of the state and the market. However, there is a sense in which this broadening of the ideological debate might be seen in itself as a new radicalism because it represents, at least implicitly, a call for a shift away from the old left–right continuum. In a review of political reactions to right-wing criticisms of welfare, Papadakis (1990) talked about these as new radical reformers; and, in a more general discussion of developments in political debate in both Western and Eastern Europe, Keane (1988) emphasised the growing pluralism in political debate that such new perspectives represented. For Keane, this new radicalism is evidence of a shift in ideological debate and political action away from the state–market conflict and into the broader terrain of civil society, where a wider and more plural range of argument would, in the future, have a growing influence on the democratic process.

This is perhaps a rather grand, and abstract, vision of the impact of these new ideological perspectives on welfare; but it reminds us that the previously rather narrow focus of debate on the four main ideological perspectives that we outlined above has severely restricted both academic study and the political process. Ideologies of welfare embrace a wide range of divisions, differences and debates; and while, as we said earlier, some perspectives clearly are more important and influential than others, the importance of these does not mean the exclusion of others. More pertinently perhaps as a final point, it is worth emphasising that, as the content of various ideologies is constantly changing, so too is their power and influence. This power and influence, however, depends not just on the theoretical debate and development of ideas but on the social, political and economic context in which these ideas operate – and it is to these changing external contexts that we move next.

8

Economic Development

The economic context

The study of social policy in Britain has traditionally focused on the development and structure of welfare services. In the case of the social administration approach this meant a fairly narrow concern with the operation and effectiveness of current social policy initiatives. More recently, social policy has been more broadly conceived and has paid attention to the wider issues of the ideologies and theories that have shaped the welfare policies and the political context in which these have developed. However, welfare policies are not just the product of a particular political or ideological context, they are also affected by the economic forces that govern the development of the society within which they are located. Indeed, because they determine the resources that are available to meet all individual and social needs, it is arguable that economic forces are the *most* important factor influencing both the size and scope of all social policy.

At a simple level at least, this is certainly true. Welfare services cost money to deliver and, therefore, economic circumstances of individuals and groups can dictate who pays for welfare and how much they pay – a question to which we shall return in more detail in Chapter 12. At a more complex level, however, social policy development is also closely dependent upon the economic structure of a society and upon the economic growth within it. Changes in such economic structure or economic growth can have a direct impact upon social policy. For instance, the declining economic growth and changes in economic structure in Britain in the 1970s and 80s resulted in significant shifts in social policy development and, in particular, in major cutbacks in many welfare services, as we shall return to discuss in a little more detail below.

However, it is not just the case that economic changes effect the development of social policy. In modern welfare capitalist societies social policies effect economic forces too. For instance, as we have seen, social security policies can maintain a reserve labour force during periods of low employment which is then ready to be re-employed when circumstances improve, and they can even operate to encourage employment through the subsidisation of wages for low-paid employees. Policies for education and training can equip, or re-equip, the workforce with the skills that they need to develop and implement new productive processes. In effect, in modern societies social and economic policies are inextricably intertwined, with changes in one area inevitably leading to changes in the other.

An understanding of social policy thus requires an understanding of the economic policy context in which social policies develop and of the interrelationship between changes in economic and social policy. The study of economic policy is a vast and complex field, however, with its own theories, concepts and literature. To understand economic policy fully, therefore, we would first need to come to grips with the basic theories and concepts of economics – an enterprise that is well beyond the scope of this introductory book. Students of social policy frequently do study economics as part of the broader social science framework in which social policy is situated, and for those who wish to pursue a more detailed introduction to the field there are some useful basic texts (Huhne, 1990; Curwen, 1992; Gamble, 1992). However, in order to provide a brief guide to the interrelationship between social and economic policy development, we shall discuss here some of the major trends in economic policy that have influenced the study of social policy in Britain, and elsewhere, in recent years, for these trends constitute a crucial feature of the context within which social policy has been constructed.

The early Fabian proponents of social policy in Britain at the beginning of the twentieth century argued that social policy was needed in order to counteract some of the undesirable consequences of economic development. In particular, they argued that the capitalist economic system, which was dominant in Britain, had resulted in the creation of significant social problems, most importantly high levels of poverty, and that social policy intervention was required by government in order to restructure socioeconomic conditions in ways that would eliminate or prevent these problems – for example in order to redistribute resources from wealthy capitalists to poor workers (or would-be workers).

As we have seen, therefore, the social policies that have been developed in Britain have been constructed within a capitalist economy, in order to mitigate some of the effects of the operation of capitalist economic forces. The consequences of such changes, however, have been to transform that capitalist economy, in particular through the introduction of an enhanced role for the collective actions of the state in exercising some control and organisation over both production and distribution. In effect the crude (and cruel) capitalist forces, which were criticised by Fabians, have been supplemented, and in part replaced, by public provision and public ownership. This has led politicians and commentators to argue that Britain no longer has a capitalist economy but rather has a mixed economy, in which private capital plays only a partial role – albeit in practice a dominating one.

Whether we conceive of Britain as a capitalist or a mixed economy, however, our understanding of the economic context that this economy provides for the development of social policy requires an examination of the basic structures of capitalist economic systems and the processes by which these have developed, and have been changed and adapted. We need to look briefly, therefore, at the recent history of capitalist economic development in Britain; and through this we will examine some of the major concepts and theories of economic policy that have been influential in this development.

Capitalism

We can trace the growth of capitalism back over at least two hundred years of British history, although, in practice, its roots extend back much further than that as the earlier feudal system was gradually transformed into an economic system based upon monetary exchange and the market mechanism. Writing over two hundred years ago Adam Smith was one of the earliest, and most well-known, economic proponents of capitalism (Smith, 1776). His argument was that the market mechanism was the proper way in which society should be ordered because it ensured that goods and services would be produced and distributed in the most efficient and effective manner. In simple terms this was because of the impartial operation of the laws of supply and demand. Goods and services would be produced and sold on the market, and consumers would go to the market to purchase what they needed or desired. Because consumers would only purchase what they wanted at a price that they could afford, only those producers who were supplying such needs would be able to sell their products. Inefficient, or undesirable, production would thus be driven out of business and the market would produce a stable balance between the forces of supply and demand.

This is a persuasive model – in theory; however, economists quickly discovered that in practice such a comfortable balance was difficult to achieve as production processes changed and consumers' purchasing power fluctuated. Even its theoretical explanation of capitalist development was questioned in the nineteenth century by Karl Marx, who produced a far-reaching and highly influential critique of the basic structure of the capitalist economy (Marx, 1970).

Marx's argument was that the basic structure of the capitalist economy was not the market mechanism of supply and demand but the wage–labour arrangement for the production of goods and services. This arrangement was founded upon the structural exploitation of the worker, who was paid less by the capitalist than the exchange (or market) value of the goods he or she produced, with the surplus value (or profit) being pocketed by the capitalist or reinvested through accumulation in further capitalist production, which would produce yet further profit. Therefore the capitalist, however morally righteous he or she might be, was inevitably motivated by the pursuit of profit for further production, with the result that the productive forces of capitalism were driven forward through the exploitation of the working class.

This process of the development of productive forces resulted in a growth in the range and scope of the production of goods and services; but it also, Marx suggested, led to an inevitable, and structural, conflict between the worker and the capitalist – or more generally between the representatives of the working class and the representatives of the capitalist class. Capitalists would pursue higher profits and workers would pursue higher wages; conflict between the two would be endemic. This conflict could lead to adjustments to profits or to wages as struggles were won or lost, or compromises reached; but the cause of conflict would always remain. Capitalism was not therefore, according to Marx, a stable economic order, but rather a fundamentally unstable one and eventually, he predicted, it would collapse and be replaced by a more stable order – socialism.

However, in over two hundred years of capitalist economic development in Britain there has been no fundamental collapse, or replacement, of capitalism with socialism. Indeed, where socialist economic systems have been introduced in Eastern Europe and the Soviet states, these have now collapsed and capitalist market economies have been reintroduced. Thus, although Marx's explanation of the driving force behind capitalist development (and of the inevitable conflicts that this produces) may have been a convincing one, his conclusions about its fundamental instability seem to have proved to be unfounded.

Perhaps the reason why the conflicts generated by capitalist development have not led to its demise is because they have led instead to its transformation. Working-class demands for higher wages (and later for legal regulation and social protection of conditions of work) have, in part at least, been successful in securing changes in the private market economic order of capitalism. As we have already discussed, the development of social policy and welfare services have displaced private markets largely, or entirely, in the provision of some important goods and services – hence the reference to a mixed economy. Another phrase which is used to describe this mixture of private production and public welfare is *welfare capitalism* – and more recently still commentators have begun to refer to such societies as *social market economies*.

This does not mean that the exploitation, and resulting conflict, which Marx argued characterised capitalist society, has been removed – clearly exploitation and conflict both remain, as low wages and industrial disputes continue to demonstrate. However, the exploitation and the conflicts are more fractured and more complex than a basic head-on battle between the capitalists and the working class.

- Exploitation is fractured – some workers earn good wages and work in good conditions, and also many workers produce no direct profit for their employer; not all exploitation at work is wage based, as those engaged in unpaid caring work often experience.
- Conflicts are complex – workers may be in conflict with each other (the two trades unions in the 1980s miners' dispute) or

with the state (teachers' and nurses' disputes over changing work practices); conflicts may be based on consumers' interests (tenants' action) or even general economic policy issues ('poll tax' demonstrations in the 1990s).

Thus social policy developments have transformed capitalist society; they have also as a consequence transformed the nature of the problems and the conflicts within it. Indeed, conflicts now occur over the impact of social policy itself. Although welfare capitalism may have mitigated some economic problems, it has not removed such problems altogether.

However, British capitalism has also changed in other ways. In the early part of the twentieth century British economic policy was largely a matter of national development – albeit that this national development relied in practice on the exploitation of a large empire. At the end of the century economic development in Britain is very largely determined by international forces within a global capital economy. Production processes are owned or controlled by worldwide corporations; goods and services are produced and marketed on an international level. In Britain economic growth and development, and economic problems and conflicts, are no longer a national affair. This has been further accentuated by Britain's membership of the European Union. As we shall discuss in more detail in Chapter 9, the EU operates a single market for production and distribution throughout its member states; economic policy planning within the Union is increasingly taken on at a supranational level.

The British capitalist economy is no longer, therefore, based on the simple process of capitalist ownership and workers' exploitation described by Marx, nor on the simple market of supply and demand advanced by Adam Smith. It is no longer exclusively *capitalist* and it is no longer only *British*.

However, it is still in large part a market economy, and one in which capitalist investment by major private corporations is a significant determinant of economic growth. Furthermore, economic growth remains a crucial factor in securing improvements in standards for both capitalists and workers and in providing the resources for the social policy developments that seek to mitigate the market's harshest effects. All major economic commentators, and certainly all important political actors, are now agreed that it is the prospects for economic growth within Britain's complex and fractured economy which are the major focus of economic policy concern – and thus, indirectly, they are the major concern of social policy too. The need to secure growth has become at least as important as the question of what to do with the fruits of it.

Classical economics

Policy based on classical economics drew on the relatively simple model of the capitalist market economy outlined by early economists such as Adam Smith. Classical economists believed that economic growth was the product of the free operation of market forces within society. Freedom did not imply anarchy of course; there was a role for the state within society to provide a secure context in which the market could operate. Thus the government had a responsibility to protect property, through law and contract, and to provide security, through policing and national defence. Beyond this, however, the laws of supply and demand would determine investment, production and distribution, and therefore also prices and wages. Efficient producers of desirable products would survive and others would have to adapt or disappear; this was a process in which government could not, and should not, interfere.

This was referred to at the time as the *laissez-faire* approach – leave alone. In the late twentieth century New Right, or neo-liberal, economists have called for a return to the policies of *laissez-faire*, because of their claims that the interventionist measures pursued earlier in the century, which we shall discuss shortly, had failed to secure growth. Neo-liberal economists such as Hayek (1944) and Friedman (1962) argued for a return to the classical economic policies of the (supposedly) free market, through the removal of government controls over investment, credit and employment relations, with the claim that this would restore the equilibrium of the market forces of supply and demand, and reproduce the capitalist economic growth that Britain had enjoyed in the nineteenth century.

It is debatable, as we shall see, how far the classical prescriptions for economic policy of the neo-liberals were taken up in practice by government in the late twentieth century, for there were many prominent economists and politicians who doubted both the desirability and the feasibility of a return to free market forces in the complex economy which Britain has by this time become. However, their assumption that the free markets of the nineteenth century had, in any event, produced sustained and non-problematic economic growth was almost certainly flawed.

In nineteenth-century Britain capitalist production certainly grew in scope and scale but at a heavy cost in terms of low wages, poor conditions and frequently high levels of unemployment for the majority of the population. At the end of the century, when the British economy was arguably at its most powerful, the early social policy researchers, Booth (1889) and Rowntree (1901), found high levels of acute poverty – even in London, the capital city of the British Empire. In fact much of British economic growth, in particular towards the end of the nineteenth century, was based upon exploitation of the materials and markets that the empire provided. Despite this, however, growth had not continued uninterrupted; for example in the 1870s the economy had experienced a major slump, leading to high levels of unemployment and threats of social unrest.

The poverty and social unrest that Britain's capitalist economy had produced in the nineteenth century were part of the pressure for social policy reform articulated by the Fabians, and orchestrated by the labour movement, in the early twentieth century. At the beginning of the century the Boer War and First World War revealed the need for the state to move in to guarantee that the working-class recruits to the army were fit and healthy and to ensure that the production processes were geared up to meet national military needs. This resulted in some abandonment of the strict principles of *laissez-faire* and the involvement of the state in social and economic planning. After the First World War, in the 1920s and 30s, the country again experienced a period of deep economic depression, which by now was a world-wide phenomenon. Poverty and unemployment again rose dramatically, as Rowntree discovered in a repeat of his 1901 study of York (Rowntree, 1941). In the face of declining economic performance, therefore, the new social policies had failed to protect a large proportion of the population from deprivation and suffering.

The depression of the 1930s was seen by many social policy reformers as powerful evidence of the failure of the capitalist economy to provide adequately for the whole of the population. Beveridge's (1942) proposals for social security reform, which followed the depression, were intended to ensure that never again would economic change result in such social hardship. It was also evidence to economists of the failure of the *laissez-faire* approach of classical economics to secure sustainable economic growth. Pressure for a change towards a more interventionist economic policy therefore began to develop. This was given greater impetus by the experience of 'total war' during the Second World War, during which government control over production and distribution throughout the economy in Britain and over relations with allied trading partners was essential to the success of the war effort.

Keynesianism

The welfare state reforms of the postwar period, associated in particular with the recommendations of Beveridge in his 1942 report, were the social policy response to the deprivations of the depression. At the same time as this change in the direction of social policy, however, the postwar period also saw a change in the direction of economic policy in Britain, associated with the economic policy recommendations of Beveridge's colleague Keynes. Indeed, the economic and social reforms of the period have sometimes been referred to as the establishment of the Keynes/Beveridge welfare state (Cutler *et al.*, 1986).

Keynes was an economic advisor to the wartime government and, although he himself died in 1946, his ideas dominated government economic policy in the two decades following the war. His recommendations had been formulated during the depression of the 1930s (Keynes, 1936) and were based upon a belief that government could, and should, intervene in economic markets, in particular to ensure that full employment was maintained. That full employment was a goal of both economic and social policy was a matter on which Keynes and Beveridge were firmly in agreement. Full employment was essential to Beveridge's recommendations for social security and family support – albeit that this was restricted to men's labour market participation; it was also the cornerstone of Keynes's prescriptions for future economic growth. Full male employment therefore became the main social and economic policy priority of the immediate postwar period.

Full employment was to be achieved, according to Keynes, by ensuring that growth was sustained in manufacturing production; and, as the depression had demonstrated, this could not be guaranteed by the free market alone. Classical economists had assumed that in a market economy supply would necessarily encourage demand – people would see goods and would want to buy them. In a depression, of course, many people could see goods that they wanted – but they were unable to afford to buy them. However, if they could be given the resources to buy the goods, they would do so – thus stimulating further production of these goods. This would lead to increased resources for those employed in the production of the goods, who themselves could then buy more goods, so stimulating yet more production elsewhere. In other words, Keynes argued that increased demand could *stimulate* supply and thus lead to economic growth.

This virtuous circle of increased demand leading to increased production is called by Keynesian economists the *multiplier effect*. The investment of an additional fixed sum of money into the economy will lead to further production, further spending and further investment that cumulatively will be of much greater value than the initial sum invested. Economists even claim that the growth potential of any particular investment can be calculated from the workings of this multiplier effect, thus giving economic planners a clear idea of how much to invest to secure any particular level of improved growth. Not surprisingly, advice along these lines would be likely to be warmly welcomed by governments, especially those promising to improve economic and social circumstances in the short term.

Keynes also argued that the means of securing such additional investment was in the hands of the government which, in times of reduced demand and supply, could afford to borrow money in order to increase government spending on public works and services, in the secure knowledge that the multiplier effect of this would be to stimulate economic growth from which the borrowed money could later be recouped and repaid. Such a period is called a *deflationary gap*, and at such times governments should increase spending or cut taxes to invest in economic growth. When full employment is achieved, however, continued growth in demand could lead to inflation (if more goods cannot be produced, prices go up – a problem to which we shall return shortly). This is called an *inflationary gap*, and at such times, Keynesians argue, governments should cut spending or increase taxes to reduce demand.

Through the application of Keynesian economic principles, therefore, it appeared that governments could control and manage economic growth through public spending and investment in the economy. This provided a great boost to the interventionist social and economic tendencies of the postwar Butskellite governments – and of course a great boost to the profession of economists. Economic advisers were now much valued by government for the guidance they could provide on how to manipulate the economy. Mathematically constructed economic models could be used to simulate the performance of national economies and the effects of different economic policy measures could be estimated in advance. The Treasury began to use such a model to calculate the effects of government spending in Britain. This economic modelling is called *econometrics*. It is a complex, and to the non-mathematically minded, daunting 'science'; but in Britain, and in other postwar advanced economies, it became more important than the political ideologies of different parties in determining major economic policy decisions – further increasing the already overpowering influence of the Treasury on policy planning.

Throughout the 1950s and 60s British governments of both political parties pursued Keynesian approaches to economic management of the economy, mirroring the political consensus that seemed also to exist in social policy over the central role of the welfare state. Indeed, state welfare spending and Keynesian economics went hand in hand, with the one naturally supporting the other. Their success seemed to confirm the view that capitalism could be transformed from within through economic and social policy reform, with politicians such as Crosland (1956) claiming that capitalism had been replaced by a new 'classless society' in which all could benefit. In 1959 the Conservative Prime Minister, Harold Macmillan, entered the election campaign claiming that the British people had 'never had it so good'.

Certainly during the first two decades after the war Keynesian economic policies did appear to be successful. Britain was experiencing one of its longest periods of sustained economic growth, wages levels were rising in value and employment levels were so high that immigrants were encouraged to come from the old imperial colonies to fill gaps in the labour market. However, in practice, the government's management of the economy fluctuated from deflationary gaps to inflationary gaps, characterised by what commentators called *stop/go* policies on spending and taxation. No attempt was made to control the rises in incomes and prices that resulted from the increased industrial power that full employment gave to organised workers in manufacturing industry.

Furthermore, in spite of the consensus on welfare, there were also problems within the mutual interdependence of social and economic policy planning. In social policy terms it was argued by critics such as Titmuss (1956) and Townsend (Abel-Smith and Townsend, 1965) that, despite improved incomes and public services, not everyone was benefiting equally from the protections of the welfare state, and indeed some were still living in poverty. Economists talked about this as the trade-off between *efficiency* and *equity* – an issue which we shall return to discuss in Chapter 12. Efficiency could be achieved by economic growth if all were better off, so that no-one's gain meant somebody else's loss. However, equity required ensuring that all needs for protection were met and this might require some redistribution of resources to those who were poor, with consequent losses for the better-off. Keynesianism appeared to assume that greater efficiency would also lead to more equity but, as continuing inequalities revealed, this might not necessarily be the case.

The collapse of Keynesianism

During the euphoria of the long postwar boom, however, these contradictions within the Keynesian approach appeared to be minor issues when compared to the overall success of sustained economic growth in Britain – but there were also other problems with this sustained growth. By this time Britain's economy was already part of a broader world capitalist economic order; and throughout this global economy economic growth was universally high. Indeed, by international standards, the growth rate within the British economy was fairly slow. Furthermore, throughout the 1950s and 60s Britain was excluded from the new international economic block in Western Europe, the European Economic Community (EEC – now the EU), which the country was not able to join until 1972. The mutual benefits that the early members of the EEC were able to secure for each other were, therefore, not automatically shared with Britain.

The international context of postwar economic policy, however, extended beyond the EEC and the general growth in international trade. Economic planning was also now undertaken at an international level by the advanced industrial nations, in particular through the organisation of the International Monetary Fund (IMF), a kind of collective international bank. In 1944 the IMF had established an agreement under which all member countries would guarantee to maintain the exchange rate value of their currencies at a particular level in relation to the US Dollar, called the *Bretton Woods* agreement. Confident of their powerful economic position in the world, the British government fixed the Pound at a relatively high level within the Bretton Woods scheme and thus were committed to maintaining this level, despite Britain's relatively slow rate of economic growth in the international arena.

The high value of the Pound internationally meant that British exports were relatively expensive for foreign buyers. It also conversely meant that imported goods were relatively cheap in Britain. These two factors together did not act positively to boost British manufacturing performance. In the mid 1960s, when the world economic boom was itself beginning to slow down, this poor performance began to be revealed in new economic problems in Britain.

The most obvious problem to flow from decreased exports and increased imports is a reduction in the *balance of payments* – that is the overall surplus, or deficit, shown in Britain's trading with other nations within the world economy. A deficit in the balance of payments can be sustained for a short period – obviously not every trader can make a profit all the time. However, a sustained reduction in the balance is evidence of poor economic performance and thus a decline in the relative international economic standing of a nation's economy. This would be likely to reduce international confidence in such an economy and make it more difficult for the government to maintain the high level of the currency within the exchange rate agreement. In the mid 1960s this applied to Britain and was revealed in international pressure on the value of the Pound.

However, balance of payments reductions do not just lead to difficulties at an international level; they are manifested in economic problems at home too. Lower exports and higher imports can lead to a decline in manufacturing activity and this can lead to the creation and growth of unemployment. They can also lead to inflation, as British manufacturers seek to off-set the loss of foreign sales by increased prices for goods sold at home. *Inflation* is a complex economic problem – and a much disputed one. In simple terms it means that the prices of goods and services, as measured by a national aggregation of the prices of a sample of major items (called the *Retail Price Index* – RPI), is rising faster than the production of them. This rise in prices leads to workers demanding higher wages to pay for the more expensive goods and services. However, if wage rises are conceded, these result in yet further price increases to meet the higher wages – leading to a spiral of rising prices and wages. Once such an inflationary spiral has taken hold, the government is brought under pressure to print more money to meet the demand for higher prices and wages. This additional money (unlike the public spending investment foreseen by Keynes) does not contribute to increased demand and supply but rather is soaked up in meeting the higher prices of existing goods, simply adding to the amount of money circulating in the economy without any increase in production or economic growth.

Such inflation, with rises in prices and wages running ahead of economic growth, had not been foreseen as a significant problem by the early Keynesian economists, who assumed that full employment and economic growth would ensure an equilibrium between prices and wages because increases in wages would inevitably flow from improved economic activity. Thus Keynesian economic policy focused upon using state intervention in the economy in order to secure full employment rather than to control inflation. However, in the mid 1960s Britain's balance of payments problems and declining international confidence were threatening this single-minded focus on the need for demand-led growth to boost manufacturing employment.

Britain's problems were serious enough at this time to encourage the Labour government to seek international financial aid from the IMF. However, the IMF were only prepared to provide this on condition that Britain devalued the Pound within the Bretton Woods exchange rate agreement, in recognition that the British economic performance could no longer justify sustaining it at the previous high level. Following IMF pressure, therefore, the government agreed to devalue the Pound; but they also hoped that the devaluation would help restore a positive balance of payments in the country by in effect reducing the cost of British exports abroad and raising the price of foreign imports in Britain, thus stimulating home production.

There was some evidence that this did temporarily improve Britain's international performance in the 1960s. Unfortunately it was a relatively minor step taken at a time when international economic forces were in any event reducing demand, and thus production, on a broad global scale. What is more, if such a devaluation had not succeeded in boosting economic growth in Britain, it could have run the risk instead of adding to economic problems. If cheaper exports had not increased the volume of sales, manufacturers might have been tempted to put up prices at home to recoup their losses. This, together with increased prices for imports, could have put pressure on workers to demand higher wages to meet these higher prices, resulting yet again in an inflationary spiral.

There is in essence, therefore, an inevitable danger that attempts to stimulate demand in a stagnant or declining economic situation will result in rising inflation rather than improved economic growth. In Britain by the early 1970s this is just what was beginning to happen, as unemployment and inflation were both rising and as on a world-wide scale the long postwar boom began to come to an end. Changes in economic policy thus began to take place as a result of this. The Conservative government of 1970–4 removed the Pound from the fixed exchange rate (Bretton Woods) agreement and allowed it to 'float' on the international currency market. This meant that the government was no longer committed to retaining it at a particular level; but it also meant that loss of international confidence in Britain could lead to a decline in the value of the currency that the government would no longer be able to resist.

However, Britain's international position was expected to be strengthened at this time by the decision to join the EEC in 1972, when the original six members finally agreed to an extension of the community. It was hoped that this would boost Britain's trade with its partner members – although of course it also opened up British markets more directly to penetration from Europe.

In the early 1970s the government also made the first direct moves to control prices and incomes in order to reduce inflation – moving the focus of economic policy away from concentration solely on the creation and maintenance of full employment. However, the statutory controls on prices and incomes introduced by the Conservative government were not popular – especially with the trades unions – and they led to significant industrial unrest, including a miners' strike that reduced British industry to working a three-day week as a result of power shortages. At the same time economic growth failed to pick up, with the result that the government decided once again to try to stimulate demand through Keynesian-style measures including tax cuts and an increase in public and private borrowing – sometimes referred to, after the Chancellor of the time, as the 'Barber Boom'.

Even if such reflation had been a judicious policy response to Britain's growing economic problems, it was in effect too little too late – and it was probably born more of political desperation than clear economic planning. Reflation did not prevent the growth in unemployment, which by now had passed the one million mark; and it also contributed to rapidly rising inflation, which by 1975 had reached over 26 per cent a year (in other words, at the end of the year prices were 26 per cent higher than they had been at the beginning of it). As if this were not enough, Britain's problems were further compounded – as indeed were those of all other industrial economies – by the massive increase in the price of oil introduced by the Organisation of Petroleum Exporting Countries (OPEC) in 1973. Oil was by the 1970s the world's major fuel for economic production and between 1972 and 1974 its price rose fourfold.

The oil price rise was a symbolic moment in the ending of the international economic boom that had followed the Second World War. In Britain, where problems were worse than in some other countries, it pushed the economy rapidly into recession, or as the economists of the time called it *stagflation* – high inflation in a stagnant economy. In the face of this, Keynesian demand management appeared to be impotent and the debate began for a shift in the focus of economic policy.

Monetarism

Throughout the period of the postwar boom the social and economic policies of the Keynes/Beveridge welfare state had appeared to be successful in securing both economic growth and social protection in Britain; and the picture was the same in most other welfare capitalist countries. In this period welfare spending grew in cash terms but it also grew significantly as a proportion of *Gross Domestic Product* (GDP). GDP and GNP (*Gross National Product*) are general measures of the activity of a national economy. They are an attempt to count together all goods and services produced *in* the country (GDP) or, in the case of GNP, including also those produced *abroad*. In a growing economy, therefore, GDP, or GNP, would be increasing each year.

In such an economy a growth in public expenditure may not be problematic – as the economy grows so we can afford better public services, and the taxes used to pay for these can be afforded relatively easily out of the improved profits and wages that growth brings. Nevertheless, a growth in the *proportion* of public expenditure suggests a change in the balance of activity within the country – more resources are going into welfare services than into industrial development. This again may not be a problem, especially in a growing economy. For example, much of the growth in public expenditure in the 1960s and early 1970s was the result of the growing numbers of public employees in welfare services, where employment increased by about a third. This helped to maintain high employment levels as well as stimulating demand through the purchasing power that these workers brought into the economy more generally.

In a declining economy, however, growth in public expenditure is more problematic. Growing levels of expenditure still have to be financed out of increased taxation and now this will compete with private investment or private consumption within a restricted overall economic climate. This may make taxes, and thus spending, less popular but, more seriously in economic terms, it may also compound economic recession by reducing investment in industrial production and curtailing consumer spending – and thus the demand for goods.

It is just such problems that new critics of Keynesian economic management began to suggest were the source of Britain's declining economic performance in the mid 1970s. Right-wing critics such as Bacon and Eltis (1976) in their book, *Britain's Economic Problem: Too Few Producers*, argued that growing public expenditure was crowding out private investment in the economy. The reduced size and scope of private manufacturing ('too few producers') thus led to economic decline, which was compounded if, at such a time, public expenditure and public employment continued to grow as a proportion of GDP.

Growing public expenditure can, of course, be financed by increased taxation – although as we have suggested this might at such times become unpopular; or it could be financed by government borrowing. Governments can borrow, against the expectation of future growth or future tax revenue; the level of this borrowing is referred to as the *Public Sector Borrowing Requirement* (PSBR). Keynesian economic management assumed that government borrowing would be needed in order to finance demand-led economic stimulation, with the borrowing being repaid, or at least reduced, once economic growth increased performance and thus raised the revenue from taxation. In the early 1970s the PSBR was rising as a proportion of GDP. However, economic growth did not now follow; and the new critics of Keynesianism pointed out that, instead of solving economic problems, the rising PSBR was contributing to them, because the growing amount of money available in the economy that resulted from it merely added to the pressures on inflation.

The conclusion that these critics were drawn to was that, at times of recession, it was not possible to stimulate economic growth through demand management, fuelled by public expenditure; and further that, if this were attempted, it would result only in growing inflation, which would make matters worse. To counteract Britain's accelerating economic decline, therefore, an alternative approach was required. This meant abandoning the policy commitment to full employment, that in any event had failed in practice, and seeking instead to control inflation in order to stabilise the economic climate and provide more security and encouragement for private investment – from which it was assumed growth would follow. Controlling inflation meant controlling the money supply and a move from Keynesianism to *monetarism* as the central plank of economic policy planning.

Monetarism was the economic policy favoured by the New Right critics of Keynesian economics, such as Friedman (1962). The 'failure' of Keynesianism appeared to confirm their views on the incompatibility of expensive welfare and an interventionist state within a market economy; in monetarism they saw a strategic means of reducing state expenditure and intervention and restoring the private market. The *narrow* goal of monetarism, therefore, was the control of inflation. This was to be achieved by restricting the supply of money within the economy, so counteracting the tendency for prices and wages to rise. The main factor leading to an increased money supply in the 1970s, it was argued, was government borrowing, as expressed in the PSBR. Thus the PSBR had to be reduced and, in order to do this, public spending would have to be cut. The *broader* goal of monetarism, however, especially for the New Right, was the general reduction of state expenditure, especially welfare expenditure, that otherwise seemed set to rise inexorably as yet more needs and demands for social protection were pressed on government.

A shift to monetarism in economic policy was not, therefore, merely a reaction to the limitations of Keynesianism in times of recession. It was a wholesale rejection of the Keynes/Beveridge welfare state partnership of social spending and demand-led economic growth. Thus the results of such a change in economic policy also had serious implications for the future development of social policy.

Of course the Labour government of the late 1970s, although it was faced with the most serious recession in the British economy since the 1930s, was not the natural political ally of New Right monetarism, and was reluctant to accept readily the anti-welfare message that monetarist economist critics espoused. Labour's first commitment, therefore, was to seek to control price and wage inflation by more direct means. Legislating against such increases had proved politically disastrous for the Conservative government in the early 1970s and so, through its partnership with the trades unions, Labour sought to secure voluntary wage restraint. The agreement on restraint was contained in a *social contract* between the government and the trades unions, in which, in return for reduced wage demands by the unions the government would introduce employment protection legislation and other social measures.

In fact this social contract approach to wage and price restraint was not a new phenomenon outside Britain. In a number of European countries, especially in Sweden and some of the other Scandinavian countries, such *corporatist* economic planning between government, trades unions *and* representatives of industry had been a feature of economic policy throughout much of the postwar period. In some of these countries this centralised bargaining had resulted in greater wage and price restraint in times of growth and recession – although usually also in a context of greater wage equality and improved welfare services. It had also secured both greater public protection and lower rates of inflation. The corporatist approach is sometimes credited, therefore, with having prevented countries such as Sweden from experiencing the worst effects of international recession in the 1970s and 80s – and certainly throughout that period levels of both inflation and unemployment remained much lower in Sweden than in Britain, although these problems have begun to develop there in the 1990s.

In Britain in the 1970s, however, the corporatist remedy was both economically too late and politically too weak. Here PSBR and balance of payments problems were so great in the mid 1970s that the government had to turn once again to the IMF for assistance. And once again the assistance granted by the IMF was tied to

required policy changes. In particular, they wanted the British
government to implement monetarist controls over the escalating
money supply and, consequently, to reduce public expenditure.
Perhaps reluctantly, therefore, the Labour government of the 1970s
was converted to monetarism, as Prime Minister James Callaghan
explained to the Party Conference in 1976,

> We used to think that you could just spend your way out of a recession
> and increase employment by cutting taxes and boosting government
> spending. I tell you in all candour, that option no longer exists...
> (Callaghan, 1987, p. 426).

In fact the Labour government of the 1970s did not whole-
heartedly embrace monetarism. It did not reduce the overall extent
of public spending but rather prevented its further projected
expansion, mainly by cutbacks in a few areas such as housing and
education balanced by continued expansion in others such as social
security and health; and it continued to press ahead with voluntary
control to reduce inflation through the 'social contract'. To some
extent these policies were successful, for inflation did start to fall
after 1976, although the world-wide recession within which Britain
was then operating meant that stimulating economic growth was not
so easy to achieve.

However, the ability of the government to sustain its voluntary pay
and prices policy was subject to significant political challenge at the
end of the decade as many trades unions, especially those representing
public sector workers, rejected the social contract and went on strike
for higher wages. The public sector strikes of 1978 and 1979, which
halted many public services in local authorities and hospitals, were
dubbed the 'Winter of Discontent' by media critics; and they
undoubtedly lost the government much political support. In the
election which followed in 1979 the Labour Party was defeated, and a
new Conservative government, under the leadership of Margaret
Thatcher, was elected to power. Thatcher was an outspoken supporter
of the policy prescriptions of the New Right and was much more
willing than Labour had been to embrace the recommendations of
the monetarists – and to reject Keynesianism.

In the early 1980s, therefore, the shift in economic policy away
from Keynesianism became both more determined and more far-
reaching; and it was accompanied by changes in social policy too.

The Thatcherite wing of the Conservative Party was closer to the welfare ideology of the New Right than to the Middle Way collectivism that had characterised previous administrations. Thus restrictions in overextensive state welfare provision were viewed as desirable goals in themselves and not merely as the necessary consequences of stricter economic policy.

Stricter economic policy was, however, pursued in the early 1980s, with monetarist controls aimed at reducing inflation now identified as the major feature of policy planning. In fact inflation rose immediately after the Conservative election victory, partly because of a concession to the public sector wage demands and a shift from direct to indirect taxation resulting in a big increase in Value Added Tax (VAT) – which together pushed up both wages and prices. After this inflation did fall significantly, reaching a low of 3.7 per cent in 1983 (Peden, 1985, p. 215).

However, the economic growth that was supposed to follow from the shift towards financial constraint and freedom for the private market did not materialise. In the early 1980s the international recession was generally getting worse rather than better, in particular as a result of another OPEC oil price increase in 1979. By the 1980s, of course, Britain was itself an oil producing and exporting nation and this did begin to provide much needed revenue for the country. Yet, despite it, the balance of payments began to decline dramatically, with manufacturing exports being particularly hard hit. Manufacturing industry in Britain experienced its worst ever period of decline during the early 1980s, with the effects of international recession being compounded by the government's policy of privatisation and the withdrawal of public support for industry, aimed ostensibly at restoring private incentives within a free market. The effect of this was a shift into the red in the balance of trade in manufactured goods between Britain and the rest of the world by the mid 1980s, and a catastrophic decline in manufacturing employment and output, especially in the heavy staple industries such as steel and coal.

Thus in the 1980s, although inflation declined, unemployment rose to two, and then three, million, with many of those leaving (or seeking to enter) the labour market facing the prospect of never securing permanent employment again. This of course created pressure on government expenditure on social security to support the new army of unemployed and, ironically, despite the espoused aims of government, public spending continued to grow – and in particular grew as a proportion of a now declining GDP (Peden, 1985, p. 225).

In the face of international recession, therefore, it appeared that – even if it was able to control inflation – monetarism, too, was unable to deliver economic growth. In fact, the ability of government to pursue an effective monetarist policy was proving to be much more difficult than some of its anti-Keynesian supporters had initially supposed. Monetarism required exercising control over the supply of money in the economy. This immediately raised the problem of deciding, or defining, what the supply of money was – and different definitions were in existence. A narrow definition (M1) included only those notes and coins in circulation in the country; but the government of the 1980s preferred to use a broader definition (M3) that also included all money held in deposit in banks and savings accounts.

However, even *calculating* the value of M3 was inevitably a problematic exercise – and *controlling* it proved to be much more difficult; especially as the main lever over which the government supposedly did have control, public expenditure, was continuing to rise. The financial planning targets for control of the money supply in the early 1980s were thus continually revised; and, in the mid 1980s, they were finally abandoned. With the British economy deeper than ever in recession in the early 1980s, it was easy to conclude that the monetarist strategy for growth had rather rapidly failed.

Supply-side strategy

Despite the rhetoric of financial control and the very real desire of the Thatcher governments of the early and mid 1980s to curtail public expenditure, at least on welfare services, their commitment to monetarism was in practice always rather faltering, and by 1985 had been officially abandoned. The government had been forced to face the reality that without economic growth, financial stringency was barely achievable and in any event was of debatable value. Thus the priority became the need to stimulate economic growth. With her strong New Right leanings Thatcher was unlikely to look to a return to Keynesianism in order to achieve this and, perhaps fortunately, evidence from a newly resurgent USA economy in the mid 1980s suggested that this might not in any case be necessary.

Implicit in New Right thinking was the plea for a return to the free market of classical economics that critics such as Friedman

(1962) argued had been progressively destroyed by Keynesian interventionism and welfare-state social protection. If economic growth was to be restored, the argument ran, freedom must be returned to the market. This twentieth-century *laissez-faire* is sometimes referred to as *neo-classical* economics but, following the terminology and the policy developments pursued along these lines by the Reagan administration in the USA in the 1980s, it was also called a *supply-side strategy.*

Supply-side economics, as the name suggests, implies something of a reversal of the demand-led strategies for growth proposed by Keynes. Demand-led strategies required government manipulation of the economy in order to stimulate growth – this was now referred to as *macro* management and it was argued to be ineffective. Instead, the neo-classical economists argued, governments should withdraw from all macro management and restrict public intervention in economic development to *micro* level strategies to respond only to particularly serious problems or blockages. Thus the Keynes/Beveridge control and protections should, as far as possible, be removed to restore the incentives to private capitalist investors to produce new goods and services in the expectation of making a profit. Incentives for profits would therefore stimulate supply, and increased supply would lead to a growth in employment, and thus greater demand, which would stimulate yet further production for supply – a virtuous circle operating in reverse of the direction put forward by Keynes.

The withdrawal from macro management, however, included more than just the limited privatisation and cuts in subsidies pursued by the Thatcher governments in the early 1980s. It required a removal of controls over the movement and investment of capital, the freeing up of financial markets, the withdrawal of restrictions on credit, the repeal of protections and regulations governing employment conditions and wage levels, the reduction in the rights and powers of trades unions, the privatisation of state assets and (perhaps most importantly) the cutting of taxation levels. Critics and supporters referred to this as 'rolling back the boundaries of the state'; and, of course, it had implications for social, as well as economic, policy as significant cuts were implied in welfare services such as housing, education and social security benefits.

The development of micro level interventions as a new role for government economic policy was perhaps less significant than the withdrawal from macro management in supply-side economics; but they included a new role for the Department of Trade and Industry in acting as technical advisor and assistant to private industry and for the Department of Employment in providing targeted training and advice to vulnerable groups among the unemployed. The idea was that government should respond to the needs of the market rather than the other way round.

By the mid 1980s, moreover, it appeared that the supply-side measures that had worked previously in the USA were also being successful in restoring growth to the British economy. British GDP began to grow, reaching an average of four per cent growth a year in the mid to late 1980s. As a result, although public expenditure itself continued to rise, it began to decline as a proportion of GDP after 1982–3. Unemployment, although still high by previous standards, also began to fall as new jobs were created, especially in the rapidly expanding service sector, which included such things as banks, insurance, communication technology, catering and leisure.

In fact the growth in the British economy was so rapid in the late 1980s, even by international standards, that government supporters began to heap praise upon the 'economic miracle' that the shift in policy direction had secured. At the height of the boom in 1988, after the Conservative Party's third election victory, the Chancellor, Nigel Lawson, continued the supply-side stimulation with wide-ranging tax cuts, especially for the wealthy from whom the higher rates of income tax were removed. Neo-classical economics appeared to have proved, finally, that Keynes was wrong after all.

Economic and social policy

Despite its apparent success there were serious problems, and indeed contradictions, at the heart of the supply-side boom in the British economy in the late 1980s. For a start, as we have mentioned, public expenditure growth had not been contained, even though it was no longer growing more rapidly than the economy itself. Furthermore, even this limited growth was being artificially restricted by the high revenue now being received from the sale of North Sea oil and by the receipts that the government was able to secure from its major privatisations of government monopolies in such things as gas, electricity and water supply. In this context tax cuts could be sustained as long as the economy continued to grow rapidly; but if it did not the PSBR would be bound to rise again.

In addition, although unemployment was falling, it still remained well above two million and the government continued to accept no responsibility for seeking to reduce it further if the market itself was unable to do so. Unemployment also was increasingly unevenly distributed throughout the country, with the highest levels being found in the still declining industrial areas in central and northern England and Scotland. This was because manufacturing industry was still producing much less than it had been in the 1970s or 1960s – and, even where production levels were increasing, this was usually a result of improved machinery or methods rather than a larger workforce. Much of the growth of jobs, therefore, was in the service sector and was concentrated in the southeast of England. Although some of these jobs were well paid and highly skilled, many were menial tasks undertaken for very low pay in restaurants or shops and were increasingly available only on a part-time and/or a temporary basis. Both socially and geographically, therefore, the economic trends of the 1980s had produced only partial success with greater divisions within British society; growing affluence for some being mirrored by growing poverty and inequality for others.

Britain's 1980s boom was not only partial, however; it was also very fragile. Increased supply of goods and services had been met by increased demand. But the growth in demand had been very rapid, and in practice much of it had been fuelled by the private credit that was now much more widely available as a result of deregulation. Furthermore, this increased demand did not entirely support increased production at home. Partly because of the poor condition of British manufacturing industry, and partly because of the wider international market in which Britain was now forced to operate anyway, increased demand led, as it had done before, to a major increase in imports. The result of this was a continuing, and growing, balance of payments deficit, which was made worse by the tax cut stimulation of the economy in 1988.

Ironically, the real problem was that the British economy was growing too rapidly and, in an international context, with a balance of payments deficit, this could not be sustained. The evidence for this non-sustainability was growing international pressure on the value of the Pound, which was of course now floating on the international currency markets; although, in the 1980s, the policy of the government had been to keep its value as close as possible to that of the strongest European currency – the Deutschmark. In the late

1980s the government formed the view that something had to be done to control economic growth; and, since the major motor for this was the rise in private credit, the interest rates for the cost of borrowing money were significantly increased.

As a result of these pressures the pace of change in British economic policy in the early 1990s was quite swift, in particular because the massive boom of the late 1980s was coming rapidly to an end. The increased cost of borrowing due to high interest rates halted the rise in credit (although in any event this could never have been sustained indefinitely); this led to a major reduction in demand. This reduction was made worse, temporarily, when the government joined the EU's exchange rate mechanism (ERM) which *required* it to guarantee the value of the Pound against other European currencies (in effect still primarily the Deutschmark) at a level which British economic performance did not justify.

This resulted in further interest rate rises, which further deflated demand; and in the end the pressure became too great. Following a shift of policy across the space of eight hours in one day Britain withdrew from the ERM and the Pound was floated once again. After this interest rates were reduced, in the hope of stimulating demand once again – but without much success, especially as, in order to minimise the growing PSBR, the government (despite its continued rhetoric to the contrary) was forced to raise taxation levels, primarily through increased indirect taxes such as VAT.

Thus the boom of the 1980s was followed by a sharp recession in the 1990s, when GDP again declined, the PSBR grew and unemployment once more passed three million. While, however, it had been manufacturing workers in the Midlands and North who had lost their jobs in the 1980s recession, it was the service workers in the South who became redundant in the 1990s as the expansion in these jobs proved to be rather short term. Therefore, while many of those those who remained in employment continued to enjoy relatively high standards of living, the social and economic divisions in society continued to grow. If the recession of the 1970s had proved Keynes wrong, and that we could not *spend* our way out of a recession, the recession of the 1990s seemed to prove that neo-classical economics was also flawed, and that we could not *borrow* our way out of one either.

In fact the major lesson to be learnt from the economic policy changes of the 1970s, 80s and 90s is that Britain had by then become a part of a much bigger, and more powerful, European and world market, over which the British government, no matter what policies it adopted, could have only limited impact. In this world market, too, this was a period of rapid and far-reaching change. International economists talk of a transformation here from *Fordism* to *post-Fordism*, by which is meant a decline in the importance of the mass-production manufacturing process (associated with Ford Motor company who developed the first mass-produced automobile) and a growth in the development of small businesses and specialist manufacturers producing small-volume goods for particular market needs.

The effect of these changes, it is argued, is a decline in manufacturing employment, especially in the older industrial countries, and an increase in specialist production methods that might result in employment which is part-time or temporary. These changes in manufacturing are accompanied by the growth of employment in the service sectors in all welfare capitalist countries. However, this employment is often low skilled and low paid and, where accompanied by deregulation of labour markets, leaves these workers with fewer rights and protections than had been enjoyed by the workers engaged in mass production in the past.

This restructuring of both investment and employment has resulted in instability on a global scale, and has been one of the major causes of the series of recessions that affected most industrial economies over the last quarter of the twentieth century. In the face of these recessions most governments have had to adjust economic policy planning and, in particular, to cut back on planned growth in state expenditure and social protection. Seen in this context, therefore, the changes experienced in Britain are but one example – albeit in practice a rather extreme one – of a more general international drift in economic and social policy.

However, this international context does not absolve the British governments from responsibility for the economic and social consequences of these major changes – much though they often seem to claim that it does. Such economic trends could, and arguably should, be identified and even predicted by government. And, if so, then measures could be taken early to minimise (at least) their most deleterious consequences. However, when faced with the changing international economic order of the late twentieth century, British economic policy appears to have lurched rather rapidly – and unsuccessfully – from one 'miracle cure' to another.

For our purposes here, of course, the most significant consequence of the rapid changes in policy that have characterised British economic development throughout recent years is the context that they have provided for social policy – and clearly the changes in this context have been significant and far reaching. The abandonment of the Keynes/Beveridge partnership between expanding social provision and demand-led economic growth in the 1970s resulted both in a growth in the need for social protection (in particular as unemployment increased) and in a reduction in the commitment by the state to expand public expenditure to meet this. In order to meet monetary targets or to stimulate private investment, public expenditure was thus systematically pared back from previous projected levels based on demand for services. Yet, at the same time, demand for services grew because of the polarisation in society resulting from the economic changes that were taking place.

The close partnership between economic and social policy espoused by Beveridge and Keynes has been replaced by an increasing disparity between economic goals and social protection. Rather than social protection helping to secure economic growth, social policy has become seen as a drain on limited economic resources. While economic growth was still pursued in the 1980s and 90s, social policy was at the same time reduced to more of a 'casualty' role – aimed at meeting only the most serious of social needs within a more divided and unequal social structure.

Whether we judge these changes positively or negatively, their significance for the longer-term prospects for social policy development cannot be understated. What is clear from this brief overview, therefore, is that the changing economic context in which Britain finds itself provides a powerful structuring influence over social policy development in the country. In the latter part of the twentieth century, as economic growth has faltered and economic policy has changed, this has resulted in retrenchment and retreat in social policy planning.

9

Europe and the European Union

The international context

The primary focus of this book is on social policy in the United Kingdom. Most social policies affecting the lives of UK residents have been developed within the country on a national basis by the British government, or at a local level by other agencies or authorities with devolved powers from national government; and by and large social policy has been studied and analysed at a national level. As we have already discussed, however, in both economic and social terms Britain is no longer, if it ever was, an isolated national social entity.

The lives of the British population are affected by international social and economic forces; and the ability of the British government to develop policies to respond to these forces is constrained by our relations with other nations – both politically and economically. Furthermore, the policies that are pursued by the British government are likely to be informed by the knowledge and experience of policy developments in other countries. We are not only affected by the actions of our international friends and neighbours; we can also learn from them. Thus social policy in Britain, like economic policy, has an international context – and overall this context is a broad and far-reaching one.

Policy development in Britain was influenced significantly in the past by the country's role as an imperial power. The growth and decline of the British Empire gave policy development in the country an international dimension from the nineteenth century onwards. After the empire was disbanded, the Commonwealth countries continued to maintain close contacts with Britain, so that policy developments in each were influenced by ideas from the others. This is particularly true of the predominantly white, English speaking nations such as Australia and New Zealand, which share much of a common policy framework with the UK, and from which policy initiatives have been adapted for implementation in Britain – for example, as we have seen in Chapter 2, the child support provisions in Australia were closely examined by British politicians before similar measures were introduced here in the early 1990s.

Britain has also had a particularly close relationship with the oldest, and most powerful, of its English speaking ex-colonies, the United States of America. The political ties between these two countries have always been strong, cemented by USA support for Britain in the two world wars; and economic trade with the USA has had a major impact on the British economy. Social policy development in Britain has also been much influenced by ideas and strategies developed in the USA. Urban policies for social and economic regeneration in the 1960s and 70s were modelled closely on initiatives that had been developed first in cities in the USA; and in the 1980s both economic and social policy advisors from the USA were given powerful and influential positions within the government, and a number of USA policy ideas were replicated in an adapted form in the UK.

Despite the close relationships and shared language between Britain and the USA, and the other former British colonies, British social and economic development has also been deeply influenced by relationships with our closer geographical neighbours in Europe. Although Europe has many different languages and has in the twentieth century (and before) been divided and devastated by war, the geographical proximity and shared cultural heritage of Europe mean that it has provided a crucially important international context for policy development in the UK. In the latter part of the twentieth century this context has taken on a much more far-reaching significance and a much sharper organisational form with the creation and expansion of the European Community (EC) and now the European Union (EU).

Social policy in Europe

Following the reconstruction after the end of the Second World War the major nations of continental Western Europe decided to join together to share and to plan economic development; and since then they have been joined by many of the other Western European nations, including Britain. What started out as a community of nations sharing economic planning has developed into a single European market for goods and services, capital and labour, with a European legislature and a massive bureaucracy responsible for a wide range of international initiatives. In the 1990s the pace of European integration has been growing ever faster with commitments made, on paper at least, to develop a European currency and ultimately a political union.

Not surprisingly, therefore, Britain's membership of the EU has had an ever increasing impact on economic and social policy – and of course on political debate and the political process within the country. It is now no longer possible to study social policy in Britain without some understanding of the structure of the broader European Union of which the country is a part, and of the impact of this structure (and the policies it has developed) on the policy process here.

The first point to be made about the impact of European social policy within Britain, however, is the rather different notion of social policy itself that is common in many of our European neighbours. As we discussed in Chapter 2, social policy debate in Britain has tended to focus on welfare services, such as education, health, housing, social security and social care and, in particular, on the provision of these services by the state. In other European countries the balance of state, private and voluntary sector provision of these services varies quite significantly, so that social policy study of them has often taken quite a different form from the statist social administration tradition of the UK.

More importantly perhaps, the different structural contexts of different European states has meant that what is understood as social policy has sometimes encompassed a wider range of issues than just welfare services, including employment relations and employment rights, family structure and family support, industrial training, health and safety, and other activities that clearly are policy driven and do affect the lives of all people, but have not been subject to policy analysis, or in some cases even policy planning, in Britain. Thus, when we examine the impact of the European context on the study and development of social policy in Britain, we must recognise first the very different scope that our basic concepts have on the broader European stage.

Despite the differences over the scale and scope of social policy within Europe, there are some important similarities in the development of welfare policies, and indeed 'welfare states', within the countries of Western Europe – in large part because of the similar, and shared, industrial history of all these nations. Although Britain was the world's leading industrial power in the nineteenth century, all the other European nations went through a process of industrialisation, and resultant imperialism, in much the same way and at much the same time as Britain. Similarly, as in the twentieth century welfare measures have been introduced to reform the basic capitalist industrial economy in Britain, so welfare reform has also been developed by our European neighbours. Partly as a result of this shared history, many features of the welfare reform of capitalism in the different European countries have similar aims and structures.

As we saw in Chapter 1, this common development is sometimes referred to by commentators as the *convergence* thesis of comparative welfare development and it might be taken to suggest that, ultimately, all EU nations will share a similar structure of welfare provision. However, these similarities should not be overemphasised, and trends towards uniformity within European welfare need to be contrasted with the *divergence* thesis, in which the differences between welfare regimes are also emphasised. Despite the similarities that exist, therefore, there are also significant differences between the welfare measures that have been introduced in the different European countries, some of which are in effect mutually contradictory. These make any simple convergence of European welfare into one supranational system unlikely – at least in the foreseeable future.

Obviously, in a general sense, both theses are true – there are similarities between welfare provisions in different European countries; but none are identical and all have been shaped, in part, by peculiar national characteristics. However, it is possible to make some sense of these similarities and differences for the purposes of both comparison and possible convergence. In particular, we can identify some general trends that explain why some groups of countries are more closely comparable than others, and how these groups have emerged.

Focusing on perhaps the most important feature of welfare policy – social security and the prevention of poverty – commentators in the past have differentiated between the *Beveridge* and *Bismarck* traditions of policy development within Europe. The Beveridge tradition is obviously that associated with the Beveridge Report on social insurance, and its aim of providing comprehensive national insurance protection for all citizens. Beveridge's recommendations informed policy development in Britain after the Second World War but they are also sometimes credited with informing the universal approach to welfare followed at much the same time in the Scandinavian countries. The Bismarck tradition goes back further to the German Chancellor, Bismarck, who was responsible for introducing social security protection in that country in the late nineteenth century. The German scheme was based on insurance, too, but protection under this scheme was limited to those within the labour market, with no intention to seek to provide universally for all; this more limited form of protection was also followed in other continental European countries.

The traditional distinction between the Beveridge and Bismarck welfare states, however, is a rather oversimplistic one and, for instance, does little justice to the significant differences that have developed between Scandinavian and British welfare provision, with the former being much more comprehensive in scope and structure. As we mentioned in Chapter 1, the work of Esping-Andersen (1990) has resulted in a number of recent advances in the comparative study of welfare provision – in particular through his notion of welfare regimes, which he describes as clusters of welfare states identified as sharing broadly similar characteristics in welfare history and policy.

Esping-Andersen distinguished, as we saw, between three major welfare regimes (the corporatist, the liberal and the social democratic) which, he argued, were exemplified by Germany, the USA and Sweden, respectively. Esping-Andersen's threefold typology has since been refined and developed by other social policy theorists, such as Leibfried (1993), to suggest that there may in fact be more than three different types of welfare regime. Leibfried argued, for example, that four regimes existed within the EU in the 1990s, which he referred to as the Bismarck, Anglo-Saxon, Scandinavian and Latin rim welfare states.

- *Bismarck* – The Bismarck welfare states are those that have closely followed the labour-market-based, corporatist tradition begun in Germany in the late nineteenth century. Welfare protection in such regimes is often closely linked to participation in the labour market with social security protection aiming mainly to preserve income levels for (past) workers, linked to an expectation that the family and other informal and voluntary sector agencies will provide protection for others, although there is generally universal provision for education and health. The type of protection provided thus can vary significantly between different groups, although overall state expenditure on welfare is relatively high. The original six EEC nations all have Bismarck-style welfare regimes, which may partly account for their early willingness to establish such a close partnership within Europe.

- *Anglo-Saxon* – The Anglo-Saxon welfare state is obviously associated with Britain, and with its English-speaking former colonies outside Europe. It is based on the Beveridge model of equal insurance protection for all, together with universal provision for education and health. However, there are also limitations on Anglo-Saxon welfare, with state benefit protection only available after a strict test of availability for work within the private labour market. Anglo-Saxon regimes have also tended to develop extensive means-tested provision, because of the inadequate coverage of insurance protection, and to permit widespread development of private welfare provision. Thus the welfare mix between state, private and other sectors is very different from that in the Bismarck countries.

- *Scandinavian* – At the same time that Britain joined the EEC in 1972 so, too, did Denmark, the only one of the Scandinavian countries to do so at the time, although in the 1990s both Sweden and Finland have joined. In Scandinavia the welfare mix is different once again, with the state sector heavily dominant. Scandinavian welfare states are the most comprehensive and universal in their protection, with state benefits and services generally going by right to all citizens and with the state acting as a major employer committed to maintaining full employment within the society. As result of such universal coverage in Scandinavia, welfare expenditure is higher in these countries than anywhere else.

- *Latin rim* – Quite the reverse is true of Leibfried's fourth group, the Latin rim countries. When Greece, Spain and Portugal joined the EC in the 1980s welfare expenditure in these countries constituted a smaller proportion of GDP than was the case in the older member states; yet at the same time levels of poverty and deprivation were much higher (Atkinson, 1991). In these countries the development of state welfare protection is at a fairly rudimentary level. Agriculture is still a dominant feature of the economy and labour-market-based protection is undeveloped.

Universal state provision is limited and there is heavy reliance upon informal and voluntary sector provision, in particular through the organised church. Since joining the EU, however, state protection and social insurance have been extended in these countries and welfare provision appears to be moving towards a more institutional basis, as found in northern Europe.

Leibfried's fourfold typology was restricted to welfare regimes within the EU. However, difference, and change, in welfare provision is also experienced elsewhere in Europe, especially in the Eastern European countries with *former communist* regimes. Many of these nations are subject to rapid social and economic transformation and some are now looking for EU membership – although it is not currently on offer. In effect they constitute yet another European welfare regime, which may at some time influence EU convergence or divergence. Here, formerly universal socialist provision, based on low-wage full employment within a planned economy, is challenged by the marketisation of the economy (Deacon *et al.*, 1992). Old forms of social protection are frequently no longer available here – or are ineffective; yet it is not always entirely clear what new forms will replace them, especially as the relative lack of a voluntary, or non-state, sector makes implementing the kind of welfare mix found in many Western European countries difficult.

One of the original aims, or at least ideals, of the founder nations of the EC was the eventual *harmonisation* of welfare provision within a single European model, perhaps as a precursor to a *federal* European state that could plan social and economic policy across the existing member nations. This is still the hope of some EU members but, as the wider range of welfare regimes now included within the Union reveals, it has become a more and more distant goal as the Union has expanded and diversified.

Furthermore, the hope that there would be a gradual convergence towards the corporatist, labour-market and family-based protection of the northwestern continental regimes now seems to be contradicted in particular by recent moves towards a more liberal or residual regime in Britain, and by fears in Denmark that their more comprehensive and universal welfare state should not be watered down by European pluralism. It is perhaps significant that in both Britain and Denmark there was considerable public opposition to the ratification of the Maastricht Treaty, which we shall discuss below, and the move to the European Union in 1994 – although in both countries ratification was eventually secured.

In the immediate term, therefore, the goal of harmonisation has been replaced by a policy of *concertation*. This is a more limited commitment by EU member states to the development of shared, or European-wide, social policy initiatives around particular issues of international importance or in areas where standardisation of practices will ensure fair competition between nations within a single economic market.

Again, the expectation of some here is that the gradual extension of concertation initiatives will introduce a wider range of common practices within the Union, which themselves will begin to reduce the policy barriers between the member states, paving the way for more comprehensive, or federal, supranational planning in the future. For the less willing federalists, however, this tendency is contradicted by another recent commitment to subsidiarity within Europe.

Subsidiarity is based on the German practice of seeking to devolve decision making and initiative taking to the smallest possible local base, thus encouraging participatory activity rather than top-down state paternalism. This strategy is supposedly now being replicated throughout the EU. However, it is largely understood by some member states (notably Britain) to mean that policy decisions taken by national governments are preferable to international directives from the EU Commission, which in effect means that federalist tendencies can be resisted at a national level.

Despite the resistance from reluctant federalist nations such as Britain, the longer-term tendencies towards European-wide planning and harmonisation of welfare regimes are clear to see. The history of the EC and EU is one of growing breadth and depth of supranational cooperation and planning. This tendency has been gathering pace as the Community has expanded – as the move from Community to Union has symbolised. It is a pressure which is almost certainly irresistible, in particular as economic development becomes ever more internationalised. Harmonisation might at the moment be off the European agenda but convergence is still the predominant driving force.

The development of the European Union

The history of the European Union is primarily a story of the gradual development of European cooperation from the limited goals of the original six members in securing some shared economic regeneration after the ravages of the Second World War, to the federalist ideals of a European superstate that would be the world's most powerful economic block – and most progressive social regime – at the beginning of the twenty-first century. This is a process during which the European Economic Community (EEC), as it was first called, has expanded in size and at the same time has increased the extent and depth of its activities and aspirations.

The expansion in size has seen the Union grow from six nations to twelve, and now to fifteen (see below) – with the pace of expansion becoming ever more rapid and the future possibility of further extension into Eastern Europe still under discussion.

- *1957* France, West Germany, Italy, Belgium, the Netherlands, Luxembourg
- *1973* UK, Ireland, Denmark
- *1981* Greece
- *1986* Spain, Portugal
- *1995* Austria, Sweden, Finland (Norway voted not to join)

Before the EEC proper was established by the *Treaty of Rome*, signed by the original six members in 1957, the same countries had already entered on limited joint economic planning to deal with socioeconomic consequences of industrial change in the form of the European Coal and Steel Community, which followed the *Treaty of Paris* of 1951. The Treaty of Rome, however, established a much more extensive base for joint economic development. There was a total of 248 articles in the treaty covering a wide range of matters of shared concern or commitment. Most, however, focused on economic policy, with only twelve (nos. 117–28) devoted to social policy (Hantrais, 1995, Ch. 1).

The Treaty of Rome began what can be categorised as the *first* phase of development of social policy within the EC/EU. This period ran from 1957 to 1972 and was characterised largely by a concentration on the promotion and regulation of movement between labour markets within the new community. At this time such social policy activity as existed was closely tied to the broader aims of economic development within the six member states with no specific social goals being pursued – hence the focus on labour mobility.

The *second* phase of development from 1973 to 1984, following the first expansion of the Community, saw a more extensive concern with employment-related social rights across the member nations. There were attempts to harmonise and upgrade basic employment rights, for example in the areas of equal pay and equal treatment for men and women. This period also saw the implementation of the Community's first social action programme which was begun in 1974. Although it was outside the formal treaty commitments, this had the political support of all members and resulted in a number of important new community-wide initiatives, such as the European Social Fund (ESF) and the First Poverty Programme (which we shall discuss below) and the establishment of community agencies to monitor and develop social issues, such as the European Foundation for the Improvement of Living and Working Conditions, established in Dublin in 1975.

The *third* phase of development, following the accession of Frenchman, Jacques Delors, to the Presidency of the Commission, ran from 1985 to 1992. Delors is credited with developing a social dimension to supplement the focus on economic development that had always dominated the EC – or *l'espace sociale*, as it was called in French. So at the same time as economic planning was drawing closer together – notably through the commitment of most nations to a European exchange-rate agreement (the European Monetary System, EMS) – social commitments to workers' rights were also placed on the EC agenda and the range of scope of Community-wide social programmes and initiatives was expanded.

In 1985 high-level talks on socioeconomic issues were held at Val Duchesse in Belgium and, following this, new legislation, the Single European Act, was signed by all countries in 1986. The Act emphasised a commitment by the Community to social cohesion as a corollary to economic cohesion, and European activities in the social field were considerably expanded, for example through a major strengthening of the ESF. The idea of social rights for citizens within the Community was taken further in 1989 by the *Community Charter of the Fundamental Social Rights of Workers* (the 'Social Charter').

The idea of a European Social Charter had in fact been initiated as early as 1961 when a charter of such rights was signed by thirteen members of the *Council of Europe*. The focus of the Council of Europe charter was primarily on rights at work (Brewster and Teague, 1989, p. 10); and this employment-based approach was also the major thrust of the EC charter of 1969 (Grahl and Teague, 1990, p. 211). It echoed the continuing domination of economic concerns over social issues within the Community and the fact that the labour-market focus remained the major focus of social policy in the most powerful nations of continental Western Europe. Like the Council of Europe Charter, the EC Charter was not legally binding on members; however, at Strasbourg in 1989, it was adopted by all member states, with the exception of the UK, and has sometimes since been referred to as the *social dimension* of the Single European Act.

The 1980s also saw a much increased use of EC structural funds and community-wide initiatives, such as the poverty programmes, to secure social policy goals and, in particular, to attempt to mitigate some of the deleterious consequences of the economic restructuring that were now being experienced on an increasingly widespread basis throughout the Community. Knowledge about these social changes was also a much more important feature of the EC agenda, not least because of the increased activity of Community agencies such as the statistical office, the Dublin Foundation and some of the newly established *Observatories* examining issues such as ageing and social exclusion – for these EC-wide agencies began to provide the Community with more extensive and detailed information about social and economic trends both within and across member states.

However, concern with social and economic trends within the community became even more significant in the *fourth* phase of development, which began after the creation of the Single European Market in 1992 and continued with the signing of the *Maastricht Treaty* on European Union that year. The creation of the single market was the logical conclusion of the plans for economic cooper-ation that had begun in 1951. All trade and tariff barriers between member states were removed; goods, labour and capital can now move freely from one country to another. For employers and employees, therefore, national boundaries within the Union no longer have any significance.

This move towards economic union prompted the member states, in 1992, to aim further for monetary union, social union and, ultimately, political union – a federal United States of Europe. Such a strategy was debated at the Maastricht Summit, which preceded the treaty in 1991; but there was not universal agreement on it. In particular, the UK expressed strong opposition to the idea of a federal superstate. Eventually it secured an arrangement which permitted Britain to opt out of the creation of a single European currency, and to opt out of the *Social Chapter*, which through a separate Protocol to the treaty committed the member states to implementing the Social Charter (Hantrais, 1995, p. 11).

Despite this, there was opposition in the British Parliament to the ratification of the Maastricht Treaty. There was also opposition in some other countries too, with two referenda in Denmark (the first producing a narrow majority to reject the treaty) and only a narrow majority voting in favour in a referendum in France. Nevertheless, the treaty was eventually ratified by all, and was symbolised by the terminological shift from European Community to European Union. Since then three more nations have been accepted for membership of the Union on the terms of the treaty. Although the UK opt-out from the Social Charter and monetary union still exists, it is debatable whether it will eventually be acted upon, especially if there is a change of government in the country – a point to which we shall return later. In the fourth phase, therefore, the shift from economic cooperation to social and political union has become complete; it is no longer possible to examine the economic or social policy of member states outside the broader policy framework of the EU.

The institutions of the European Union

Because the EU, and the EC which preceded it, is constituted by the coming together of initially separate member states, it is still predominantly run – or 'governed' – by the representatives of the member governments. The forum for the meeting of these representatives is the *Council of Ministers* (which meets in Brussels) consisting of the relevant ministers, depending on the business in hand, from each country. The heads of government also meet twice a year to take major policy decisions. The presidency of the Council rotates on a six-monthly basis between all the member states, providing an opportunity for all the different influences to be brought to bear at different times.

The Council determines policy for the Union, based primarily on the proposals made by the European *Commission,* which in effect operates as a kind of civil service for the Council. The Commission is also based in Brussels and comprises a vast administrative network, headed up by permanent Commissioners appointed by each member state, and a President, who from 1985 to 1995 was Jacques Delors and is now Jacques Santer, a Belgian. The Commission initiates and implements EU legislation, which is approved by the Council. An early example of this process in the social policy field was the approval by the Council of Commission of recommendations for *directives* on equal pay and equal treatment between men and women in the 1970s. These then became binding on member governments, forcing some, such as the UK, to alter legislation in their countries to bring it into line with the directive.

The vast administrative machinery of the Commission is divided into a number of departments, or Directorate Generals (DG), with responsibility for different aspects of EU policy development and implementation, the main one in the social policy area being DG V which is responsible for employment, industrial relations and social affairs. The Commission has also established a number of other bodies operating to develop, implement or monitor policy on a community-wide basis. These include the EU statistical service (*Eurostat*), the research *Observatories* comprising academic representatives from all member states (such as the Observatory on National Family Policies) and various European *Centres* (such as the one for the Development of Vocational Training [CEDEFOP] in Berlin).

If the Commission is the EU's civil service, then the *European Court of Justice* (which sits in Luxembourg) is its judiciary, acting as the guardian of the treaties and the enforcer of legislation and directives. The court is controlled by judges appointed for six-year terms of office and it operates as an autonomous legal system over and above the legal systems of the different countries. All citizens, and member states, can use the court; and, if the court finds a country to be acting in breach of treaty commitments, that country must change its legislation to comply – as happened in the UK to equal pay legislation in the 1970s.

In terms of constitutional theory, therefore, we might expect that the *European Parliament* (sitting in Strasbourg) would be the legislative body of the EU – especially as since 1979 its 518 members have been directly elected by all EU citizens. However, the member governments have not ceded any real political power to the European Parliament and continue to exercise control through the Council of

Ministers. In practice, therefore, no new legislation can be initiated in Strasbourg. Nevertheless, the Parliament does have something of a blocking power, by refusing to support a Commission proposal, and it can require the Commission to answer questions or supply information. Furthermore, as the Union develops, it seems likely that the powers of the Parliament will expand.

The other major EU institution is the *Economic and Social Committee*, which comprises direct representatives of employers, workers and other interest groups throughout the community. Like the Parliament, the Committee has no power to initiate legislative change but it does provide a forum for consultation and representation on a range of social and economic issues, including, for example the ESF and the Social Charter. In effect, the Committee has something of a 'watchdog' role situated within the complex set of institutional checks and balances which seek to ensure that policy making within the EU follows the wishes and interests of a broad spectrum of the population across the community.

European social programmes

As the EU has developed from economic cooperation to social partnership, and ultimately perhaps political union, the concern of the Council of Ministers, and more especially the Commission, has focused increasingly upon the European-wide consequences of the economic development that the Union has fostered. In particular this concern has been directed towards the deleterious social consequences of economic development and the inequitable distribution of these consequences throughout the different member nations. What is more, the development of European Centres and Observatories to examine these social trends has created internal pressure within the Commission to act to redress some of the worst and most pressing of these developments; this in turn has resulted in proposals being brought before the Council for action at a European level. The result of this pressure has been the establishment of an increasingly expensive and far-reaching set of community-wide social policy initiatives, or programmes, designed to counter – or at least to alleviate – the growing social problems that have been recognised.

The main initiatives used to counteract the consequences of social and economic restructuring have been the *European Structural*

Funds. There were initially three separate structural funds (Teague, 1989, Ch. 3):

- the *European Social Fund* (ESF) for employment and training initiatives
- the *European Regional Development Fund* (ERDF) to improve infrastructure in depressed regions
- the *European Agricultural Guidance and Guarantee Fund* (FEOGA) to assist in rural change and development.

However, after the Single European Act, these separate funds were extended and integrated in order to maximise their impact within member states. In effect the funds now operate as one general programme for employment, infrastructure and agricultural change providing support for projects initiated or supported by national governments in areas of established social need. The targeting of funds is now determined by the designation of specific regions within countries as priority areas for European support, against a series of criteria, or objectives, agreed by the Council. These include *Objective No. 1* regions, which are areas in which the average GDP *per capita* over the last three years is less than 75 per cent of the national average, and *Objective No. 2* regions, which are areas of high unemployment due to industrial decline.

A large part of the budgets of the structural funds are now concentrated in these two groups of priority regions. In overall terms, however, the budget has also been growing significantly – although by the end of the 1980s it was still less than ten per cent of total community-wide spending. Furthermore, structural fund spending requires the support of national governments; yet in theory it should not be used merely to replace investments that national governments would otherwise be making. This has sometimes led to controversy – especially with the UK government, which has objected to the Commission appearing to determine spending priorities within the country; although Britain, because of the depressed state of many of its older industrial regions, has in effect been a significant beneficiary of both ESF and ERDF funding.

The structural funds have acted indirectly to counteract the social deprivation which may have resulted from economic change within the community; but they have not been directly focused on the problem of growing poverty. However, data from Eurostat, from the

European Observatories and from various member governments has revealed that poverty has become a growing problem within the community, especially since the 1970s. Thus in 1975 the Council decided to act directly to do something about poverty within the community through the establishment of a *European Community Programme to Combat Poverty*.

This *first* poverty programme ran from 1975 to 1980 and consisted of a small amount of Commission funding to support a number (21) of small-scale, local action (or pilot) research projects aimed at combating poverty within particular communities. The idea was not that this would lead to any significant reduction of poverty within the community but rather that it would provide some examples of local initiative that, where successful, could be copied or reproduced elsewhere on a much wider scale. This view was encouraged by an official evaluation of the programme carried out on behalf of the Commission by academic researchers (Dennett *et al.*, 1982). In practice, however, not much was done by way of reproduction of the first poverty programme initiatives; and after the end of this first period the whole programme went into abeyance for four years.

In 1984, however, the initiative was resurrected with the establishment of a *second* programme, again running for five years, through to 1989. The second programme was in fact very similar to the first, being based on support for a number of small, local action research projects – initially 65 – later supplemented by a further 26 based in Portugal and Spain, following their entry into the EC in 1986. Once again the programme was subject to research evaluation both on a national basis within each country and across the whole community programme (Room, 1993); once again, little was done to extend the work beyond the projects funded within the programme.

Nevertheless, the second programme was followed immediately by a *third*, sometimes now referred to as *Poverty 3*, which ran from 1989 to 1994. Poverty 3 was slightly larger than the previous two programmes, with a total budget of 55 million ECUs (European Currency Units – equivalent to around £38 million) – still a minuscule amount when set against overall EC spending. It was based on fewer, larger, local projects (a total of 39 across the 12 member states), although still within an action research framework; again, it was subject to national and European-wide monitoring. There were four Poverty 3 projects in the UK, three larger ones based in parts of Belfast, Edinburgh and Liverpool, and a smaller lone-parent action group project based in Bristol.

The expectation in the Commission was that Poverty 3 would be followed immediately by another five-year programme beginning in 1994. However, this did not happen for the Council refused to ratify the programme proposed by the Commission, and once again it went into abeyance.

There is no denying the fact that the EU poverty programmes have done little or nothing to combat the growing problem of poverty and social exclusion within the Union. Their focus has been restricted to small-scale, isolated, pilot initiatives – backed up by academic research and monitoring. However, their symbolic importance as European social policy programmes, initiated and implemented through the offices of the Commission, far outweighs their immediate practical achievements. The poverty programmes are perhaps one of the clearest examples of European social policy making in embryo. The fact that they have, thus far, grown in scale and profile suggests that they may provide a model for future policy initiatives which aim to target priority issues and priority areas throughout the Union.

Furthermore, it is not strictly true to say that the Commission has done nothing to support anti-poverty activity within Europe outside the poverty programme projects, for they have also provided a small amount of funding for the *European Anti-Poverty Network* (EAPN). This is an umbrella organisation providing coordination and information for a wide range of locally based anti-poverty projects throughout the EU. EAPN produces a regular newsletter, and organises conferences and seminars, using EU funding; and it acts as a pressure group on the Commission to further the cause of locally based anti-poverty activity. This, too, may be a precursor of the policy developments to come within the new Union in the early twenty-first century.

The European Union and the UK

As we have seen, Britain was not a member of the original 1951 Coal and Steel Community or of the EEC which was established by the Treaty of Rome in 1957. During the 1960s the British government sought to alter this isolation and applied on several occasions to join the Community but their application for entry was vetoed by France. So when Britain did eventually join in 1973 it was after a decade of waiting; thus it might be expected that there was widespread political support and enthusiasm for membership and future European cooperation within the country. However, this was not the case.

In the 1970s the Labour Party, which was in government from 1974 to 1979, was split over the question of EC membership. Partly in order to quell the divisions within the party, the Prime Minister, Harold Wilson, organised a referendum in 1976 on the question of whether or not to continue membership. This resulted in a significant majority in favour of continuation, thus isolating Labour's anti-Europeans. Some of this early Labour opposition to the Community was based on its initial predominantly economic focus and narrow labour-market concerns. When this focus began to change, with the development of a stronger social dimension in the 1980s, the Labour Party (now in opposition) adopted a much more united policy of support for continued membership of – and even extension of – the EU.

At the same time in the 1980s, however, the Conservative Party, now in government, began to divide over Europe. A significant, and vocal, minority of Conservative MPs became overtly hostile to the extending powers and influence of the European Commission – in particular in the social policy field; some of this hostility was also shared by Prime Minister Thatcher, who led Britain into a much more oppositional role within the Council of Ministers, frequently speaking out against new policy initiatives and far-reaching federalist plans. Britain did not join the European Exchange Rate Mechanism in the 1980s, preferring to pursue a separate monetary policy; and, although this changed with membership being agreed in 1990, Britain quickly withdrew again when the 1990s recession began to bite. This new British role as the reluctant member of the EU was continued in the 1990s by Prime Minister John Major, represented in particular by the opt-out arrangements negotiated over the single currency and the Social Chapter in the Maastricht Treaty of 1992.

Britain's reluctance to participate in more rapid moves towards a united, or federal, Europe has led commentators and politicians in some of the other countries to suggest that the Union should develop a *twin-track* strategy for development, in which closer union is pursued by some, more willing, members while other, more reluctant, ones maintain a more cooperative than collaborative approach. The expansion in size of the Union may well operate to reinforce such a twin-track strategy; but it could be a rather controversial development – and, for Britain, a potentially damaging one.

If Britain, and perhaps some others, remain behind, or outside, the social and political harmonisation of EU policy, it is possible that they will be excluded from, or at least disadvantaged within, economic policy development too. Social policy has always followed on from, and been closely related to, economic policy planning within the EU. It is not at all clear that it would be easy for countries to opt out of one and yet remain in the other. It is likely that the political implications of pursuing a policy of opt-out, in practice would be to create divisions and hostilities within the Union, as a result of which reluctant partners might find many potential benefits reduced or withdrawn.

Such fears have certainly not been lost on the Labour and Liberal Democrat opposition in the UK. In the 1990s both opposition parties have been openly critical of the Conservative government's limited approach to European union – in particular the reluctance to embrace social policy commitments; and both have promised to follow a more collaborative strategy within the EU if power were to change following an election. It may be, therefore, that the reluctance which has characterised British involvement within the EU in the 1980s and early 1990s could be abandoned in favour of a more whole-hearted European vision before the end of the century.

Of course, even the reluctant strategy of the 1980s did not prevent British social policy, and economic development, being significantly affected by membership of the Community. On the economic front, although Britain did not join the Exchange Rate Mechanism (ERM) in the 1980s, British economic policy was forced to adapt to the currency regime being followed by the European partners, which in effect meant seeking to follow the lead of the major ERM currency, the Deutschmark. In social policy, directives agreed by the Council of Ministers had the effect of requiring changes in UK social policy legislation. For example, in 1986 a case brought by a woman carer, Jackie Drake, under the Equal Treatment (Social Security) Directive of 1978, forced the government to alter British law to permit married and cohabiting women to claim Invalid Care Allowance – a benefit paid to those caring for disabled adults at home, from which they had previously been excluded.

More generally, however, the existence in the 1990s of a single market for goods, capital and labour within the EU has begun to lead to a rapid acceleration of the process by which all economic trends and developments take on a European-wide dimension, over which individual national governments can have little direct (or even indirect) control. The social policy consequences of these developments will inevitably require European-wide initiatives and commitments too.

Economic commentators have already begun to suggest that the effect of the single market will be to concentrate the power, and the advantage, of economic development into a small central core within the EU, sometimes referred to as a *golden triangle* based between Frankfurt, Paris and Milan (Cameron *et al.*, 1991). If this happens, the peripheral regions around it, including probably all of Britain, will experience relative economic decline. This could only be counteracted by the use of European-wide social policy initiatives to redirect resources and investments towards the periphery, such as the extended use of EU programmes and structural funds. In this scenario the importance of linking economic development with collaborative social policy activity is manifestly clear, and makes any strategy of partial opt-out of social policy planning an extremely risky one.

The concentration of economic power and benefit is not, however, the only likely European-wide social policy implication of the single market and the future of EU development. There are also fears that employers within the Union seeking to reduce costs through the use of cheap labour will transfer capital resources around the new Union in order to employ those workers with the worst pay and conditions, and the least expensive social protection – a process sometimes referred to as *social dumping*. The effect of this over time could lead to a general downward drift in conditions and protections throughout the Union if all countries or regions ended up seeking to compete with each other by lowering standards. Again, a response to this requires European-wide commitments to minimum standards and enforceable rights for workers, as represented, for instance, by the Social Charter.

A reverse tendency to the problem of social dumping is the accompanying fear of *social tourism*. Workers, or more especially non-workers, in disadvantaged regions with poor social protection are likely to be encouraged to exercise their rights to move around within the new European Union in order to seek improved protection in other countries where this exists. Thus those nations with better social welfare protection may find increased pressure of demand on these protections from the mobile population of countries with less well-developed social services. This is a fear that has in part been responsible for restrictions on social security entitlement in Britain for those not 'normally resident' within the country. However, only enforceable European-wide planning and European standards could counteract these tendencies effectively across the Union – providing yet another source of pressure for integrated social policy development.

When viewed in this light, the greater integration of European social policy across the member nations of the new Union seems to be an inevitable process – and, from the point of view of the majority of workers and citizens throughout the Union, a desirable one. For without the attempt to guarantee social standards across the member states, there may be pressure on all governments to reduce protections in order to secure short-term economic advantage.

Economic concentration is therefore almost bound to be followed, ever more rapidly, by social concentration – or concertation – and it is unlikely that any British government would be able, or willing, to resist such a process for a significant period of time. In social policy terms, as well as in economic policy terms, membership of the EU is in effect a 'one-way street' – even though we may try to stop, or even engage reverse, we are not able to turn around and go back. Already social policy in Britain has been indelibly imprinted with the stamp of European initiative and intervention; in the future such initiative and intervention is likely to extend both further and deeper into the lives of *all* citizens of the Union.

10

Local Control of Welfare Services

The central–local dimension

Much debate about, and analysis of, the development and implementation of social policy focuses upon the national context in which policy issues arise. Even where this *national* context is placed within a broader international, or supranational, context, it often appears to be assumed that it is the policies and practices of national government that are the basis of international comparison – or interference. In the earlier chapters of this book we have tended to assume that social policies within Britain have been developed through national political action as part of a single welfare state and yet, in practice, this is far from the case.

Indeed a closer examination of the historical development and current organisational structure of welfare services in Britain reveals that it is *local* initiatives that have frequently been the driving force behind the establishment and extension of many major services, and that the local administration and delivery of services is still a major operational feature of the twentieth-century welfare state. In fact, as we shall discuss shortly, in many ways it would be more accurate to say that the modern British welfare state has its roots in the initiatives and activities of local, *rather* than central, government within the country.

The history, and current state, of the relationship between central and local government in the development of welfare services is, however, a complex – and at times a conflictual – one. In particular in organisational terms, the extent of devolution of power and

192

responsibility that can be made to the local level is fraught with difficulties and contradictions. For instance, if local administrators have the power to determine the shape, or size, of local services, how can consistent standards of service for users be maintained between different areas? And, if local responsibility for services is based upon the power of locally elected representatives, does this not provide a basis for inevitable political conflict between local and central government?

Both of these are problems that have dogged the relationship between central and local government in Britain in the latter half of the twentieth century, and we shall return to discuss each in a little more detail below. As a consequence, however, the central–local dimension of social policy development is both complex and fraught – and, as a consequence of this, it is also constantly changing. The process of achieving a working balance between central and local control of policy in the context of potential, or actual, political conflict between the two has therefore been in a near constant state of flux. We can only understand the current distribution and operation of responsibilities by recognising that these are the products of such a process of change.

In examining the central or local balance of policy control, however, it is important to distinguish between the local administration and delivery of welfare (or other) services and the local government of such services. Of course, most welfare services are delivered, and thus administered, on a local basis – even where all aspects of policy and practice are determined directly by central government; citizens using such services on a day-to-day basis are likely to have access only to their local area office.

However, for services which are governed nationally this local *administration* of central welfare services is merely an organisational feature of the structure of delivery to users, who need a local point of contact with those providing the service. For instance, the local benefits agency office provides a base from which claimants can pursue their entitlement to social security benefits, and the GP surgery provides a local point of entry into the NHS.

By contrast the local *government* of welfare services means that these are the direct responsibility of a set of politicians elected by the local population, operating with powers and duties that are quite separate from those of national politicians in the central state – and may even conflict with these. For instance, education services, although they are constrained by statute to provide certain standards in teaching and learning, are controlled by local councillors who can set the policy priorities for development and delivery of these within their local area; and local authority housing is planned, designed and built according to policies set by local politicians, sometimes against central government priorities. Local government is thus, in effect, a separate sphere of the state, with a guaranteed constitutional status. Some commentators have referred to it as the 'local state' (Cockburn, 1977).

In fact, most welfare capitalist countries have local, as well as central, state machinery as a constitutional feature of their political make-up, and these enjoy clear, yet delineated, powers over both policy development and implementation. The central–local political divide is a widespread international phenomenon; and in comparative terms this divide can take a number of different forms. In particular it is important to distinguish between two broad categories of central–local structure – unitary states and federalist states.

- *Unitary* states have a central government which has historically been the major political base of the country and has the exclusive power to legislate and thus determine the broad structure of policy throughout the country – although in unitary states some powers and responsibilities are usually devolved by legislation to local government. Leaving aside for a moment the devolution of powers to subnations such as Scotland and Northern Ireland, the UK is an example of a unitary state – and it is clear within the UK that central government politicians have greater power and influence than local politicians.
- *Federalist* states are generally the product historically of the coming together of a number of smaller administrative regions, each initially with their own autonomy – and, although there is now a central government covering all such regions, this autonomy is preserved to some extent, for example by the retention of law-making powers by local states. The USA is the major example of a federalist state, where law-making powers over major aspects of social policy have been retained by individual states. Here, by contrast, the power of local state politicians is such that they are considered some of the most important political actors within the country.

However, even between unitary states the extent and amount of devolved power and control varies significantly. For instance, in Europe, countries such as France and Germany have devolved control to local government to a much greater extent than is the case in Britain, with the German *Lander* appearing in some cases to have almost as much power as USA *States*. In fact, in such comparative terms Britain is not just a unitary state, it is, among unitary states, one of the most centralised – and it has become more centralised as its welfare services have developed.

This recent increase in centralising tendencies in Britain, and the contrast that this reveals with other welfare capitalist states, including our most important European partners, has raised the profile of the central–local debate within social policy, and within the political arena, in this country. This has also been compounded by the impact of EU policy making on Britain, because many European policy initiatives are directed towards local policy development or are targeted upon particular regions or areas within member countries. Thus the devolution, or non-devolution, of powers has become a major party political issue in Britain in the 1990s; and local government has been subject to a major structural review and reform. The proper role of local government in social policy has therefore become a matter of academic concern and political debate in a way that had not been the case before – although, as we can see from the history of local government in Britain, in practice its role in policy development has always been an important one.

The history of local government

The history of local government in Britain, in the context of social policy, is one of structural stagnation – and yet policy initiative. It is also a story of rapid local growth followed by a gradual loss of powers to central government – although this is a much more complex and fluctuating picture than it is sometimes presented as being. For instance, especially since the Second World War, the loss of powers has been accompanied by a significant growth in local government expenditure; and in recent years the centralising thrust of national government policy has been counteracted by the extension of local political activity into new and innovatory areas. As Stoker (1988, p. 6) argues in his textbook on local government, the view of the development of local government as a history of decline is at best a one-sided one.

The rise of local government in Britain was initially closely linked to the growing impact of the process of industrialisation. The creation of new, large, urban populations led to local problems, to which the existing minimalist central state was unable to respond. The initial reaction of central government to this was to establish bodies at a local level, such as the Poor Law Boards and the Improvement Commissioners, to deal on an *ad hoc* basis with different social problems as they arose. In 1835, however, elected municipal councils were established in the new urban towns and cities. As the century progressed, these authorities gradually acquired responsibility for a range of local social services, such as health and housing. At the same time, however, the *ad hoc* bodies continued to grow, in particular through the establishment of School Boards to run local primary schools.

In 1888 local government was extended by the establishment of County Councils in rural areas and Municipal Borough Councils in the larger non-industrial towns. A separate London County Council, covering the whole of the London metropolitan area, and operating above the 28 Borough Councils, was also established, providing some much needed coordination over local services within the capital. Between 1894 and 1899 this structure of local government was completed, and in places revised, in particular through the creation of new multipurpose authorities (District Councils) operating below County Councils in rural areas and with responsibility for a separate set of powers and services. Similar developments also took place in Scotland. Thus throughout much of the country there were, by the end of the century, two tiers of local government, with a larger County Council including within it a number of smaller District and Parish Councils with various powers over different services. In the larger urban towns and cities, however, there was unitary political control within the Municipal Borough Council.

The structure that emerged from the 1890s was thus a complex – and frequently overlapping – one. Nevertheless, it remained the structure of local government throughout the development of the welfare state in the first three-quarters of the twentieth century and was not reformed until 1974 (1975 in Scotland) – following the recommendations of the Maud Committee of 1967. Since then, however, structural reform has taken place each decade with some authorities being abolished in the 1980s and a range of others restructured or abolished in the 1990s.

In the early part of the twentieth century, however, despite an unchanging structure, local government initiative and influence within social policy grew dramatically. During this period the functions of local government also changed and expanded.

- Control of health, highways and housing remained but the latter grew significantly in importance after the development of municipal housing for rent in the 1920s.
- In 1902 the School Boards were abolished and control over education passed to local authorities.
- In 1929 local authorities acquired responsibility for Poor Law relief and for local hospitals and their responsibilities for children were expanded.
- In the early twentieth century local councils controlled and developed major infrastructural services such as gas, water and electricity.
- Finally, by the late 1940s local government had acquired more general control over all physical development through responsibility for town and country planning.

The first half of the century was therefore a period of municipal enterprise and municipal development, to some extent pioneered by Joseph Chamberlain (the Mayor of Birmingham) who, as leader of the largest local authority in Britain, proudly boasted that the lives of all citizens of the city had been 'improved' by the development of local services. The model of Birmingham was followed in particular by a number of other larger municipal authorities, for whom the power, for example, to build local authority housing allowed them to transform both physically and socially the circumstances of local people. This also resulted in a massive growth in the extent of local government activity; and between 1900 and 1938 local authority expenditure increased fourfold.

The period up to the beginning of the Second World War is sometimes referred to as the heyday of local government in Britain, because it was a period of almost uninterrupted expansion on all fronts and was followed after the war by the gradual loss of many of the functions that had been created and developed in this early period. In one sense this is clearly true:

- control of gas and electricity was lost in 1947
- control over mainstream health services was lost in 1948 when these were transferred to the NHS
- control over water services was lost in 1962
- control over ancillary health services was lost in 1974
- in the 1980s control over housing, education and personal social services was much restructured and reduced (an issue to which we shall return later).

This loss of local government services during the postwar period was made all the more significant because this was the period of the major growth of the welfare state in Britain. For the Labour government of 1945–51 (the creators of the welfare state) in particular, the vision of social policy development was one of national, rather than local, responsibility for the welfare of citizens. This can be seen most obviously in the establishment of the NHS, which took functions away from local government, and of the social security system, although many functions here had effectively been lost in the 1930s. Both the NHS and the National Insurance and National Assistance schemes were predicated upon the establishment and enforcement of national standards for all.

It is clear that there was little effective voice from local government within the Labour administration of the postwar period and the implicit distrust of the local state to deliver national services evenly on a high-quality basis was undoubtedly compounded by the rather outdated structure within which it was trapped. Yet, although there was pressure from some quarters for reform of local government structure, this was never accorded sufficiently high political priority during the welfare reform years of the early postwar period (Stoker, 1988, p. 7).

However, the centralising tendencies of the postwar period can be overexaggerated. Of the five major welfare services, three (education, housing and personal social services) remained, or in the latter case were placed, in local government hands. The Education Act of 1944 was the first of the welfare reforms and it placed almost total control over the establishment and running of primary and secondary schools on local government – a situation that was to lead to conflict in the 1960s and later when central government sought to change the structure of secondary education in particular, and many local councils refused to implement the required changes. In housing, too, the major power remained with local councils, even though in the 1940s and 50s central government provided heavy subsidies to ensure that the high targets set for public sector house building were met. Social work was to a large extent a creation of the postwar period and the new Children's Departments and Mental Health Departments which led to its growth were established in local authorities while local Welfare Departments took over some residual Poor Law functions.

Before the reforms of the postwar period, education and housing had already become established as the major items of *expenditure* for local government (Dunleavy, 1984, pp. 52–4). Throughout the 1950s and after, the rapid growth of these services fuelled a continued growth in local spending, with the result that, even though functions had been lost, local authority expenditure continued to increase – both absolutely and in proportion to overall national expenditure growth. Between 1955 and 1975 local authority expenditure increased threefold, and rose from 28 to 30 per cent of overall expenditure. Furthermore, much of this expenditure was represented by an increase in employment in local authority services (Stoker, 1988, pp. 9–11). In terms of Keynesian economic policy, therefore, local government remained a central feature of both service delivery and the generation of economic growth.

Alongside the continued increase in local authority expenditure in the immediate postwar period, however, was a shift in the financial base for such expenditure – although this shift had already begun to take effect before the war. Local authority expenditure was, and still is, financed by income from three sources: local *rates, charges* for services (such as adult education or planning applications) and central government *grants.* Originally the local development of services had been financed primarily out of local taxation through the rates, with central government money constituting only a minor source of income, and charges, providing around 30 per cent, somewhere in the middle.

Although the role of charges remained almost constant, at least until the 1990s, the relative balance between rates and grants changed dramatically over the postwar period, with central government grants replacing rates as the major source of income by the 1950s. The reason for this was the greater importance of national services, locally governed, such as education and housing, within local expenditure and the concern of central government to ensure that adequate provision of these services was secured in all areas.

However, the consequence of this was to provide central government, potentially at least, with much greater (indirect) control over local government. This was a factor that was to become of major significance in the relationship between central and local government in the 1980s.

Between the 1950s and the 1970s, therefore, the gradual expansion of the welfare state was mirrored by a gradual expansion, and enhancement, of the role of local government. Not only did the numbers of teachers, planners and social workers grow, so too did their professional prestige and influence. With the support of their increasingly powerful public sector trades unions, local authority employees enjoyed secure employment and extensive (perhaps even paternalistic) control over local services. So, although functions had been lost, it is these postwar years that were perhaps the real heyday of local government – at least in the social policy field.

Towards the end of the 1970s, however, this began to change. As we have seen, the major fuel for local government expenditure and influence was by this time the provision of welfare services; the freezing – then cutback – of these services after the onset of recession was therefore bound to lead to pressure for reductions in local authority spending and local authority influence. In the late 1970s cash limits were set for future house building and for education spending; and in the 1980s these cash limits became cash cuts.

As we shall discuss shortly, the attempts by central government to secure reductions in local government expenditure on welfare service in the 1980s led, in practice, to major conflicts between central and local government. In the face of cuts the natural opposition of local service providers to threats to service standards led to resistance by local government to reductions in their service role. This was fuelled by the party political differences between Conservative central government and the Labour controllers of many of the major local authorities.

Partly because of this political conflict central government in the 1980s introduced a number of significant changes in the structure of relationships with local authorities, although some of these changes were also a product of the more general strategy of redrawing the boundaries of state welfare services and encouraging private or independent provision. The most significant of these changes, however, were those affecting central financial support for local government services.

Throughout the earlier postwar period central support had taken the form of a *Rate Support Grant* (RSG) from central government to supplement local rates and to ensure that service spending commitments could be met. The problem with this, in the new policy climate of the 1980s, was that it left the determination of local commitments in the hands of local government, and thus cuts in the RSG would be likely to be received by local government, and local people, as cuts in service commitments. Therefore this was replaced after 1980 with a regime of financial support determined on a standardised basis through the use by central government of a list of indicators of local service needs. This was called the *Grant Related Expenditure Assessment* (GREA). It was determined directly by central government and, in a climate of cuts, it was frequently well below the assessments of need made within authorities by local politicians.

The initial response of many authorities to the reduced levels of central support through GREAs was to increase local rates in order to maintain services at the levels that they felt were necessary. This, however, meant the government's overall targets for reduced public expenditure were still not being met because, in effect, they were thwarted by the continued spending of local authorities. Central government therefore sought to control the powers of local authorities to expand expenditure through increased local rates.

At first this was attempted by setting spending targets for authorities, which were enforced by reductions in the government grant if the targets were exceeded. But this did not prevent some authorities defying the government by exceeding the targets and paying the penalties through yet further increases in the rates. The government therefore sought to prevent rate increases altogether in some authorities through the introduction of *rate capping* (setting a limit on the amount of increase in the local rates); but even this was difficult to enforce in practice, and was unpopular with local electorates. So eventually the whole rating system was replaced by a new form of local taxation, the *community charge* (or 'poll tax'), which was paid by all individuals living in the area, who, it was thought, would thus be less willing to vote to elect high spending authorities.

In fact the poll tax proved to be a hopelessly ineffective and widely unpopular form of local taxation. It was difficult to collect money from all individuals and it provoked popular resistance to payment in many areas. It was introduced in 1990 and by 1993 had been replaced by a new *council tax* based, as the rates had been, on payments made by all property owners or occupiers. By the 1990s the GREA had also been replaced by a reformed, but similar, form of centrally determined expenditure calculation called the *Standard Spending Assessment* (SSA). By this time also, however, political opposition to local spending cuts had largely dissipated, and the new financial regime began to operate more or less effectively – with the result that local government expenditure commitments were significantly reduced.

During the 1980s, however, local government did not just experience reductions in its expenditure base; there were also attempts to remove important aspects of service provision from authorities, primarily though measures requiring or encouraging the privatisation of local government services. This process was begun, most dramatically, in 1980 by the granting to all council house tenants of the 'right to buy' their rented home from the local authority – a right which by the end of the decade over a million former tenants had exercised. By the end of the decade, too, legislation had been introduced to permit whole estates to 'opt out' of council control. A similar power had also been given to local authority schools, which could leave local authority control and receive their public funding direct from central government.

In addition to the provisions for opting out, local authorities were also required in the 1980s to offer certain services, such as cleaning or refuse collection, to commercial operators through a process by which contracts for the delivery of local services were put out to tender on the private market. This was a process which was extended further in the 1990s to a wider range of local services, including housing management. In some cases these contracts were 'won' by the existing local authority workforce, in competition with commercial tenders. However, on occasions they were not; and in such cases service provision was removed from direct local government control.

Unlike the earlier losses of functions in the 1940s, this reduction in the scope of local government in the 1980s and early 1990s was somewhat piecemeal in its effect, with the extent of opting out and contracting out varying from one authority to another. In general it was also nowhere near as extensive as some of the protagonists of the 'contract culture' on the political right (both in and out of government) might have hoped. Nevertheless, it was a significant accentuation of the gradual trend towards a reduced role for the local control of service provision – yet at the same time it was accompanied by *expansion* of local authority activity in other fields, as we discuss below.

The enabling authority

During the 1980s, and after, local authorities that were worried about the impact of cuts in welfare services in both local and central government provision – and about the more general consequences for their local populations of the serious economic recessions of the 1980s and 90s – began to look to new ways in which they might act to protect local people. Some of this protective activity involved a new, or renewed, commitment to working with local communities; and it resulted in a shift away from the authority as a provider of services to local people, towards a role in which local government would provide support for voluntary sector and community-based activity.

David Blunkett, leader of Sheffield City Council in the 1980s, for instance, referred to this as 'Building from the Bottom' (Blunkett and Green, 1983). In many areas it consisted of the targeting of local government resources onto particular groups of people known to be experiencing much of the brunt of economic and social hardship, such as ethnic minority communities and women's groups. As well as such targeted support, however, many local authorities also sought to encourage the more general economic regeneration of their areas through the use of local government knowledge, resources and influence to work in partnership with local private industry to create, or protect, local jobs.

Economic development strategies, focused on industrial (or service) development and job creation, became an important feature of local government activity in the 1980s, particularly in the declining industrial areas of the Midlands and North – in some ways returning local authorities to the pioneering role as the champions of local prosperity that they had enjoyed at the beginning of the century. However, seeking to secure local economic regeneration in the face of international economic recession, and frequently without national government interest or support, was not always a readily achievable goal – and in many cases, despite the intentions (and the interventions) of local government, local unemployment and deprivation grew. By the 1990s many local authorities were extending (or replacing) their economic regeneration policies with strategies for social regeneration, or with more wide-ranging attempts to develop *anti-poverty* initiatives at the local level (Alcock *et al.*, 1995).

Thus, by the mid 1990s, local authority involvement in the control of welfare services had changed significantly from both early twentieth-century days of municipal development and postwar years of comprehensive service provision. Many functions had been lost and others restructured. Yet at the same time local government had begun to extend into new areas of activity, in particular through seeking – in partnership with other local agencies – to develop a strategic response to the needs and problems of local people (Cochrane, 1993). This change has been described both by government and by academic commentators as representing a significant shift in local government from a *controlling* role over the provision of local services to an *enabling* role working with both other service providers and local citizens.

Local authority structures and powers

One of the problems for local government in their struggles with central government over the devolution or the centralisation of powers has been the complex, and frequently outdated, structure of local authority organisation across the country. As we said, the structure of local government is the product of historical process. It is not therefore the product of logical planning; and, despite a number of supposedly comprehensive reviews of the structure especially in the latter part of the century, it remains dominated more by current vested political interests than by any future vision of the proper role for localism.

In reality, of course, what might properly constitute the 'local' area for the purposes of devolved government or community control is far from clear. The local dimension is perhaps best seen as something of a continuum rather than a clear-cut distinction; it ranges from the small village or neighbourhood community (where in theory at least everybody knows everybody else), through the parish or small town, to the city, county or metropolitan area, and then to the region or quasi-independent nation (see Figure 10.1).

Smallest					**Largest**
Neighbourhood	Parish	District	City	County	Region
Belgravia	*Beverley*	*Bournemouth*	*Birmingham*	*Berkshire*	*Northeast*

Figure 10.1 The different levels of local government

There has never been local government at neighbourhood level in Britain. At parish level, however, local councils have existed in rural areas since the nineteenth century and most remained after the local government reforms of 1974, although their powers are very limited (Elcock, 1982, pp. 35–7). District councils cover all towns and some smaller cities, and usually share the powers of local government with the county council which extends over a number of district areas. Larger cities, however, often have single local authorities which enjoy the full range of local powers. Regional government does not exist in the UK, although it is common in some other European countries; but there is an element of devolved government over the subnations in the UK – Scotland, Wales and Northern Ireland. Furthermore, within both Scotland and Northern Ireland the organisation of local government itself is significantly different.

Thus the structure of local government does not follow a simple logic of devolution of different powers down to different local levels on a consistent basis. In particular, since the changes made by the abolition of the metropolitan counties in the major urban areas, such as London and Merseyside, in the 1980s, there has been a somewhat arbitrary divide between those large industrial towns and cities, such as Newcastle or Oldham, and the London boroughs, such as Islington or Tower Hamlets, which have unitary authorities providing all local government services, and those more predominantly rural areas where powers are divided between a district council and a larger county council. Until the 1990s county councils also included some large cities, such as Bristol or Nottingham, which were larger than some of the single-tier authorities in places like Oldham.

Beginning in 1996, however, most of the larger towns and cities were given single-tier status – although dual authorities remained throughout the rest of the rural areas in England, despite initial hopes in some local government quarters that this dual structure might have been abandoned altogether. In Scotland and Wales the larger regional and county councils were removed and replaced with smaller, unitary, district authorities.

After the mid 1990s reforms, therefore, local government in Britain remained a mixture of single-tier authorities in the larger towns and cities – plus the London boroughs and all of Scotland and Wales – where all locally devolved powers are concentrated in one elected council body; and dual-tier authorities in the predominantly rural counties, where some powers (such as housing) are the responsibility of a local district council and others (such as education and social services) are the responsibility of a larger county council covering a number of districts.

As we said earlier, during the welfare state reforms of the 1940s control over heath and social security was placed in the hands of central government departments, although the services that these departments administer are, of course, delivered locally by hospitals, doctors and social security offices. Despite the centralising tendencies of the postwar reforms, however, control over education, housing and personal social services, as well as a range of other powers, remained in local government hands.

- *Education* is the most important of local government services, both in terms of expenditure and numbers of service users. It was passed to local government following the abolition of the School Boards in 1902. In 1944, when a comprehensive provision for primary and secondary education, up to age 15 (later 16) or 18, if desired, was introduced, virtually all aspects of curriculum development and school organisation and management were placed in local authorities – or local education authorities (LEAs), as this aspect of their work was called. Local authority control thus restricted central government influence; and in the 1960s when the Labour Government wished to convert all secondary education from the 'tripartite' (grammar, technical and secondary modern) scheme to a comprehensive system, many LEAs resisted and continued to maintain a version of the old system.

  However, in the 1970s and 80s central government began to increase its influence over the structure and delivery of school-based learning through the introduction of restrictions in LEA powers and budgets. After the reforms in education in 1987 a national curriculum and national tests – determined by central government – were established and schools were given the power to opt out of LEA control. LEA control over further education for 16- to 19-year-olds, and higher education in the old polytechnics (now universities), was also removed from LEAs in the late 1980s and early 1990s and placed under the control of new national bodies directly controlled by central government.

- *Housing* is the second largest aspect of local government service provision. Local authority powers here date back to the nineteenth century and to their concerns through control of housing to improve standards of sanitation. However, it is council housing, built for rent from the 1920s on, that has been the major feature of the local development of housing policy. During the course of the twentieth century, local authorities have become the major landlords of rented housing, controlling around 35 per cent of the national housing stock by the 1970s.

Following the postwar housing boom, however, local development has concentrated more and more on slum clearance and inner city development, including the controversial development of high-rise and system-built blocks of flats. These flats in particular, and local authority somewhat authoritarian management of its housing stock in general (for example restricting improvement or even redecoration of council tenancies), had secured a somewhat negative impression for council housing in some quarters by the 1980s. Since then the right to buy and the estate opt-out provision, together with massive cuts in local authority house building programmes, have reduced the scale of council house provision both absolutely and relatively. Now less than 25 per cent of dwellings are in local authority control, and housing association building has outstripped councils in the provision of new homes. Furthermore, it is now generally speaking the poorer quality dwellings occupied by poorer households that remain in the council sector, and local authority provision has been reduced to something of a residual role catering largely for the less well-off.

- *Personal Social Services* – often also referred to as *social work* – is the other major area of welfare service controlled by local government. Local authority social work dates back to the Children's Departments and Welfare and Health Departments of the late 1940s. However, in 1971, following the Seebohm Committee report of 1968, these were extensively reformed and combined to form new integrated social service departments (SSDs). Since then local authority SSDs have been responsible for the delivery of a range of services for vulnerable and needy individuals and communities, including monitoring child abuse and neglect, services for the chronically sick and disabled, community care for mental patients and provision for the frail elderly.

Since 1993, however, the role of SSDs as service providers has been replaced by a new role as the organisers of community care for many of these groups. The idea now is that social workers should identify the needs of their vulnerable clients and then seek services to meet these needs by packaging together services from the state, private, voluntary and informal sectors – although, as we have seen, this is a process that in practice is frequently fraught with difficulties, especially where local community provision is limited (Means and Smith, 1994).

In addition to the major services of education, housing and social work, local authorities also have responsibility for a range of other service provision, which, in part at least, is encompassed within the field of social policy. These include leisure services (such as sports facilities, museums and parks), consumer protection, maintenance of highways and street lighting, and emergency services (such as policing and fire fighting). The latter services, however, are under the control of separate bodies of councillors sometimes covering more than one authority in urban industrial areas; and in London the Metropolitan Police are separately controlled by statute.

The devolution, or development, of control over these services by local government does largely mean, however, that to some extent their administration is accountable to local people through the mechanism of local council elections. Of course, the complex structure of responsibilities, especially in county and district areas, may be beyond the comprehension of much of the local electorate. What is more, local control can lead to some important, and in some services unavoidable, problems over what should be the appropriate local focus for service accountability.

For a start, not all local authorities provide a local base for political accountability that is popularly understood by local people. For instance, when local government was restructured in 1974 some authorities were merged with their neighbours, much to the disappointment of local people, and some new authorities were created to which local electorates did not feel any allegiance – for example the new county councils of Avon and Humberside. Such opposition to local change is of course inevitable, and there is in many cases no organisational structure that would capture the full support of all local people. However, fear of possible structural exclusion can also act as a block to future restructuring or reorganisation, even where this might in the longer term be more efficient – and even more accountable, and popular.

This fear of change in organisational boundaries is only one example of the inescapable issue of *boundary problems* in local democracy. Lines on a map must be drawn somewhere; and wherever they are drawn they are likely to separate some areas or communities that might, geographically, historically or culturally, feel that they belong together. Where there are such divided populations, the existence of different authorities all covering a part of a local area can make the development of any coherent overall strategy difficult, if not impossible. This has been true, for instance, in an area of South Yorkshire known as the Dearne Valley, which is split between Barnsley, Doncaster and Rotherham Borough Councils.

Even where the lines of division are not problematic or controversial, however, they can still lead to boundary disputes. For instance, families living near the boundary of one authority might wish to send their children to a school nearby in a neighbouring authority. Prior to the education reforms of 1988 they would not have been able to do this; and they still may not, in practice, today if the school will not accept children from another local council. Similarly, an urban local authority wishing to demolish the inner city slums and rehouse their inhabitants in new housing estates in the countryside may be unable to build such houses because the neighbouring countryside it wishes to use is part of a different authority. In some cases neighbouring authorities are able to cooperate successfully over issues that cross their respective boundaries – in London in particular this is common and essential – but it does not always happen; in practice it requires both careful management and political support.

Cooperation between authorities is required in country areas, however, where powers are shared between county and district authorities. To many local people here, the difference between the county and the district authorities in their area may be an obscure, and even an unjustifiable, one. All they know is that they need to contact different officers in different council buildings, probably in different towns, in order to make use of different local services – and, if the officers of these two authorities whom they contact turn out to know little or nothing about the structures or workings of the other (a not uncommon problem), this is unlikely to extend the popularity of local government to local service users. If they are in conflict (which sometimes they are), it is likely to make the experience of local accountability both a negative and a frustrating one.

Even where there are no such boundary disputes or interauthority conflicts, however, the experience of local government services has not always been a positive one for local service users. The idea of local government accountability is based upon the assumption that local elections provide a basis for communicating the views of local people to the local councillors who represent them, so that these councillors can then ensure that the officers providing the services follow the dictates of the local electorate. As we shall discuss shortly, however, the political process of local government does not in general operate in such a directly responsive way to pressures of local democracy. In a number of authorities councillors from one particular political party have been in control of local government for decades or more, and in such cases they often rely heavily on the advice and guidance of the senior officers within the authority – rather than on any changing views among their local electorate.

Partly because of the rather limited nature of democratic accountability, therefore, local authority services have often in practice been developed within highly bureaucratic, and heavily paternalistic, frameworks. A typical example of this would be the local housing department of the 1960s or 70s with its long waiting lists for new properties and its strict controls over the rights and responsibilities of tenants – even down to the colour of paint on their front doors. In circumstances such as this the attractions of the local control of welfare services may turn out to be more apparent than real.

Such paternalism and bureaucracy can of course also be found in central government services – indeed, arguably, it is an even more extensive problem there. What is more, the undesirability of such aspects of state welfare services is now widely recognised by commentators and by politicians on both the right and the left. As a result, the privatisation measures of the Thatcher governments of the 1980s made a significant impact on this paternalism within local government. For instance, faced with the prospects of right to buy and estate opt-out, local housing management had to alter its practices to become more responsive to tenants' demands and, faced with policies for community care, local social work departments had to develop new relationships with voluntary sector agencies and community organisations.

Indeed, in general over the 1980s and 90s, local government has moved more and more rapidly from the paternalist model of service provider towards its new role as an enabling authority, with a more strategic view of local needs and a more complex interrelationship with the private, voluntary and informal sectors of welfare provision within its area. This has resulted in some loss of employment in local state service provision and in some loss of power and influence for local councillors and officers; but it has also seen an enhanced focus on accountability to local service users and empowerment of local community representatives within the democratic process. In the longer term, therefore, such changes may even provide a more secure base for local democracy than the restricted – and conflictual – electoral party politics that had come to dominate local government by the 1980s.

Political conflict

Within any democracy political conflict is inevitable – indeed arguably, it is desirable, for it is evidence of healthy political debate. However, the separate electoral base for local government from central government creates a specific context for potential political conflict between the two, since there are likely to be a range of issues, particularly those relating to local government powers and resources, over which they may not agree. Furthermore, these conflicts are likely to be exacerbated in a party political electoral system, where at different times different parties may be in control of central and local government.

Despite this potential, however, the history of local government is not in particular a story of party control and party conflict. Even by the time of the Maud Committee of 1967 only around 50 per cent of local authorities were under party political control (Stoker, 1988, p. 38), with the majority of these being in the larger urban areas. Since that time, however, local government has become much more widely politicised and now control of virtually all councils is the subject of party political struggle and competition – although often competition has to be followed by compromise and cooperation if the election is 'hung' and no one party is successful in winning enough council seats to exercise overall control.

If, however, party control is a relatively new phenomenon for many rural authorities, it is a much more established tradition in the larger urban areas. Following the lead in municipal development taken by Birmingham in the early part of the twentieth century, many of the larger city authorities elected parties into power based upon radical manifestos for local development. The Labour Party in particular was instrumental in using such local government manifestos as an early base for demonstrating the potential achievements of democratic socialism; in cities like Sheffield, where Labour has exercised control on an almost uninterrupted basis since the 1920s, a programme of 'municipal socialism' based on public house building and infrastructural improvement was pursued by the new council regimes of the early half of the century (Blunkett and Jackson, 1987).

Of course the local pursuit of municipal socialism was likely to bring such Labour councils into conflict with a Conservative-controlled central government, for whom such socialism was definitely not a part of the political agenda. In the 1920s, for instance, conflict arose in a direct form within the London Borough of Poplar (now Tower Hamlets) where the Labour council was pursuing a policy of paying higher wages to its workers and higher levels of poor relief to its benefit claimants. This led to legal action being brought against the council as a result of which some councillors were eventually sent to gaol. Although the imprisonment of elected representatives in Poplar was a rather extreme consequence of such political conflict, other authorities, too, pursued radical policies that did not have the support of central government and resulted in political conflict with it. This form of local political challenge began to be referred to as *Poplarism* (Ryan, 1978; Holman, 1990).

After the war, however, the welfare state reforms of the 1940s removed some of the political impetus for Poplarism from local government, as the major concern of central government at that time became one of ensuring that recalcitrant Conservative local authorities were required to meet national standards of service delivery in areas such as education and housing. Since then, however, the growth in the size and importance of these local authority welfare services has been accompanied by an increasing politicisation throughout local government and, as a result, conflicts between central and local government have again become common. In the 1960s there was conflict between the Labour government and a Conservative authority over comprehensive schooling in Tameside, near Manchester (Hill, 1993a, p. 160), and in the 1970s there was conflict between the Conservative government and a Labour authority over increases in council house rents in Clay Cross, in Derbyshire (Elcock, 1982, pp. 48–9).

In the 1980s, however, the politicisation of local government, and the conflicts between local and central government, reached new levels. For a start, the growth of party politics within local government resulted in new challenges to some of the apparently established bastions of one party control, with the Liberals (now Liberal Democrats) winning power in London in Labour Tower Hamlets and Conservative Richmond. Even within established party strongholds, however, the political climate of local government began to change. In particular, in the large urban councils, where Labour had traditionally been in control, there was a dramatic move to the left in many areas – at the same time as the central government, under Conservative control, was moving to the right.

Commentators referred to this shift as the development of a new *urban left*, committed, as their predecessors in Poplar in the 1920s had been, to the development of a kind of 'local socialism' (Boddy and Fudge, 1984). This urban left began to exercise power in the West Midlands, in Manchester, and in London boroughs such as Hackney and Lewisham – and, most notably, in Sheffield, under the leadership of *Blunkett*, and in Greater London, under the leadership of *Livingston*. The latter two figures in particular became dominant spokesmen for the new local politics of Labour. Blunkett wrote about the renewed importance of local democracy (Blunkett and Green, 1983; Blunkett and Jackson, 1987); and Livingston was instrumental in extending the range of local government activity in London to cover economic development, support for minority groups and local anti-poverty initiatives. Both are interviewed in Boddy and Fudge (1984, pp. 242–83) – although both later left local government and joined national politics as Labour MPs in Parliament.

The local socialism of the 1980s urban left was in fact a complex political affair. It was in part based upon attempts to realise a new role for local democracy by recreating accountability to local communities and populations, and in part based on an attempt to save locally controlled welfare services from the effects of central government spending cuts. These two aims, however, were not always shared by all the authorities who came into conflict with central government during this time – many were concerned only to protect services. And in any case they were not always in themselves mutually compatible aims. For instance, the defence of local services often turned out in practice to be primarily a defence of the jobs of local service workers; yet in some cases the services that these workers were delivering were not entirely welcomed by all local people. Conflicts thus sometimes also arose between service providers and service users, where interests in jobs and services did not coincide; there were even strikes by some local authority workers who ended up in dispute with their local 'left' Labour council – for example in Sheffield in the mid 1980s.

Nevertheless, the primary local conflict in the 1980s was that between local Labour councils and the Conservative government; and it was a conflict that central government was ultimately better placed to win.

- Grants to local government for service provision were cut.
- The power to raise money through the rates was restricted and rates were finally abolished.
- Local government political campaigns against central government policy were made unlawful.
- New service initiatives developed by some authorities in defiance of government were stopped – such as the subsidisation of public transport, begun in Sheffield and copied in Greater London in the 'fares fair' campaign which reduced tube and bus fares in the capital.
- Some councils, notably the Greater London Council itself, were abolished and their powers transferred to smaller authorities.

In one sense, therefore, the new urban politics of the 1980s was, in terms of broad policy delivery, a failure – central government cuts in welfare service were eventually implemented and, in most cases, Labour councils were forced to abandon their politics of confrontation. However, the renewal of local democracy, which was bound up with much of the enhanced profile for local politics during this period, did have a broader long-term impact. The 'building from the bottom' championed by Blunkett and Livingston did renew support for community activity within many authorities and encouraged them to adopt a more strategic approach to identifying and meeting the needs of local people – and these have, perhaps ironically, been given further impetus by the shift in the 1990s from the provider to the enabler role for local government.

The political conflicts of the 1980s also saw the rise in importance of the umbrella associations which coordinated the general interests of all local government and represented these within national politics. In spite of their differences, all authorities do have a number of common or shared interests and concerns, in particular arising from central government determination of financial support. The umbrella associations enable them to pool knowledge and experience of such issues and to act collectively to put pressure on central government. The main representative bodies for local authorities are the joint associations: the Association of Metropolitan Authorities (AMA), the Association of County Councils (ACC), the Association of District Councils (ADC), which merged into one association in the mid 1990s, and the Conference of Scottish Local Authorities (CoSLA). Training and research functions for local government are also carried out by the Local Government Management Board (LGMB), and political campaigning by the Local Government Information Unit (LGIU).

Despite its loss of financial support and political power, therefore, local government did experience something of a democratic renaissance during the 1980s. However, it is important not to overestimate the strength, and depth, of the political climate within local government. The turn-out of electors in local council elections is still well below that in national elections; only around a third of those entitled to vote do so – far fewer than in most other European countries, for instance. It is also still difficult in some cases for parties to find candidates to stand for election in their local wards. Thus in some local wards councillors are still elected unopposed, and in some authorities one party retains a stranglehold on political power. Local democracy may indeed have been revitalised in the 1980s but its future nevertheless remains uncertain.

What role for local government?

At a general level, however, despite the political conflicts of the 1980s, and the low profile still enjoyed by most local politicians, the future of local government probably does remain quite secure. Authorities may be further denuded of functions, and of finance, and moved more towards an enabling role – but they are extremely unlikely to disappear altogether. Indeed, this new enabling role may help to ensure the development of a more strategic base for local government in planning for social and economic development across its area. Such a base could also be enhanced by supranational policy developments within the European Union in the 1990s, for cross-national policy initiatives within the EU are frequently focused upon localities or regions within member nations and require the active participation of local government.

On the other hand, despite the limited reforms of the mid 1990s, the structure of local government in Britain remains both complex and contradictory. Local government structure is still a product of history rather than logic and, apart from a general commitment to local democracy at council level, it is not informed by any clear principles specifying the appropriate balance between local and central control. This can be contrasted with some other European countries, such as Germany, where the principle of *subsidiarity* has long operated to provide a logic – and a pressure – for devolution to the appropriate local level.

The development of principles to inform local democracy, however, requires answers to some difficult (and perennial) questions – for example, what should be the appropriate balance between central and local control over welfare services? There are arguments here in favour of moves in either direction.

- *Local control* ensures a closer relationship of accountability between elected representatives and local people; it permits knowledge of local conditions and local preferences to inform policy development and delivery; and it encourages a strong sense of identity and community to support local initiatives.
- *Central control* can be more efficient, ensuring economies of scale; it can ensure uniformity of services throughout the country so that school children in Birmingham get as good an education as those in Bournemouth; and it can permit redistribution of resources from wealthy areas to poorer areas to prevent geographical inequalities being replicated in local service provision.

There is no obvious right or wrong solution to this problem of uniformity versus flexibility within the control of social policy, and this perhaps explains why past changes have shifted in different directions at different times. When the political context of local, and central, government is added to this organisational conundrum, predictions of future developments become tentative indeed – for political prediction, at any level, is a hazardous science. However, there is no doubt that thus far local government has played a critical role in the development and implementation of social policy in Britain – and, despite all its recent changes, continues to do so.

Section Four

Issues

11

Social Divisions

A divided society

We usually conceive of British society, or indeed any society, as providing a uniform social structure in which we all live. Within this social structure we are bound together by a common democratic and political structure and by a shared cultural experience and heritage, exemplified perhaps most strongly in modern times by the national media (television, radio and newspapers) which provide us with so much of our knowledge of the rest of our social world. In particular from the point of view of social policy, we are also subject to the same policy developments and legal rights and responsibilities. Thus when we read about the 'British Welfare State' we generally assume that it refers to a body of social services that function within society to provide social rights and social protections for all in the country.

However, as some sociologists are quick to point out, this monodimensional and *functionalist* model of British (and other) societies is in fact a rather partial one – and in many senses is a fundamentally flawed one. While there may be much that unites us as British citizens, there is also much that divides us. We do not all have similar needs and interests and our experience of the, supposedly shared, social services of the welfare state may in practice be a widely varying one. Against the assumption that society follows a functional model, therefore, sociologists argue instead that we should adopt a *conflict* model. A conflict model highlights the different circumstances and different experiences of social groups within society both in the production and consumption of resources, and recognises that the

218

needs or interests of some will conflict with those of others. Thus from such a perspective, the development and the consumption of welfare services is not a product of improved social functioning – it is a focus of social struggle.

In a broad sense, of course, both approaches have some truth in them. We do all share a social and cultural context as British citizens; yet at the same time we are members of different groups with different and sometimes conflicting interests. However, where there may have_been a tendency in some of the more traditional social policy and social administration literature to emphasise the shared – even supposedly universal – nature of welfare services (Crosland, 1956), there is now an increasingly widespread recognition in social policy debate of the fact that we live, and function, within a divided society (Williams, 1989).

In understanding the development and operation of social policy, therefore, it is essential to recognise, and to study, the issue of social divisions. The social groups to which people belong will structure their experience of social policies, and the political processes by which policies are developed will be determined by the differential power and influence of different groups. Furthermore, these experiences and processes are intertwined – marginalisation or exclusion from the process of policy making is also likely to lead to disadvantage or discrimination in the receipt of services. However, in Britain, as in most other welfare capitalist countries, the welfare state has in practice been constructed largely by certain social groups, who have consequently benefited disproportionately from it. The model of universalism on which it is supposedly based is therefore essentially a flawed one and needs to be replaced with a recognition of diversity and difference.

The most widely recognised and debated social division is probably that of social class. Class is also still the most important social division, although in modern welfare capitalist societies class differences have become more complex. Class divisions are a way of making sense of the inequalities of socioeconomic circumstances within society by reference to people's position within the labour market or production process and, as we shall see, such divisions have long been debated and argued about. However, inequalities are not just the product of the labour and production processes. Class differences also arise from consumption patterns; and in addition there are broader aspects of inequality than simply cash income and access to material resources. Social status, life chances, life choices, and cultural freedom are also inequitably distributed, and differences here are not only structured by the economics of class.

Gender differences clearly affect all of these issues, as well as structuring economic inequality independently of class. In a multicultural and multiethnic society such as Britain differences in racial or cultural background also lead to a range of inequalities, although here, as we shall discuss, it is really the rac*ism* which reacts to such differences which is the cause of the inequity and disadvantage. Gender and 'race' are discussed by Williams (1989) in her critical review of the discipline of social policy; she argues that these are dimensions that have frequently been ignored in both academic analysis and policy development in the past. However, there are other divisions, too, that have also remained hidden in – or hidden from – social policy debate.

Differences of age can also affect both involvement in, and experience of, welfare services, as do differences of physical ability, or disability – and we shall discuss these further below. Sexual orientation may also influence experience of social policies, especially perhaps for gay men since the growth of AIDS. Family circumstances, language differences, geographical differences and many other circumstances also lead to different needs and experiences. Indeed in all sorts of ways we are divided from each other through our membership of different social groups, with their different experiences and different needs.

Furthermore, as we shall also return to below, welfare services are not only affected by social divisions – they also frequently reaffirm and reinforce these divisions. Indeed, the structure of welfare provision itself may *create* social divisions. For instance, as authors such as Dunleavy and Husbands (1985) have argued, the consumption of welfare services can create *consumption cleavages* between different user groups, such as the different material interests of owner-occupiers and tenants within different sectors of housing provision. The receipt of services from different providers itself also creates divisions, such as those between pupils in 'public' (private) schools and pupils in the state sector. Finally the very process of delivering services creates divisions and conflicts of interest between the providers of services and the consumers of them that is perhaps most starkly symbolised by the plastic screens separating social security officers from the claimants who come to see them.

Recent, *postmodernist* theorising in social science stresses the complex nature of such social divisions and social processes within welfare capitalist societies – and the interrelationship between such divisions and processes. The simple functioning model of a social order in which all is shared equally from those able to provide to those most in need, or the simple conflict model centred only on the struggle between those who own and those who work, cannot be applied to Britain in the late twentieth century. Our society is much more complex – and much less united – than such models of social functioning or class conflict might suggest.

However, the complexity of social divisions does not mean, as some postmodernist thinking suggests, that these differences and divisions are almost infinite; nor does it mean that all divisions are equally important. Indeed, there is a fair amount of agreement among social policy analysts that, within the complexity that can be found, there are some significant structural factors which mean that some divisions are more important and more far-reaching than others. Class is still certainly a major social division; but so, too, as Williams (1989) has demonstrated, are gender and race; and so, too, it is increasingly recognised, are age and (dis)ability.

Class

Theoretical and empirical debate about the structure of social class in Britain, and other modern societies, is both wide-ranging and long-standing. Indeed it is probably true to say that the concept of class is one of the most critical, and most contested, issues in social science. Most social scientists have something to say about it. At an introductory level, however, Abercrombie and Warde (1994, Ch. 30) provide a useful basic summary of much of the empirical evidence on class composition and division, and Crompton (1993) provides a useful guide to theoretical debates.

Theoretical differences over how to define, and how to determine, social classes have their roots in the major theoretical traditions stemming from the work of Marx and Weber – the former arguing that social class is determined only through relationship to the means of production, and the latter arguing that differences of occupational status are also important in separating people into different classes (Sarre, 1989, pp. 84–96). Not surprisingly therefore, it is not possible to extract one agreed model of class structure from these traditions and disagreements will always remain. Nevertheless, there is a fair degree of consensus over major class groupings, and we shall follow a class division based on such well-established distinctions here (see Figure 11.1).

Upper Class	aristocracy, capitalists
Professional Middle Class	doctors, lawyers, managers
Petty Bourgeoisie	shop-keepers, self-employed business people
Lower Middle Class	nurses, teachers, secretaries
Working Class	factory workers, hairdressers
'Underclass'	unemployed, part-time workers

Figure 11.1 The different social classes

The classes in Figure 11.1 are clearly presented in a hierarchical order. The upper class, at the top, have most wealth, privileges and power; and the 'underclass' at the bottom have least – and in many cases have little indeed. In between, the middle classes generally do better than the working class, although this is not always the case – some factory workers, for instance, are paid much more than some secretaries. And of course the boundaries between the classes are not fixed or watertight, as the distinctions and similarities between head teachers (perhaps members of the professional middle classes) and other teachers might reveal.

Also, and perhaps more importantly, the size and make-up of social classes is constantly changing. In Britain in the latter part of the twentieth century, the size of the working class has been declining and the size of the middle classes, with the possible exception of the petty bourgeoisie, has been increasing (Abercrombie and Warde, 1994, p. 123). There is also some debate about whether or not a new 'underclass' has been emerging below the working class in modern Britain, as a result of de-industrialisation and the restructuring of the labour market to create a more or less permanent group of people who are unemployed or can only get limited part-time and/or temporary jobs (Smith, 1992; Morris, 1994).

Of course, it is not only the case that class categories are overlapping and constantly changing; membership of social classes is also subject to change. In most societies there is likely to be significant *class mobility*, with individuals moving up, and down, between classes. For instance, someone from a working-class family may, through achievement within the education system, secure a job in the professional middle class or may start up a successful small business; conversely, someone who is self-employed may see their business fail and may become unemployed and unable to secure future permanent work. Class mobility is, in part, the means by which such a hierarchical class structure retains a level of legitimacy within any society – we all might hope one day to join the higher classes. Such mobility, and the gaps between social classes, have also been the major foci of social policy development.

The introduction of welfare provision through social policy in Britain was clearly intended by some of its promoters to *reduce* the inequalities between class categories. For instance, social security policies were intended to prevent an underclass developing as an impoverished group cut off from the rest of society; and the NHS was intended to provide equal medical care and cure to all, reducing the differences in health and illness that might otherwise exist between classes. However, social policies may also promote social *mobility* by making it easier for people to move between classes, especially in an upward direction. For example, one of the aims of education provision has been to ensure that all are given an equal opportunity to reach their full potential in learning, and thus progress to a potentially higher class status than they might otherwise have achieved.

However, the continued existence of stark divisions of class within welfare capitalist countries such as Britain suggests that social policies have not been effective in achieving such goals. Social security may have prevented extreme hardship, but the low level of benefits that it provides still mean that those dependent on them live at standards significantly below those of the majority of the working population. Indeed, in relative terms the position of social security claimants has remained more or less constant as a proportion of average wage levels throughout most of the twentieth century in Britain (Atkinson, 1990). Despite the success of the NHS in providing free health care for all, class difference in the experience of ill-health (morbidity) and the risk of early death (mortality) also remain (Townsend *et al.*, 1988). Equality of opportunity in education has also not prevented class inequalities being reflected in levels of achievement (Halsey *et al.*, 1980).

These continuing differences between social classes might suggest that social policies in the areas of social security, health and education have failed. Such a judgement is supported by some of the studies that have been made into the access to, and use made of, welfare services, that reveal that many supposedly universal services are in fact used more widely by the middle classes than the working class – and are of more benefit to them. Le Grand's (1982) study of health and education revealed that these services were frequently of greater benefit to middle-class users, and were not effective in promoting greater equality within British society.

However, this judgement presumes that the aim of welfare services *is* to promote class equality. While this may have been the hope of some of their supporters, it is clear, as we discussed in Chapter 1, that welfare services are the product of more complex social forces than a simple Fabian 'strategy for equality', and also that they have contradictory aims – within which the maintenance of divisions and differences may be as important as the delivery of services to all. In social security, for instance, strategies of division and control are a central feature of the benefits system, for example low levels of unemployment benefit and strict requirements to seek even low-paid employment create pressures on both claimants and those on low wages.

That welfare services have not succeeded in removing class differences is not really such a surprising conclusion to reach. Social policy in welfare capitalist societies like Britain has been constructed and implemented within a continuing complex and divided socioeconomic structure. Those in positions of power and wealth within such a structure have obviously sought to ensure that these privileges are not destroyed by the development of improved welfare for all. To put it simply, welfare services have been in part a victory for the lower classes; but they have also been in part a benefit conceded grudgingly by those higher up the social order.

Furthermore, the development of welfare services themselves, while delivering benefits to users and securing (sometimes well-paid) employment for providers of services, has also created its own differences of power and privilege. Within the health service, for example, hospital consultants – and now even more so hospital managers – have become influential arbiters of people's health needs, involving decisions even over life and death. And yet at the other end of the spectrum a new section of the lower working class, such as hospital cleaners and porters, has been created often with lower pay and poorer conditions than those working in 'exploitative' capitalist private industry.

Class differences, therefore, may have been influential in creating pressure for the development of social policy in welfare capitalist countries; and clearly class structures have been significantly affected by the development of welfare provision within all such countries. However, class differences have not been removed by social policy, nor indeed would it be at all realistic to have expected them to be. Furthermore, in some cases existing differences have been accentuated, and also new divisions created, as a direct result of policy development and implementation. Class differences thus remain at the centre of any understanding of the operation of social policy in Britain and elsewhere; but they are not the only differences that must be understood and studied.

Gender

Gender differences, in particular the greater power and privilege of men over women, are as deep-seated and as long-standing as differences of class in British society, and in other welfare capitalist countries too. Furthermore, these differences have not only survived but have also in part been accentuated by the development of welfare services – and they remain central to our understanding of the operation of these. However, unlike class, gender has not always been a central feature of debate about the development or the delivery of welfare services – indeed, as Wilson (1977), Pascall (1986) and others have argued, the different experience of welfare for women has frequently been marginalised in mainstream social policy debate.

This is because, in a society in which men hold most of the dominant positions of power and influence, it is also men who have dominated the development, and the study, of social policy. However, in recent years there has been a growth of academic interest in the gender dimension of policy development and delivery; and, at the same time, a growth in the political activity of women seeking to challenge male domination of our social services. Thus we now know much more about the different experiences, and needs, of men and women within welfare capitalist societies; and what we know confirms feminist suspicions that gender inequalities remain sizeable and significant – and that within this it is women who are disadvantaged.

The most obvious evidence of women's disadvantage in British society generally is the continuing differential between women's and men's average rates of pay. In 1992 women's weekly average rate of pay was 71 per cent of men's (Abercrombie and Ward, 1994, p. 213).

This is a significant difference. It means that women are less able to provide for themselves, or for their families, and thus are more likely to rely upon social security. It means that they are also less likely to be able to buy things that they need through the market and so are more likely to need to rely upon state or voluntary sector welfare services. For instance, only 37 per cent of women, compared to 61 per cent of men, have private or company pensions (Abercrombie and Ward, 1994, p. 213). Furthermore, it means that women are, in practice, likely to have to rely upon men to provide some things for them, a point to which we shall return shortly.

The differential between women's and men's rates of pay remains despite the introduction of policies designed to eliminate such inequalities in the Equal Pay and Sex Discrimination Acts of the 1970s. In fact the differential has declined to some extent since then – in 1970 women's weekly average pay was only 55 per cent of men's. But it has not been eliminated. This is because, although the numbers of women in employment have been increasing steadily since the Second World War, many of the jobs into which women have been recruited are different jobs from those traditionally done by men. Within the labour force women are *horizontally* segregated from men (they are doing different jobs) and are *vertically* segregated from men (they are generally at lower grades in the career structure).

These differences in women's employment circumstances have not been altered significantly by the development of welfare services. Indeed, to a large extent the growth of welfare provision, including in particular state welfare, has often reinforced occupational segregation through the creation of jobs that have been occupied almost exclusively by women, such as nurses, primary school teachers or social workers. In Britain these jobs have usually been associated with low status and low pay compared to those occupied characteristically by men, such as doctors, lecturers and service managers. Thus, while welfare services have created employment opportunities for women, they have also reinforced employment inequalities, although in some other countries, for example Sweden, such occupational inequities are much less marked.

Despite this growth in women's employment, which has been stimulated in part by the development of welfare, women are still less likely to be *economically active* than men. In 1992 women constituted 43 per cent of people in employment, although they made up over a half of the working age population (Abercrombie and Ward,

1994, p. 216). Signing on and claiming benefit as unemployed is generally taken as evidence of economic activity in addition to employment. However, although women are less likely to work than men, they constitute a minority of the official unemployed because they are also less likely to be entitled to benefits when out of work, especially where they are living with an economically active man. Thus women are more likely to remain outside the formal structures of both employment and unemployment.

Because they are less likely to be economically active, women are also therefore more likely to be dependent. Women constitute the majority of those who are dependent upon social security benefits, especially among the poorest groups such as lone parents and the single elderly (Alcock, 1993, Ch. 8; Oppenheim, 1993, Ch. 5); and, as the contributors to Glendinning and Millar's (1992) collection of papers on women and poverty point out, women are more likely than men to be at risk of poverty. However, women are not only more likely to be dependent upon state benefits; they are also frequently dependent, too, upon male spouses or partners.

The mutual dependency of close family members is a central feature of much policy planning within most welfare capitalist countries. In social security it is sometimes referred to as *aggregation*: the assumption that all the income and wealth of a family or household can be aggregated and treated as the shared resources of all members. In practice this often means that the main 'breadwinner' in the family is expected to provide for the rest; and in many families men, and women, assume that this breadwinning role should be occupied by the man. Women are thus presumed, and pressured, to accept a family role as dependent upon a man. This may partly explain the differential, referred to above, between women's and men's average rates of pay – women put their husband's careers before their own; but it is at the same time a fallacious assumption – in part because most married, and unmarried, women do engage in paid employment and do contribute towards household costs.

It is a myth therefore to believe that men are the only breadwinners. Many women are also providers for their families – although, because of lower pay and lower rates of employment, they often, nevertheless, remain dependent upon men. It is also a myth to believe that household and family resources are equally shared among members. As Pahl (1989) and others have shown, patterns of distribution of family income vary significantly; and in most cases women are not the major beneficiaries. What is more, in many other ways, too, women's family dependency may reduce the standard of living that they are able to enjoy when compared to their male partners – for instance, it is still women who do the majority of unpaid work *within* the home, even when they are also engaged in paid employment *outside* it.

Women's role as unpaid workers in the home is also reflected in their greater involvement as service providers in the informal sector. The vast majority of informally delivered welfare is home-based caring work. This is sometimes seen as predominantly 'women's work' – and in practice it frequently is. Childcare has always been predominantly provided by women at home; and the growing amount of care for dependent adults provided at home is also primarily done by women. For instance, although, as we mentioned in Chapter 6, men do provide care for adult dependents, throughout Europe the main carers for elderly people are women (McGlone and Cronin, 1994, Ch. 3). The differences between men and women as service providers within the welfare system are not restricted, therefore, to the differences between doctors and nurses within the state sector.

However, the gender differences within service *provision* are perhaps not as significant as such differences in the *access* to, or *use* of, welfare services. Feminist critics of traditional social policy have pointed out that most welfare services have in practice been constructed by, and for, men, with very clear assumptions made within them about the roles that women are to be expected play in this (Dale and Foster, 1986). As a result of this, women's experience of the welfare state is rather different to men's. This can be seen most clearly in the assumptions made about women's role within Beveridge's influential report on social security.

Beveridge's primary assumption was that married women's main role would be as housewives and mothers within the family, and that they would therefore make 'marriage their sole occupation' (Beveridge, 1942, p. 49). He thus excluded married women from insurance protection within his social security proposals through the offer of reduced contributions without an entitlement to benefits, because he assumed that their husbands would be able to provide income support for them. Although since then equal treatment directives from the EU have ensured that women are no longer excluded directly from benefit protection within social security, indirect disadvantages still remain – for instance, within means-tested provision women are still assumed to be able to rely upon support from a working partner (although this also applies where appropriate to unemployed men). In addition, assumptions which Beveridge made about women's family 'responsibilities' still dominate many other areas of social policy planning.

The provision (or non-provision) of nursery education and care for young children and the organisation of the school day and school year for older children assume the availability of women at home to care for children outside school hours. Community care within health and social services is also, as we have discussed, largely predicated upon the availability of women as providers of informal care, in cases of both acute need and chronic illness. Such assumptions have also influenced other service delivery in ways that have often overtly disadvantaged women. For instance, in education in the 1950s and 60s girls were required to achieve higher standards in the 'eleven plus' examination in order to progress to grammar school – and yet once there achieved lower standards, in part because they were subject in places to a separate curriculum designed to prepare them for their role as mothers. Such differentiation is now unlawful and the achievements of girls in school examination have overtaken those of boys (Abercrombie and Ward, 1994, pp. 232–5), suggesting that past inequalities were a product of institutional discrimination rather than actual gender differences.

As feminist critics such as Williams (1989) point out, therefore, the expectations that men have of women as housewives and mothers have structured the way in which welfare services for women have been developed and operated. In many cases, of course, these expectations are also shared by women, who are willing to shoulder the burdens of family responsibility, despite the disadvantages to which this inevitably leads. However, the growth of feminist criticism itself is evidence that women are not entirely passive, or subservient, recipients of gendered welfare policies. Academically and politically the rise of feminism in the last quarter of the twentieth century has seen a mounting challenge to the disadvantage which women experience within welfare services.

This challenge is not just an ideological, or theoretical, one either. Although in practice evidence suggests that generally welfare services do involve a net transfer of resources from men to women (Hills, 1993), feminists and others have been active in campaigning for improved, or restructured, welfare provision and in establishing separate services for women where male dominated provision was felt to be inappropriate or undesirable. Campaigning activities were discussed by the *In and Against the State* authors in the 1970s (LEWRG, 1979); and examples of separate services include women's aid refuges for victims of domestic violence and 'well women's clinics' for health promotion and medical care.

As Williams (1989) recognises, however, feminists do not all agree on their criticisms of the male welfare state, nor on what should be done to change this. There are different theoretical traditions within feminism, for example between the liberals and the radicals, and these differences lead to different strategies for challenging male domination within social policy, for instance between working with men and developing separatist women-only services. And, of course, there are also differences between women themselves – not all experience disadvantage within welfare in the same way or to the same extent.

Williams (1989, pp. 75–81) discusses the different experience that black women have of welfare services in Britain, for example their experience of some aspects of birth control as threatening to their role as mothers; and she points out that such differences have sometimes led to the development of services specifically designed for black women alone, for example the Asian women's refuge in Brent (Williams, 1989, p. 71). But it is not just race that divides women. Class clearly divides them, too, with some professional middle-class women benefiting significantly from their role within the welfare state. Age also divides women, with older women often experiencing disadvantage compared to their younger sisters. Gender differences are thus compounded, and cross-cut, by other social divisions.

Race

The importance of racial or ethnic differences in the experience of welfare services has, like those of gender, been marginalised within mainstream social policy in Britain, and in most other welfare capitalist countries. This marginalisation is now being exposed, and challenged. Like class, however, debates over divisions of 'race' depend to some extent upon how racial differences are perceived and defined and, more importantly, upon how the whole issue of race – or racism – is approached.

Britain is, and always has been, a multiracial and multicultural society, as flows of immigrants and emigrants have altered the composition of the indigent population. In the nineteenth and early twentieth centuries people came to Britain from Ireland, and Jewish emigrants arrived, in particular from Eastern Europe. Following the Second World War, Europeans, notably Poles, established themselves in Britain, and immigration was encouraged from Britain's former imperial colonies, such as the West Indies, India, Pakistan and Bangladesh. Immigrants have also arrived at different times from Africa, the Middle East and the Far East; and, since Britain's membership of the EU, significant numbers of people have come to this country from other member states.

There is thus a wide range of ethnic minority groups in the UK, some of whom have retained, or developed, relatively close community ties among themselves. Many of these ethnic minority groups have also been subject to discrimination and ill-treatment by other sections of the indigent population. The Irish, Jews, Poles, Pakistanis, and others, have all been the victims of negative attitudes and hostile reactions. These ethnic differences have also sometimes been reflected in disadvantage within welfare services. However, there has been a significant difference between these disadvantages and the discrimination experienced by the black immigrants who came from Britain's former colonies to settle in the UK in relatively large numbers in the 1950s and 60s. These immigrants were readily identifiable because of their black (or brown) skin colour and this became a source of hostility – and identity – that was independent of, or additional to, any other cultural or ethnic differences.

The hostility to black people coming to live in Britain is _racism_; it extends not only to immigrants but to all black people living here, an increasing proportion of whom, of course, have been born and brought up as British citizens. The racism that black people in Britain experience is thus not the same thing as reaction to ethnic differences, in part of course because it is quite independent of any such differences. The distinction that it creates is one between black people and white people, in which the former, whatever their origins, are frequently seen as undeserving interlopers. Despite recognising the differences of ethnic and cultural background that exist within the country, therefore, it is this racist distinction between black and white that has become the major force dividing the British population on the basis of race in the latter half of the twentieth century, and that is most important for our understanding of divisions within welfare services. It means that the focus of our analysis is thus not _race_, but racism (Solomos, 1989).

Williams points out that the marginalisation of race within traditional social policy means that knowledge about the circumstances, needs and problems of Britain's black population is frequently absent from policy debate. As she discusses, however, there is a more developed literature outside social policy, where these issues are more directly addressed (Williams, 1989, p. xiii). Thus we know that there are now around 2.6 million black people living in Britain, compared to around 100 000 before 1950 and that over 40 per cent of these were born here (Abercrombie and Ward, 1994, pp. 249–53). Black immigration to Britain took place mainly in the 1950s and early 1960s, when people were encouraged to come to Britain to supplement the labour force here during a period of economic boom – in many cases to take low-paid jobs within the expanding public services such as health or transport.

Black workers in Britain were thus immediately segregated within the broader labour market, generally occupying the lowest status jobs with the worst conditions and pay. This segregation and disadvantage has remained since, with black workers earning less on average than their white counterparts, as confirmed by later studies of economic activity among the black population – in the 1980s West Indian men earned on average only 85 per cent as much as white men, and Asian men 86 per cent (Brown, 1984; Robinson, 1990). Growing levels of unemployment have also affected black people differentially, with rates of unemployment in the early 1990s for West Indians (11 per cent) and Pakistanis (17 per cent), for instance, being much higher than those for whites (7 per cent) (Abercrombie and Ward, 1994, p. 256). As a result of this, black people in Britain have always been at greater risk of poverty and deprivation, and this risk has continued into the 1990s (Amin and Oppenheim, 1992). Their need for welfare protection is thus arguably greater; but their access to such protection has in practice often been more restricted.

In the mid 1960s recruitment even to low-paid jobs in Britain began to decline and, after legal changes in 1962, immigration was restricted to those who could first demonstrate a guarantee of a job on arrival. As the boom turned to recession in the 1970s, it was mainly only spouses and children joining their relatives here who were able to secure entry to the country. This process of restrictions on immigration has in itself created many problems for black people who have had difficulty proving their rights of entry into Britain (Moore and Wallace, 1975). Immigration restrictions have thus kept black families apart and have created a climate of suspicion and distrust that has in effect been visited on all black people living in Britain, whatever their national origins. They have also compounded the problem of anti-black racism, which was already present among the white British population, providing fuel for the suspicion that black people do not 'belong' in the country.

This suspicion has spilled over into the delivery of both public and private services to black people, operating in practice to restrict their access to them. For example, where services are only available to those with a legal right of residence in the country, the suspicion that black people may be illegal immigrants without such a right means that those delivering services may unjustifiably extend suspicion of non-entitlement to all potential black service users. There is evidence of such anti-black hostility and distrust in all major welfare services in Britain, including health services and public sector housing; but perhaps one of the clearest examples of it has been the requirement by some local benefit office staff for black – but not white – claimants to produce their passports as evidence of entitlement to social security benefits (Gordon and Newnham, 1985).

The exclusion of black service users from welfare provision in Britain is not, however, just a product of racist discrimination fuelled by suspicion of illegal immigration. At a more general ideological level it runs much deeper than that. One of the great strengths of the British welfare state, according to many commentators, is its development throughout the twentieth century as a joint product of political struggle and enlightened reform within the country – in particular during the important formative years of the 1940s. At that time it was presented as (and since then has often been praised as) a major national achievement – and thus a source of national pride.

As we have already discussed, however, many of these struggles and reforms were dominated by men and resulted in welfare services that reaffirmed, and reinforced, inequitable gender relationships within society. They were also struggles and reforms dominated by the political parties and campaigning organisations of the white British population. The national welfare state was a (white) British achievement – and as such was presented as a model to many of Britain's black colonies and former colonies. Most of the black people resident in Britain in the 1960s and 70s thus arrived in the country after the establishment of this national welfare state, from countries that had not themselves developed such structures. This invited an assumption by some that Britain's black population had not contributed to the development of the country's welfare services, and thus were not interested in using them – or even were not *entitled* to use them. From such a (racist) ideological perspective the welfare state was not intended for black people in Britain, and as a result their attempted use of it justified both suspicion and discrimination.

In the case of entitlement to some services such an exclusion was not just a product of certain ideological attitudes; it was also incorporated into the eligibility criteria for access to services. For instance, the National Insurance scheme, the centre-piece of the postwar social security system, based entitlement to benefit upon past contribution through employment. In the case of pension entitlement this meant contributions over the majority of a working life from the age of 16 to 65. This link between contribution and benefit was a central feature of the welfare reforms of the 1940s but, at least initially, black immigrants coming to Britain in the 1950s and 60s could not benefit fully from it, and were thus excluded from proper pension protection.

In the case of access to public sector housing similar exclusions also operated. Throughout most of the postwar period new council houses were a scarce resource and allocation of houses to local populations was in effect a rationing process. Most local authorities operated such rationing through the use of a waiting list. Frequently only local people with a number of years' residence in the authority were admitted to the waiting list, to ensure that houses went first to such local people. In practice, however, this discriminated against black people moving into local authority areas in the 1950s and 60s with no housing, and yet no history of local residence. They were thus effectively refused access to public sector housing for some years, and as a consequence forced into poorer, less secure, properties in the private sector.

In both of these cases rules and practices controlling access to welfare services were intrinsic – and in some ways understandable, or even desirable – features of entitlement that in fact operated to make access for black people more difficult. They did not *directly* discriminate against people on the basis of skin colour – NI contribution conditions and council house waiting lists technically applied equally to all. However, they did constitute a form of *indirect* (or *institutional*) racism, because of the much greater likelihood that black people would experience reduced access as a result of them. By operating in effect as indirect forms of discrimination, they also fuelled the more direct hostility and suspicion that black people often experienced in using these services which resulted from the assumption that they had not contributed towards the development of them.

Of course one of the effects of such institutional discrimination was that Britain's new black population of the 1960s and 70s was unable to benefit equally from the social services which had been developed as a result of the policies of the national welfare state, and thus had to provide for themselves in other ways. In the case of housing, for instance, their exclusion from public sector housing, and the direct discrimination that they also often experienced from private sector landlords and vendors, meant that black ethnic minority groups were forced into some of the worst private rented and private owner-occupied housing in Britain's inner cities. Together with their concentration in certain sectors of the labour market, this meant that black populations were thus not evenly distributed on a geographical basis throughout Britain. In practice they have lived and worked in particular urban areas, such as London, the Midlands, Lancashire and West Yorkshire; and within these urban areas they are concentrated in poorer, inner city districts where housing conditions, and other service provision, is much below average.

Such race, or ethnic, concentration is common in most other welfare capitalist countries, too, and it is particularly stark, for example, in the USA. However, it also further compounds the discrimination and disadvantage experienced by the black people living in such inner city 'ghettos'. This operates both directly because both public and private provision in such areas is often inadequate, and indirectly because residence within a deprived district may lead to further discrimination by external service providers. For instance, banks and building societies have been known to discriminate against residents of certain districts in their policies of granting (or not granting) mortgages to house buyers – sometimes called 'red-lining'.

The reduced access of black people to welfare services is thus compounded by their geographical isolation within local communities. This fuels direct racism against black residents here. It also forces black communities to seek protection and provision outside the formal welfare services. It is no coincidence, therefore, that community-based voluntary organisations have always been significant sources of welfare and support within black communities; and that informal provision, through the family and community, has also been of vital importance for them.

What is more, the need for such forms of 'self-help' has been further accentuated by the more general failure of formal welfare services to recognise many of the specific needs and problems of black individuals and groups. Welfare services designed by, and for, Britain's white population have ignored the different physical and cultural needs of different ethnic groups. This is revealed in the inattention given by health services to diseases specifically affecting black groups, such as sickle-cell, rickets and hepatitis; and in the more general inequalities in health revealed in Townsend *et al.* (1988). It is also found in the reluctance to recognise and provide for religious or cultural differences in education, such as the need for Muslim children to have halal meat in school meals and to subscribe to strict dress codes in girls' clothing.

It is not just that different needs have been ignored, however. Different social or cultural practices have also led to condemnation and stigmatisation. For instance, different family structures and family practices among the black population, such as the greater incidence of lone parenthood among Afro-Caribbeans, have sometimes been characterised as inappropriate or inadequate and have resulted in suspicion and pathologisation of black families (Williams, 1989, p. 188). This can mean that black clients are more likely to end up as 'problems' on social service caseloads, for example mixed-race children are over-represented among those in local authority care (Bebbington and Miles, 1989).

Ironically, however, the development of voluntary and informal support to replace the inadequacies within, and exclusions from, formal welfare services has in some ways compounded the discrimination experienced by black people. For the existence of self-protection can act as a confirmation that formal services are not needed by black communities, because they can be relied on to 'provide for themselves'. Exclusion from welfare services thus becomes translated into apparent disinterest in them. This is a view that can encourage both direct and indirect discrimination by white service providers.

However, it can also lead to further, strategic, separatism by black communities, which respond to exclusion from 'white' welfare services by the conscious development of *black-only* separate provision. Williams (1989, pp. 100–10) discusses some examples of this black autonomy, such as the Asian Women's Refuge (referred to earlier), black housing associations, and the issue of the adoption of black children in care only by parents who are black. These are obviously to some extent controversial issues, for black-only service provision can operate to confirm, rather than reduce, divisions between black and white users of welfare – although they may for many black people be the only way of meeting some current needs.

The relative exclusion of Britain's black population from welfare services is curiously contradicted, however, by the involvement of black people as workers within such welfare services. As we said, many black people came to Britain in the 1950s from the former colonies to work in the growing public services such as health and transport; black people have thus always occupied a strategic, if undervalued and low-paid, role within many welfare services (Doyal *et al.*, 1981). As in other developed countries, therefore, migrant and immigrant populations thus contribute as service providers, even though they do not always benefit as service users.

Age

Discrimination by age within social policy is in one way significantly different from discrimination on the basis of class, gender or race. Despite class mobility, the latter are all very largely closed categories; thus to a large extent we can explain the discrimination between them in terms of self-interest – for example powerful white men benefit at the expense of poor black women. In the case of age, however, the differences are stages in a lifecycle through which most of us will inevitably go – and all of us will presumably expect to. If self-interest is at play here, it is a very shortsighted self-interest indeed – and yet the evidence, especially of more recent analysis and research, suggests that this is just what is the case.

Discrimination by age adversely affects the young and the old. Children, because they are unable to provide for themselves, must be provided for by others – they thus need welfare services. In Britain, as in all other welfare capitalist countries, the expectation is that these services will be provided predominantly on an informal basis through the family, and this is largely what happens in practice – the most notable exception, of course, being the provision of free education through the state. However, families need support to care for their children, especially where income is low, and the cost of providing for children is likely to push such families into deprivation.

The costs of providing for children within families were a major focus of social policy campaigning in Britain in the interwar years, resulting in the introduction in the 1940s of Family Allowances to cover some of the costs of family child-rearing (Macnicol, 1980). Family Allowances, and the former tax allowances for children, have now been replaced by *Child Benefit*, a direct subsidy towards the additional costs of children. However, Child Benefit does not (and is not intended to) cover all of the additional costs that families face in providing for their children. Thus it has left families – and consequently the children within them – at greater risk of poverty than the rest of the adult population (Oppenheim, 1993, pp. 35–6).

The disadvantage that we face as dependent children is also continued into early adulthood. Sixteen- to eighteen-year-olds are now largely excluded from benefit protection within the social security scheme and are expected to continue to rely on their parents if they cannot find paid work. If, after the age of 18, young adults are still unemployed they are effectively excluded from NI protection, because they have not been able to make the requisite contributions, and they are paid at a lower rate of Income Support until the age of 25. Since the rise in levels in unemployment in the 1970s, young people have also been at greater risk of unemployment and low pay (Lee, 1991). Thus the discrimination against children as dependants, extends also to young adults both inside and outside the labour market.

Discrimination against the young in social policy is not, however, as marked as discrimination against the elderly. Older people experience a range of disadvantages within policy development and delivery, which are the direct result of assumptions that younger policy makers make about their circumstances and needs. It is only relatively recently that the particular problems experienced by older people as a result of 'ageism' within social policy have been widely debated and analysed within the discipline. It is now, however, sometimes referred to as a specific area of study called *gerontology*. In their collection of papers on ageing and social policy, Phillipson and Walker (1986), two of the most prominent contemporary gerontologists, discuss a number of the important aspects of age discrimination within welfare, in particular the myths about dependency and need in old age.

Dependency

The myth of dependency is based upon a fear among policy makers that the growing numbers of elderly people will constitute a financial burden upon the rest of the population, as a result of which provision for them needs to be curtailed. Certainly the numbers of older people in society have been growing in Britain, and in most other developed countries, throughout the twentieth century – and they are set to increase further in the early twenty-first century. This is in large part, of course, a product of the success of other social policies in prolonging life expectancy. It is presumably welcomed by all at an individual level; but at a collective level it changes the balance of age distribution within the population, and this is seen as a problem by some.

Demographic trends (the changes in the size and distribution of the population) allow us to make fairly accurate predictions about the current and future balance between age groups within the population. As Tinker (1984, Ch. 1) discusses, in practice the picture in Britain is a more complex one than just a growth in numbers higher up the age profile. Shifts in fertility patterns and the effects of war and economic depression have meant that the numbers born, and surviving, in each generation throughout the twentieth century have varied; and thus, as each generation (or *cohort*) gets older these variations affect the balance between young and old in different ways – although overall the trend in growing numbers of older people remains a relatively constant one.

In the early half of the twentieth century the growth in numbers of the elderly was not seen as a social problem; and, although older workers were sometimes seen as inefficient, they were also valued for the experience that they could share with new recruits. However, two policy developments in particular have conspired to change the value placed on age and experience. These are the provision of pensions for older people as a substitute for wages and the establishment of retire-ment (and increasingly earlier retirement) as a means of removing older people from the labour market. Retirement is now a well-established lifecourse event. Men expect to retire, or are required to retire, at 65 and women at 60, although women's retirement age is now to be raised to 65. With high levels of unemployment in the last quarter of the century, however, many men and women working in areas where labour is at a surplus have been persuaded or coerced to take earlier retirement in order to leave jobs for younger people, or have effectively retired early themselves after becoming unemployed in their fifites or sixties.

Retirement is seen as justified by many, and may be welcomed by some, because pension provision means that those who do retire can continue to enjoy an income after employment. State pensions were the first of the new social security benefits to be introduced at the beginning of the twentieth century and were a major feature of the postwar Beveridge insurance scheme, under which contributions made during working life entitled all workers to a basic pension on retirement. This basic state pension is still the largest social security benefit, in expenditure terms, and it has been supplemented since 1978 by an additional earnings-related element – the State Earnings Related Pension Scheme (SERPS).

However, many workers, and increasing numbers of pensioners, are now also contributing to, or receiving money from, private or occupational pension schemes that act as a supplement to the basic state pension, and usually a substitute for SERPS. Private and occupa-tional pensions are in effect a form of deferred wages, and they mean that some older people can enjoy a significant income from them after retirement, with state pensions as an additional bonus – these people have sometimes been called *Woopies* (Well-Off Older Persons). But it is only a minority who are so well-off. Most occupational pensions provide only small additional benefits; and many pensioners have not been part of such schemes at all. For most older people, therefore, it is the limited state benefits that provide the bulk of their income after retirement. This means that their average standard of living is much lower than the rest of the population and their risk of poverty much higher (Walker, 1990; Alcock, 1993, Ch. 10). Indeed, throughout the whole of the twentieth century the elderly have constituted the largest group among the poor; as Walker (1986) argues, this is because of the role of pensions policy in producing poverty in old age.

The differences between Woopies and poorer pensioners do reveal, however, that the circumstances of the elderly are not identical; in fact differences within old age are structured by social divisions experi-enced earlier in the lifecycle – in particular those between class, gender and race. Thus it is working-class older people, women and black elders who are least likely to be benefiting from private or occupational pensions and thus most likely to be dependent upon basic state provision. There are even further differences by *age* here, too, with the 'young old', who have recently retired with private pensions and assets purchased while in employment, being better off than the 'older old', who have been on low incomes for much longer and whose working life preceded the relatively recent period of the rapid development of private and occupational pension provision.

Dependency in old age is thus a product of policies of pension provision and retirement. Consequently so, too, is the fear that a growing proportion of elderly people requiring pensions will constitute a burden on the rest of society, which society will not be able to afford. Of course, this fear is unfounded in policy terms for, although high unemployment has created pressure for retirement for older people, the funding of, and entitlement to, pensions can be changed as circumstances change, as indeed could policies on retirement age and the employment rights of older people. Thus the burden of provision – if indeed it can be characterised as a burden at all – can be reduced or transferred depending upon economic circumstances and political priorities.

Welfare needs

This dependency myth, however, is confounded by the assumption that older people have more extensive, and more expensive, welfare needs than the rest of the population; and that, as a result of this, they are less able to provide for themselves and more likely to require support from social services. Underlying this assumption is the presumed frailty of older people, as result of which it is anticipated that they will be unable to work and will require health and personal care. While it is true that older people do consume a larger proportion of health and personal social service spending than the younger population (McGlone, 1992), this is because when people are older they are more likely to experience physical disability, especially over the age of 75. In other words, their welfare needs arise because of physical or other disabilities – not because they are old. This is a crucial distinction; yet it is unfortunately frequently disguised in the classification, by health and social service providers, of all older service users as *elderly* – even though the services that they use are based upon their specific and identifiable needs for care or support.

In fact, the majority of older people do *not* have extensive needs for health and social services. More than half of those over 65 do not have any disability and a further 20 per cent have only slight disability; even among the over 75s, over a half have no disability or only slight disability (Phillipson and Walker, 1986, p. 8). The vast majority of older people live alone, or with partners, in private homes within the community. Furthermore, despite retirement, many older people still are still engaged in part-time paid work – and most are capable of employment. Also many undertake voluntary work; and virtually all (well at least all women) continue to do unpaid work in the home and family. Indeed, Finch (1989) found that older people were generally the givers, rather than the receivers, of informal services within families.

The discrimination against older people within social policy, therefore, and the fears of the 'burden' of an ageing population, may both be seen as products of social policy – rather than problems for it. Retirement has excluded able older people from paid employment, and inadequate pension provision has left them in, or at risk of, poverty as a result. And the categorisation of all older service users as 'elderly' has created the myth that old age is a cause of disease and disability. However, gerontologists are now challenging such myths within social policy and, as a result of this, recognition of discrimination by age has now become an essential feature of policy analysis.

Disability

Discrimination and disadvantage experienced by people with disabilities is, like that experienced by the other social divisions discussed above, a long-standing feature of policy development and delivery in Britain – and, as in the case of older people, the disadvantages experienced by disabled people also cut across these other social divisions. Like race and age, however, disability has frequently been absent from mainstream social policy debate and analysis, even in relatively recent times; thus the policy implications of recognising the importance of disadvantage among the disabled are still sometimes ignored as a focus of study.

As in the case of older people, too, the numbers of people with disabilities has been growing – although again this is largely a product of more general successes within social policy which should be welcomed. Furthermore, the increased consciousness of disabled people of their disadvantaged state, and their more vocal demand for services, have both challenged the paternalistic approach towards disability that had often characterised service provision in the past (Oliver, 1990). Such paternalist approaches have generally characterised disabled people as the clients of welfare services, whose needs are provided for by others on the basis of professional assessment. The new political campaigners for disability, however, present themselves as citizens with rights, which they are demanding, but are being denied by discriminatory practices and inappropriate professionalism among service providers. Disability is thus forcing itself into a different place on the social policy agenda.

From a policy perspective, however, there are some definitional problems of both an analytical and a practical nature that complicate the debate about policy development for people with disabilities. Most fundamentally, there is no clear agreement about what constitutes a disability, or what degree of disability is likely to lead to disadvantage. Clearly degrees, and consequences, of disability vary widely from a minor loss of functions or physical features, which may often be undetected by others, to complete paralysis and dependency. This has resulted, for instance, in attempts to classify degrees and types of disability, such as the social security regulations which provide a percentage scale which is used to determine the amount of benefit due to people with certain disabilities, and the elaborate definitions of care and mobility needs which are used to determine entitlement to benefits intended to meet the extra costs associated with such disabilities – notably the Disability Living Allowance (DLA).

These definitional issues were taken up most significantly, however, in 1985 and 1986 in a major study of disabled people in Britain which was carried out by the Office of Population Censuses and Surveys (OPCS), based on interviews with 14 000 adults and 1300 parents of disabled children. The findings from this were published in a series of research reports, and they are discussed and summarised by Dalley (1991). The OPCS divided their disabled respondents into ten different categories, depending upon degree of disability; from this they estimated the numbers of people in each category in the population as a whole. For the highest category, the most dependent group, there were almost 250 000 in Great Britain; and for all categories together (that is all those with some level of disability) there were over 6.5 million. Taking this broader definition, therefore, disability is clearly a major issue for social policy, with the discrimination and disadvantage experienced by those with disabilities extending to over ten per cent of the population.

Part of the disadvantage of disability is obviously a result of the loss or impairment of function which disabled people experience. For instance, blindness or paralysis mean that people cannot readily move around without guidance or assistance. Of course there are aids, such as guide dogs or wheelchairs, that can help to overcome such problems. But such aids cost money to purchase and maintain; in effect they mean that people with disabilities frequently require a larger income to enjoy the same standard of living, or quality of life, as others.

These extra costs of disability were recognised and discussed within the OPCS survey; they calculated these at between £5 and £12 a week at 1985 prices for those in the most disabled categories. However, these were notional – and controversial – calculations. The Disability Income Group (DIG), a campaign organisation for people with disabilities, put the cost at between £28 and £146 using a different measure of weekly needs (Large, 1991). These are significant disagreements, about which arguments still continue; but in all cases they represent significant additional weekly costs, suggesting that people with disabilities thus need to receive relatively high incomes – or significant support in the form of cash benefits or service provision.

In fact, however, people with disabilities generally have lower, not higher, incomes than the rest of the population, primarily because they experience inequality and discrimination within the labour market. Less than a third of disabled people of working age are in paid employment, compared to over two thirds of the general population; and even where they are in employment, disabled people earn, on average, lower wages (Dalley, 1991). This discrimination in employment continues despite the existence since 1944 of a statutory requirement in the Disabled Persons (Employment) Act that all employers over a certain size employ a specific quota of people with disabilities (Prescott-Clarke, 1990). The quota system is quite ineffective in securing equal employment opportunities for disabled people and this has contributed, in the 1990s, to campaigns for more effective anti-discrimination legislation similar to that dealing with sex and race.

Their relative exclusion from, and disadvantage within, employment thus means that people with disabilities are more likely than others to be dependent upon benefits, especially Income Support. In fact, as we mentioned, the social security system in Britain does include within it specific benefits targeted at the needs and costs experienced by disabled people. These include higher rates of standard benefits for those who are out of work due to chronic sickness or disability, such as Incapacity Benefit (formerly Invalidity Benefit, which was actually paid at an even higher level) and additional non-contributory benefits aimed at meeting the extra costs of disability, such as the Disability Living Allowance, which includes payments for the costs of providing mobility and home care.

None of these benefits is paid at a very generous level, however, and they do not bring the majority people with disabilities anywhere near the average income levels enjoyed by the bulk of the rest of the population. Yet evidence suggests that even some of these benefits are not claimed by all of the disabled people who may be entitled to them, in part because of their highly selective focus on specific disability needs and the complex process that must be undertaken to claim them. Despite the apparent good intentions, benefits for disability, therefore, do not in general operate to counteract the low income levels and additional living costs experienced by many disabled people (Walker and Walker, 1991).

Inadequate incomes could be compensated, in part at least, by the provision of services for people with disabilities – and provision is made for disabled people through both health and social services. Statutory requirements exist for the provision of services for disability through the Chronically Sick and Disabled Persons Act 1970 and the Disabled Persons Act 1986. In the 1990s much of this service provision has been restructured within the joint health and social service planning for community care. Community care planning was intended to reduce reliance on residential provision for people with physical and mental disabilities and, as a result of this, all people needing caring services within the community now have a right to an assessment of their needs and to the planning of a package of care to be carried out by a social worker.

This move towards assessment and planning of care from the perspective of the consumer of services (the citizen with a disability) rather than the provider of services (such as the local residential home) is no doubt welcomed by many disabled people who are concerned to gain more power and control over their lives; and the demand for more 'independent living' has been a focus for campaigning among some groups of disabled people. The development of community care is intended to coordinate service provision across the public, private, voluntary and informal sectors, and yet it was implemented at a time of cuts in the resources provided to public services and to voluntary sector support. In many cases, therefore, it has resulted in more reliance being placed on informal providers, further accentuating the family pressures that many disabled people and their caring relatives experience; and in greater expectations being placed on disabled people to purchase private services, or pay charges for public services, out of their already inadequate incomes. Service provision does not always compensate for low income and high costs therefore – and may indeed exacerbate the problems of these. As a result, the means by which the quality of life for people with disabilities might by raised to nearer that of the rest of the able-bodied population is still largely absent from social policy provision.

What is more, the disadvantage flowing from inadequate income and lack of services is compounded for many disabled people by their daily experience of the frustrations and exclusions of living within an able-bodied world. Lack of wheelchair access keeps many disabled people out of public buildings; lack of information in other than written form keeps blind people underinformed about events and services. Other barriers and exclusions exist throughout all public and private service provision.

However, it would be quite wrong to suggest that it is the disabilities from which people suffer *per se* that prevent them from competing, and succeeding, equally with their able-bodied colleagues and neighbours. Indeed, it is clear here that the interrelationship between disability and the disadvantages of class, gender and race intersect. The Houses of Commons and Lords, the seats of government in Britain and arguably the most powerful policy-making institutions in the country, contain members in wheelchairs and members who are blind and deaf. These politicians are no less capable or effective than their colleagues as a result of these disabilities, because they have the resources to ensure that, with appropriate support and assistance, they are able to avoid or overcome the problems they face. If the policy makers can overcome social divisions in this way, it suggests that the policies which they might develop and implement could help others to do so too – but so far this hope has not been translated into reality for all.

12

Paying for Welfare

The cost of welfare

The economic context in which social policies are developed and implemented is important in determining the scale and the scope of welfare services. As we discussed in Chapter 8, economic trends influence both the need for social services and the ability of a country to afford to provide them; and thus the shifting patterns of economic growth in Britain, and in other welfare capitalist countries, over the last century or more have had a significant impact in controlling the development of social policy. At the same time, however, it is now widely recognised that the provision of welfare services can also influence the patterns of economic growth – both directly, for instance by providing employment in welfare services, and indirectly, for instance by stimulating demand for goods and improving the quality of the workforce. Social and economic policy interact; therefore they need to be planned and developed together – and in practice in Britain, and elsewhere, this is just what happens.

This means recognising the important role that welfare plays in securing economic growth; but it also means planning to ensure that the costs of welfare services are identifiable and measurable, and can be met from within current economic resources. For, even though welfare services may be desirable in both social and economic terms, they still have to be funded. Welfare costs money – or at least it consumes resources, whether or not those resources are provided in the form of cash. Thus the money, or the resources, must be identified and collected; and must be distributed to those providing, or consuming, welfare services. In all cases, therefore, the study of social policy involves not just undertaking an examination of the structure and the use of welfare services but also understanding the means of *paying for* these.

Given the importance of welfare to economic and social development in advanced industrial societies, we might expect that all such countries would be required to address the question of paying for welfare in similar ways. To some extent this is true; international comparison reveals that all European countries, for example, spend roughly between 20 and 30 per cent of their gross domestic product (GDP) on social protection (Glennerster, 1992, p. 15). However, there are differences within this range; and there are some countries outside it – for example Sweden with 35 per cent and Portugal with 17 per cent in 1988. Such a difference, with Sweden dedicating twice the proportion of its resources to welfare that Portugal does, suggests significant variation around the norm. On this international scale Britain is revealed to dedicate a relatively small proportion of resources to paying for welfare, providing 23.6 per cent of GDP in 1988 – some way below the European average.

As we shall discuss shortly, the picture is more complex, however, than these broad overall comparisons might reveal. This is because there is variety not just in how much is spent but also in how this money is collected and distributed. Different models for financing and distributing welfare are also likely to produce differences in the structure, and the effectiveness, of welfare services; and these are independent, at least in part, of overall costs. In other words, the same overall amounts of resources can be spent in different ways, some of which may deliver similar, or better, services for the same cost. Thus comparisons based only on overall expenditure may not tell us much about the extent of welfare. We need to look in addition at how effectively the money is spent.

The debate about the effective use of resources in providing welfare services has sometimes been presented as a balance, or a conflict, between 'equity' and 'efficiency' in paying for welfare. A concern with the *equity* of welfare services focuses attention upon whether services are provided adequately to consumers and, in particular, whether individual needs for social protection are being met. Whereas a concern with *efficiency* focuses attention upon whether the resources that are consumed in service delivery are being used for maximum effect and at minimal cost.

Economists have therefore sought to evaluate the effectiveness of services in quantifiable terms, by contrasting equity gains with efficiency costs. They have sometimes suggested that pressure on efficiency resulting from the broader context of economic growth means that there is an inevitable 'trade-off' between the two, in which equity gains must be scaled back to meet the need for more efficient use of scarce resources for social protection (Okun, 1975). However, as Le Grand (1990) points out, the inevitability of such a trade-off is in practice a misleading notion, for the goal of securing equity in the meeting of needs is rather different from the aim of ensuring that the delivery of services is cost-effective. Pursuing efficiency can result in a maintenance of quality at reduced cost (Le Grand, 1993); thus it does not also prevent the securing of equity – indeed arguably improved efficiency in service provision could in fact contribute to greater equity.

Certainly attempts to contrast the two in quantifiable terms, and to set the costs of one against the other, are fraught with both conceptual and practical difficulties. Economists may argue that judgements about how, and how much, to pay for welfare should be subject to efficiency criteria. But efficiency alone cannot be the basis for making judgements about paying for welfare, for we also need to determine the social policy goals for which services are developed and delivered. Efficiency and equity are twin goals for social policy that must be considered together, not mutually exclusive poles that we must choose between – as recent attempts to control the costs of welfare in Britain have revealed.

The pursuit of efficiency

Following the economic recession of the 1970s and 80s, the growing costs of welfare services, which were providing for a wider and wider range of social needs, began to be seen as a more and more costly burden on a weakening economy – the costs of welfare were growing, and the means of paying for them were in decline. There was thus an increasing pressure within economic and social policy planning for greater efficiency in welfare services that, in part, gave rise to the false concerns about the need to review the pursuit of equity in the light of this. The main form that this concern took, of course, was the attempt to contain, and later to cut, the levels of public expenditure on welfare services, so that taxes could be reduced in order to stimulate economic growth.

We have already discussed in Chapter 8 the more general consequences of this shift to monetarism within economic policy and its inability to generate growth in the face of international economic recession. Despite this failure, however, the greater attention focused on curtailing the costs of welfare in the 1970s and 80s did lead to an enhanced profile for the assessment of efficiency within service delivery. This took the form of the setting of cash limits for annual expenditure both for central and local government, where previously expenditure targets had been adjusted to reflect spending patterns based on the demand for services. It also resulted in concerted campaigns to reduce waste and duplication in public services, through challenges to existing bureaucratic procedures and the imposition of 'savings' targets on the managers of service departments.

Cash limits and savings were aimed at driving down costs in the public provision of welfare, in order to meet efficiency targets. Cost cutting also extended to the use of private sector provision to replace state services, and the use of the competition of the private market to secure more efficient delivery. For instance, central government departments and local authorities were required to put the delivery of public services out to competitive tender between public and private providers, with contracts being awarded to those offering the most cost-efficient tender. Even where market competition with private sector providers could not be developed, efficiency through competition was pursued within state services through the introduction of *quasi-markets*, as we saw in Chapter 4.

Thus the costs of welfare, especially publicly provided welfare were reduced in the 1980s, for example through reductions in the costs of cleaning and catering services within the NHS. However, the overall impact of such cuts – or efficiencies – is more complex. The reduction of costs in one area can often merely lead to a transfer of these costs elsewhere. In effect, the cheaper services such as cleaning and catering were paid for by reductions in the wages paid to the workers employed by the new contractors, resulting in an increase in the need to provide benefits for these low-paid workers through Housing Benefit and Family Credit.

Moreover, not all of the market, and quasi-market, changes in the means of paying for welfare did lead to reductions in costs. In the health service, for instance, the 'transaction costs' implicit in the operation of the new internal markets – the need for service providers and purchasers to negotiate about transfers of resources between them – undermined any overall expenditure savings that competition might have been able to achieve (Baggott, 1994, p. 199). Thus in some cases at least, efficiency was *reduced*, without any compensating equity gain.

As a result therefore, despite the changes made in the pursuit of greater efficiency in the 1970s and 80s, the overall costs in terms of the *absolute* levels of public expenditure continued to rise gradually; and even when assessed *relatively* against the growth in the economy, as measured by GDP, they remained more or less constant at just above 20 per cent of GDP (Glennerster, 1992, pp. 65–6).

In part this continuity in public expenditure levels was a product of the failure of welfare reforms to produce efficiency savings but the predominant reason for it was the continuing real need for welfare provision. In other words, the pursuit of equity still remained as the major determinant of welfare costs. What is more, it still remained popular with the public – with gradually increasing numbers of people saying that they would be prepared to continue to pay taxes at current, or increased, levels in order to maintain welfare services (Taylor-Gooby, 1991). It is probably no coincidence, therefore, that the collection of taxes as the major means of paying for welfare has also remained at more or less constant levels throughout this period – although, as we shall see shortly, the balance within society between those who pay these taxes has changed significantly.

The growth of public expenditure

In fact in historical terms, the use of public expenditure to provide for welfare services has been a relatively recent development. Its growth, in Britain and elsewhere, has been largely a twentieth-century phenomenon, and in particular has been linked to the development of state welfare services after the Second World War. As we have seen, right-wing critics of extensive public expenditure have often suggested that such collective provision of welfare stifles the individual responsibility to provide for oneself and one's family and diverts resources from an efficient private sector to wasteful public bureaucracies. In practice, however, the relationship between public and private welfare expenditure is more complex than this, for the two are always inextricably interlinked.

At a fundamental level, of course, it is not at all clear that private expenditure better meets individual needs and desires than public expenditure. Individuals may welcome, and support, public spending both for altruistic reasons (because of their concern to remain members of a society in which the basic needs of all are met), and for reasons of self-interest (because of a recognition that collective provision can frequently provide protection that individuals could not purchase on a private market – for example social security benefits for unemployment). The balance between public and private expenditure of welfare is thus in large part a pragmatic affair rather than a matter of principle – based on planning for both equity and efficiency within social policy.

In practice this balancing act has meant that both public and private funding for welfare have been maintained and planned together, although the relationship between the two has changed in different areas over time (Glennerster, 1992, Pt. IV). The uses of public and private funding also frequently overlap. For instance, where payment for welfare is privately organised, state funding may be used to subsidise private costs, such as in the tax subsidies for mortgage costs for owner-occupiers of property or the subsidisation of assisted places for certain children in private schools. Conversely, where welfare is predominantly publicly funded, private charges may operate for some services, such as for prescriptions for drugs in the NHS; or users may be able to top-up state service with private additions, such as private rooms in NHS hospitals.

Despite the recent, unsuccessful, attempts to contain public expenditure, however, the trend throughout most of the twentieth-century development of welfare services has been for public expenditure on welfare to grow. In addition much of this growth has resulted from the collectivisation and take-over of previously private or voluntary provision. For instance, in the early part of the twentieth century public provision of primary education replaced the schools that had previously been run by voluntary organisations such as the Church; and in the welfare reforms of the 1940s the National Health Service replaced the old voluntary hospitals and much of private health care.

Public expenditure has grown in part because it is more effective, and more efficient, at providing for many social needs (what economists would call the effect of *market failure*) and in part because a wider range of social needs and public services have resulted in demands for overall improvements in collective welfare (what economists would call the impact of *public choice*) (Glennerster, 1992, Ch. 2). Despite criticisms of both market failure and public choice justifications for state welfare expenditure as an interference with natural economic forces of a market economy, they have nevertheless resulted in an inexorable growth throughout the century in the proportion of total resources being devoted to welfare from around 3 per cent to 23 per cent of GDP (Glennerster, 1992, p. 64). Of course, supporters of public welfare would point out that this has resulted both in improved economic growth and higher levels of social service – even if these are not so high by international comparison.

As we suggested above, however, it is not just the total level of expenditure that determines the equity or efficiency of public, or private, welfare but rather the way in which such expenditure is distributed and consumed. As well as the disparities in levels of expenditure, there are also disparities in the patterns of distribution and consumption between different welfare capitalist countries. Even within Britain in the 1990s, patterns of distribution and consumption vary both between different welfare services and within particular areas of provision.

The distribution of public funding

State expenditure on welfare services in Britain takes a wide variety of forms. For a start, as we have discussed in Chapter 10, not all expenditure is made by central government – much takes place at a *local* government level too. Thus, although central government raises 90 per cent of taxation for public expenditure, 25 per cent of expenditure is made by local government, with major areas of state expenditure such as education and housing being largely in local hands. The balance between central and local welfare expenditure has, of course, been changing throughout the last century; and it has been subject to much policy debate, and conflict, in recent years as a result of central government attempts to curb local expenditure growth. Despite this, local spending remains a significant aspect of overall state welfare costs, and is likely to continue to do so into the future.

Both central and local expenditure on welfare services may sometimes aim to cover the *full cost* of service delivery, such as funding for state schools and hospitals – although, in practice even such 'full cost' provision frequently requires additional private expenditure on related, but essential, factors such as uniforms, sports kits and textbooks for school children (Bull, 1980). In some cases, however, state expenditure does not aim, even in principle, to provide the full cost of services but operates only as a *subsidy* to private or voluntary provision.

Subsidies may be direct, as in the case of grant aid from government to voluntary sector organisations such as Citizens Advice Bureaux, or subsidisation of private developers to build houses or public buildings. But subsidies may also be indirect. The assisted places in private schools, mentioned above, is an example of indirect subsidisation of private education provision. There have been proposals from some to extend this principle much further through the provision to all parents of a *voucher* representing the cost of school education that could then be used to place a child in any public or private school (Glennerster, 1992, pp. 219–21).

Subsidisation of private provision through the use of tax relief for payments towards the cost of private welfare protection is already very extensive, for instance through reliefs for mortgage interest payments and private pension contributions. In 1955 Titmuss (1958) talked about the importance of such 'fiscal welfare' and pointed out that it was a major feature of state welfare expenditure that, in practice, operated primarily to benefit the middle classes. Public benefits for the middle classes may of course be a desirable goal of state welfare expenditure. However, the widespread effect of indirect state expenditure in benefiting primarily the better-off is often disguised within social policy debate because tax allowances and reliefs such as these are excluded from some calculations of the overall cost of public welfare, since they involve non-collection of resources rather than redistribution or spending by the state. Nevertheless, they are an important, and a planned, feature of the balance between the public and private funding of welfare services, and should be included in any assessment of the operation of these.

Even where state expenditure is provided on a full-cost basis rather than through subsidisation, however, the basis for distributing such funding may vary. In particular, state funding may be used directly to meet costs of those responsible for delivering state services (payments to *providers*); or funding may be given to users who can then choose which providers they will receive their services from (payments to *purchasers*). Payment of public money directly to purchasers of services has always been a significant feature of welfare provision, despite the growth of publicly delivered services in the latter half of the twentieth century. For instance, social security benefits like Child Benefit allow parents to use public money to purchase goods and services for their children.

However, the purchaser–provider division in the public financing of welfare services has become much more important both politically and in policy terms in the last twenty years or so. For example, direct subsidisation of the costs of building and maintaining public housing has been largely replaced with social security benefits targeted on poor tenants who cannot afford to pay for such costs through their rents in the form of Housing Benefit. And social security benefits for people with disabilities have provided such claimants with cash benefits with which to buy goods or services to help them with mobility or personal care needs, where previously these might have been provided directly by local social services. In both cases these were the result of deliberate policy decisions to shift the focus of state support from service providers to service users – in the case of housing, from bricks and mortar to tenants.

This policy change has been accentuated even more in the 1990s with the more widespread development of *quasi-markets* within state services in the areas of education, health and personal social services – as we saw in Chapter 4.

Quasi-markets are intended to ensure that the purchasers, rather than the providers, have power over services; but purchaser power does not always mean that the purchasers, or the users whom they represent, end up getting the best services. In the case of health and social services, for instance, judgements about the choice of health or social care require a knowledge and understanding of medical diagnosis and treatment that most ordinary people will not have. In these areas, therefore, the quasi-markets that have been introduced pass the control over purchaser resources not to the users themselves but to professional agents who can make purchasing decisions on their behalf – either GPs or social workers (Bartlett and Harrison, 1993; Means and Smith, 1994, Ch. 5).

Furthermore, the use of professionals as proxies for users in the purchase of welfare services – together with the financial incentives that flow inevitably from the purchaser–provider split – have resulted in the development of perverse, yet unavoidable, incentives within quasi-markets that disadvantage potential users. These include 'adverse selection' or 'cream-skimming'.

Adverse selection is prompted by the pressure placed on providers and purchasers to secure their income from the resources that users bring to 'buy' their services. Health service providers, such as hospitals, will thus want to attract purchasers, such as GPs, who have resources to spend; so they will not want to be drawn into providing expensive services that purchasers either cannot, or in practice do not, pay for. Patients with illnesses that are expensive to cure, and especially those with chronic conditions that require extensive treatment but offer little prospect of cure, are thus not likely to be attractive to the GPs who must purchase health care for them. As a result, GPs may refuse to accept such patients onto their caseloads, because they will reduce the amount of resources available for other patients; and consequently, the hospital providers will no longer make the treatments they need available to them.

Cream-skimming is the other side of this coin. While some users may be unattractive to providers, others may be very attractive indeed. For instance, schools who expect to be judged by parents on the basis of exam performance may seek to attract only those pupils who demonstrate good prospects of high examination achievement, and to encourage these pupils at the expense of others. The effect of this will be that high-performance schools can attract the best pupils from the surrounding area, skimming off the cream and thus perpetuating their success – and condemning other schools, and their pupils, to lower and lower standards.

Such cream-skimming has only been introduced into school education since the 1988 reforms; it has, however, been operating in higher education throughout its development, with the more prestigious universities, such as Oxford and Cambridge, being able to attract the most talented candidates. Because places at universities are restricted, this has meant that many people who have wanted (and probably would have been able) to study for a degree have been refused entry because they do not meet the university's entry qualifications. In higher education, which has always been largely regarded as an expensive privilege only available to a few, this may be understandable, and even acceptable – although in the 1990s higher education has been expanded to provide opportunities for a much higher proportion of the population. However, in school education, or in health service provision, cream-skimming and adverse selection could mean that some people are effectively denied essential services because of the perverse incentives of the purchaser–provider split.

Related to the issue of the purchaser–provider split in the distribution of public resources is the distinction between the distribution of *cash* resources and the provision of services in *kind*. In the case of disability benefits, for instance, cash payments have partly replaced some provision of goods and services, such as aids for mobility or personal care services. The distribution of cash does provide users with more apparent control over services – always assuming of course that they can purchase the things that they need with the cash resources they receive, which is not always the case given current levels of disability benefits. But it also means that users may need to be provided with assistance in securing the cash resources to which they are entitled, and in budgeting to make most effective use of those resources. This interface between support in cash and kind has always been an important issue in the provision of care by local authority social services (Baldwin *et al.*, 1988) and it is one to which we shall return in Chapter 13.

The cash–kind division is also part of a broader distinction within the distribution of public resources between the *consumption* of resources and the *redistribution* of them. Services provided for users generally involve people in the consumption of public resources – for example hospital patients consume drugs and equipment, and the time and skills of hospital staff; and children at school consume textbooks and the time of teachers. The public money spent on doctors and teachers does of course find its way into the broader economy through the spending activities of these state employees but, generally speaking, its value as a public resource is gone once the service provision has been made.

However, the provision of state resources in the form of cash involves a transfer rather than a consumption of resources. All that the state is doing here is taking spending resources from one individual or family, in the form of taxation, and transferring it to another, in the form of state benefits. This is revealed most clearly with the social security system, which is basically a scheme for redistributing money between sections of the population, rather than a means of consuming public resources.

The redistribution of public resources through social security can take a number of forms, depending upon how the money is collected and distributed. Although such social security is common in all welfare capitalist countries, these forms vary significantly. They also vary within countries, and especially so within Britain. For instance, as we mentioned in Chapter 2, redistribution may be *horizontal*, taking resources from people at one part of their lifecycle (during employment) and returning it to them at another (on retirement), or it may be *vertical*, taking resources from one group (the employed) and redistributing it to another (the unemployed). However, the differences between these two forms are not just technical; they each spring from very different notions of the problems of poverty and inequality and the proper role of the state in responding to these (Alcock, 1993, pp. 215–16).

The redistribution of resources through social security may also be based on *hypothecated* (or earmarked) taxation or contribution, or on general taxation. Hypothecated taxes are collected only in order to be redistributed as social security payments, whereas general taxes are collected to support any aspect of state expenditure of which social security benefits will only be one part. Hypothecated taxes are relatively rare within social policy; but they are used extensively for social security provision.

In Britain, and in most other Western European countries, the differences between horizontal and vertical redistribution, and hypothecated and general taxation, are reflected in the differences between social security protection based on social *insurance* and social *assistance*. Social insurance provides benefits for people in specified circumstances, such as retirement or short-term unemployment, and is based on entitlement determined more or less directly by the contributions which they have made into the social insurance scheme (called National Insurance [NI] in Britain) – that is horizontal redistribution through hypothecated taxation. Social assistance provides benefits for those with no other adequate source of income, whatever their circumstances; it is financed indirectly as part of public expenditure and is paid to claimants irrespective of whether any past contributions have been made by them – that is vertical redistribution through general taxation.

Social assistance benefits are generally *means-tested*, that is claimants have to establish entitlement to them by demonstrating that they have no means to provide for themselves and thus need state support to survive. Whereas insurance benefits are paid to those entitled on a *contingency* basis, so that all pensioners who have made sufficient contributions will receive their retirement pension whatever other income or savings they may have. Social assistance benefits are also sometimes called *selective* benefits, because claimants are selected for entitlement on the basis of proof of poverty. They are not generally as popular with claimants, or with the population at large, as contingency benefits (or as universal benefits such as Child Benefit) because of the operation of the proof of means and the consequent problem of stigma (Page, 1984; Spicker, 1984); and they generally are less effective in ensuring that the redistribution intended does reach all who might be entitled to it (Deacon and Bradshaw, 1983; Hill 1990, Ch. 7). Official estimates of the numbers receiving selective benefits to which they might potentially be entitled – the levels of *take-up* – put these at only between 75 and 90 per cent of the possible total number of claimants (Department of Social Security, 1995).

The advantages and disadvantages of different forms of social security protection are beyond the scope of this brief discussion here (for a fuller discussion see Hill, 1990; Alcock, 1993, Ch. 14). However, we can see that different models of protection do involve different means of redistributing state resources through taxation and benefit payment. Clearly, different groups, both among the poor and within society more generally, will gain or lose, relatively speaking, under different schemes. In general, of course, policies for redistribution of state resources have sought to reduce inequalities within society and to prevent, or alleviate, the problem of poverty. Over recent decades, however, social security policy in Britain has been shifting from a scheme based largely upon insurance benefits towards one based largely upon means-tested, or assistance, benefits; and this has been accompanied by growing levels of inequality between benefit recipients and the better-off employed sections of the population (Hills, 1995).

Just as with the distribution of those resources which are consumed therefore, policies for redistribution through social policy – or the *transfer* of resources, as they are sometimes called – can, and do, change direction over time. These changes involve changes in the groups of beneficiaries of redistribution, and shifts in the sources of funding for redistribution from taxation or contributions. Taxes and contributions are the major sources of funding for the distribution and redistribution of resources through the state; but they are not the only means of paying for welfare, as we shall see in the next section.

Sources of funding

In his book *Paying for Welfare*, Glennerster (1992) distinguishes between three main sources of funding for social services: taxation, fees or charges, and gifts or charity. To some extent these three different sources reflect the differences between the three organised sectors of welfare provision: the state, the private sector and the voluntary sector. However, in practice, the use of these various sources across the different sectors is more complex than such a simple three-way division, for funding of state services includes both charges and charity, and taxation is used to support both private sector and voluntary sector services. The mix of funding is thus as complex as the mix of services, if not more so. Nevertheless, state funding, financed through taxation, remains the most important source both in terms of its impact on tax payers and its support for a wide range of service provision.

Taxation

Taxes are a compulsory payment to the state which are used by government to fund public expenditure. Payment of taxes is generally made to the Treasury, and the policies for determining both the collection, and expenditure, of taxes is announced once or twice a year through the *Budget*, presented to Parliament by the Chancellor of the Exchequer. In effect this means that the Treasury is the most powerful and influential of all government departments, because it exercises control over the spending decisions of other departments; and that, after the Prime Minister, the Chancellor is the most important of government ministers.

Payment of taxes is compulsory and, in theory, should be popular – for they supply the funding for the services that the electorate have decided they want the government to provide. There is, however, a strong ideological current of hostility to taxation; and this has been encouraged in the 1980s and 90s by government claims that there is a need to reduce tax burdens in order to 'return' control over spending to individual earners and so, it is argued, stimulate economic growth.

What is more, there is significant evidence that people do seek to *avoid* the payment of taxation, by arranging their affairs within the law to minimise the amount of taxation they are required to pay; and to *evade* payment, by illegally disguising taxable resources from the

Inland Revenue, which is responsible for collecting tax payments. However, this should not be taken to suggest that the payment of taxation to support social service is genuinely unpopular. For instance, attitude survey evidence continues to demonstrate that a majority of people support current or increased levels of taxation to maintain or expand some major welfare services (Taylor-Gooby, 1991).

The main aim of taxation, of course, is to raise revenue for government expenditure. However, its importance as a feature of policies for the redistribution of resources should not be overlooked; and in particular, as we shall discuss shortly, the varying burden of taxation on different sectors of society can be a very effective means of reducing the gap between the rich and the poor. As well as raising revenue and potentially achieving greater equality, taxation can also be used to influence behaviour. For instance, high levels of taxation on the purchase of cigarettes and tobacco are intended to reduce consumption of these because of the danger of smoking to health; and high levels of taxation on petrol and diesel are intended, in part, to reduce incentives to use road transport because of the effect of this on the environment.

Taxes on cigarettes and petrol are paid by those purchasing these goods. They could be, and are, avoided by not smoking or driving a car. Such taxes are called *indirect* taxes. They include other customs and excise duties (such as the taxes on alcohol), the road licence (which is a flat-rate tax on owners of vehicles) and most importantly Value Added Tax (VAT – which is a percentage tax, currently 17.5 per cent, levied on the purchase of a wide range of goods and services). The impact of VAT has expanded substantially since the 1970s (Glennerster, 1992, p. 114) and, together with the expansion of other direct taxes, this has led to a significant shift in the burden of taxation from direct to indirect taxation in Britain. Thus, although the VAT level in Britain is still lower than that in a number of other European countries, the overall proportion of taxation levied through indirect means is greater here than in most other major advanced industrial societies (Hills, 1988, p. 14).

Payment of indirect taxes is determined by spending patterns, not by overall income or wealth. Although those with more wealth do have more to spend, indirect taxes can in fact constitute a significant part of the spending of even low-income families – for example cigarette taxation disproportionately affects people in the lower classes where smoking is more prevalent. In 1994 the government's decision to extend the full rate of VAT to domestic fuel consumption was abandoned by Parliament because of the fears that its impact would be felt too harshly by poor households. In general, therefore, the effect of indirect taxation is likely to be *regressive* – reinforcing or accentuating existing income inequalities. Direct taxation, by contrast, is generally *progressive* in its effect – levying higher rates of taxes from those with greater incomes or capital wealth.

The most substantial aspect of *direct* taxation is income tax: a proportion of income, currently between 15 and 40 per cent depending on the level of earnings, that must be paid over to the Inland Revenue. Income tax is what most people understand as taxation, although it currently constitutes less than 30 per cent of the overall burden of taxation. Payment is due on all earnings over a certain level – referred to as the 'tax allowance' or 'threshold'; and this may be extended, for example, for people paying interest on a mortgage, some of which is exempt from income tax. In most cases payment is made direct by deduction from earnings by employers, called pay-as-you-earn (PAYE), although for the self-employed, for instance, payment must be made by individuals at the end of each tax year.

In addition to income tax, most employees and the self-employed must pay National Insurance contributions (NICs). These are a direct tax on earnings, which are also paid by employers, to provide for the cost of some social security benefits, notably retirement pensions and unemployment benefit (or the job seekers' allowance). Liability for NICs is calculated separately from income tax. It operates on a weekly, rather than an annual basis; and, although like income tax liability it is based on a percentage of earnings, in practice it is much less progressive, because those on higher earnings are exempt from paying contributions on earnings above an upper earnings limit. However, like income tax, for employees it is deducted from pay at source and many workers may not, in practice, appreciate the difference between the two.

Income tax, like indirect taxes and most other direct taxes, is a general form of taxation, with the revenue raised being used to contribute towards the full range of public services. NICs however are different. They are, as we discussed above, a form of earmarked, or *hypothecated*, taxation which has been collected only for the specific purpose of providing for social security benefits. Such hypothecation is in fact relatively unusual within the taxation system, and in this case is linked to the insurance roots of NI, where entitlement to benefits is linked to the past payments of NICs. In reality this relationship is a fictitious one because contributions are not actually saved to meet future benefit entitlement but are used to pay current benefits. By contrast, in some other European countries, such as Germany, the insurance relationship is less fictitious; and, interestingly, here such contributions constitute a higher proportion of overall taxation levels.

Another form of direct taxation, which operates to some extent as a hypothecated tax, is *council* tax. This is the tax levied by local government on all households within their local area. In 1993 council tax replaced the community charge (or 'poll tax') which was a local tax on all individuals, and this itself had in 1990 replaced local rates which were a tax on property owners. Council tax provides a proportion of local government revenue, as we discussed in Chapter 10, and, as local government is responsible for a restricted range of service provision, it operates in effect as a hypothecated tax for these. This is certainly the way that council tax, and before it the rates, have often been seen by local government which makes a political appeal to the local electorate by explaining the services that it will be providing out of the tax it is asking local people to pay.

Income tax, NICs and council tax are the main forms of direct taxation in Britain, but there are others. These include corporation tax, on the profits of businesses; capital taxes and capital gains taxes, on private wealth holdings; and stamp duty, on the transfer of land and buildings. However, altogether these constitute around only 12 per cent of total tax revenue. Furthermore, although income and capital taxes are more progressive than indirect taxes, the bulk of direct taxes, too, are paid by the average and lower paid – and this weight of direct taxation on these groups has been growing significantly over the last two decades (Hills, 1988, Ch. 2; Glennerster, 1992, p. 124). Despite the views that are held in some quarters (including some government circles) therefore, lower-paid people pay a higher proportion of their income in taxes – and this proportion has been increasing towards the end of the twentieth century.

Fees and charges

Provision of most private welfare is based upon the payment of a *fee*, calculated to cover the cost of the service provided, and perhaps to include an element of profit for the owners of the service. However, access to public services, too, sometimes involves the payment of a fee. For instance, fees are charged for the use of leisure services, such as public swimming pools; and sometimes fees are charged for welfare services too, such as for the use of a day centre or for the provision of meals at such a centre. However, it is more common for payment by consumers of public services to take the form of a *charge* rather than a fee – the difference being that, unlike a fee, a charge is not intended to cover the full cost of providing the service but merely to require users to make a contribution towards such costs.

Charges have existed for a long time in state welfare services – although their role was initially a minor one, with most services being provided free to users. For instance, the payment of charges for prescriptions for drugs was introduced in 1951, very soon after the NHS itself had come into operation in 1948. This was a controversial measure at the time, leading to the resignation of Bevan, the minister largely responsible for the NHS. Nevertheless, charges for prescriptions have (apart from a brief period in the 1960s) remained ever since; and in recent years the level of the charge has been dramatically increased. Furthermore, charges for other services, such as dentistry and optical treatment, have also been introduced. In the 1980s and 90s in particular, the role of charges for public services has been expanding quite rapidly, in large part because of the cuts in direct funding for service provision flowing from policies to reduce public expenditure.

Charges in the health service, such as prescriptions, have been increasing and the use of charges within education and personal social services has also been growing. Charges are made for non-statutory education services such as adult education and community activities, and charges are made by social work departments for services such as home care, 'meals on wheels' and day centre attendance. These are mainly charges imposed by local government providers; but they are the direct result of financial and legal pressures from central government, for instance the assumption that 9 per cent of the cost of local domiciliary services to adult community care clients will be met by the levying of charges for use of services. As a result of this, most local authorities now charge for such service provision, and in the mid 1990s the level of charges increased significantly.

Although the scope of charges has been increasing, however, the structure of charges and charging policies has remained uncoordinated and, as a result, somewhat complex. The types of charges used by public service providers vary, with some making flat-rate charges to all service users and others grading charges either according to the level of service use or according to the circumstances of the client. The levels charges are fixed at also vary widely. Some charges are based on an attempt to secure an approximate contribution to the cost of the service provided but many have been priced at quite nominal levels – for instance the £1 a week charged for home care services by Bradford City Council in the early 1990s.

The growth in charges within state services in the 1980s and 90s was primarily the product of reductions in the direct funding base for such services. However, the use of charges for services does serve other purposes than direct revenue raising from consumers. Charges can reveal the real preferences and priorities of consumers, by discouraging abuse of free services by those who do not really need or want them; and they can act to raise the status of service users by providing them with a feeling that they are paying for services and thus can expect these to be delivered effectively to them. On the other hand, charges, even nominal charges, can act to discourage genuinely needy, and often vulnerable, users from gaining access to services; and they are likely to impact particularly harshly on poor users who cannot afford to pay charges out of their limited incomes.

The problem of the impact of charges on poor service users, however, can be mitigated by the introduction of rebates from charges for those with low, or no, incomes. Rebates may remove the charge altogether or reduce it, perhaps according to the level of income received by the user. Rebates are widely used both by central and local government to mitigate the impact of charges on poor users. For instance, NHS prescription charges are removed for children, pensioners and some people on low incomes; and most local authorities operate rebate schemes to reduce or remove the charges for education and social services for certain groups of poor people.

One of the problems with such rebate schemes, however, is that they introduce a further layer of complexity into the provision of welfare services – users have to identify their right to the service, understand the nature of the charge, and then recognise and apply for any possible rebate. This can accentuate the already problematic issue of ensuring access to welfare services, a point to which we will return in Chapter 13; it can also lead to many people failing to identify and take up their entitlement to rebates.

The use of rebating also leads to a further expansion of the role of means-testing within service provision, and this is likely to accentuate the 'poverty trap' problem associated with means-tested provision more generally. Because means-tested rebates are targeted on users with low incomes, when, or if, income rises, entitlement to rebates is lost, or reduced, thus undermining the effective gain that results from increased income and trapping users at the same overall state of poverty (Alcock, 1993, pp. 232–3). The wider is the range of rebates operated by central or local government, the greater is the loss experienced by those whose income rises and whose entitlement is thus removed – and this problem has been fuelled dramatically by the rapid growth of charges and rebates in the 1980s and 90s.

Gifts and charity

Charitable actions and gifts are probably the oldest form of welfare provision; there is, therefore, a view amongst some supporters of state welfare services that reliance upon charity for welfare is anachronistic in a modern welfare state. However, as our discussion of the voluntary sector of welfare provision in Chapter 5 revealed, giving remains a central feature of the modern welfare mix and, although state support for the voluntary sector is often now an essential part of the resourcing for independent and community-based organisations, most of these still rely very largely upon the time and money donated to them by voluntary activists or by the public at large.

However, it is not just voluntary sector organisations that benefit from charitable sources; gifts are also made to public service providers. For instance, money is sometimes left as a bequest in wills to central or local government departments; and in 1994/95 Sheffield City Council managed to persuade many of its council tax payers to forgo a reduction in their payments, ordered by central government, in order to support local education and leisure services. Volunteer time is also utilised by public service providers, for example volunteers of all ages, including school children, are used by local social service departments to work with vulnerable clients.

Charity and gift giving also take a variety of forms across the voluntary, private and public sectors. Volunteer time is obviously of particular importance as a resource for voluntary organisations, although time can also include skills – for instance lawyers or accountants may have much to offer to many voluntary agencies by way of unpaid professional advice and assistance. Gifts may also be made in kind – for instance the provision of equipment, or computer software, or the use of a telephone or fax line. Such gifts in kind are made by individuals but they are often a form of corporate support for voluntary agencies provided by commercial companies in the private sector. Gifts like this may even take the form of 'sponsorship', where a commercial company provides goods or services in return for their name being publicised as a supporter of the voluntary welfare agency.

Of course, most such sponsorship arrangements take the form of cash donations made in return for publicity for the corporate donator. However, cash donations without such 'strings' attached are also made by commercial companies to voluntary welfare agencies. Such support is indirectly encouraged by government through the granting of exemptions for liability for direct taxation for money made as charitable donations by companies or individuals; although, perhaps, this should more accurately be seen as a form of state subsidy that operates in addition to any corporate or private decision to give.

Cash donation is the central feature of charitable support for welfare services; and cash donations themselves take a wide variety of forms, including regular donations, one-off gifts, and contributions to street collections, charity fairs, jumble sales or charity shops. However, overall levels of cash donations to charities in Britain are not great, averaging a mean of less than £8 a month for all households in 1989/90, and they have not been increasing (Glennerster, 1992, pp. 145–6). Compared to the money collected and paid out in taxation this is a very small amount indeed; it suggests that, despite its continued importance, there are clear limits to the role of charitable giving in the funding of welfare services.

The very nature of charity itself, its unorganised and voluntary structure, may prevent some from giving because in practice they have not been asked; it may lead others to feel uncomfortable about this form of moral pressure to support welfare. What is more, different people may give different levels of support at different times and in different areas, and usually this bears little relation to individual income differentials. The moral pressure may also apply in reverse to the recipients of gifts – users of charitable services may not feel that they have the rights and entitlements that the users of public services, or the purchasers of private welfare, can command, and thus may not use them so readily. Charitable support for welfare is thus inevitably uneven in nature, both over time and across place. However, the services which rely on such inequitable and uneven support require some level of consistency over time and equality across different places both to employ workers and to guarantee services to all users.

Paying for welfare on a voluntary basis, therefore, cannot always operate to support regular service provision in the way that public taxation or private market fees can. As a result, charitable funding is often used to supplement other sources of support, in particular state funding, or to provide very specific, and adaptable, local services where flexibility and fluctuation in activity are not a limitation on provision – and may even, of course, be a virtue.

The implications of different models of funding

As with the development and delivery of services therefore, the funding of welfare in Britain operates in practice on a mixed economy model – with state, private and voluntary funding overlapping across the sectors and areas of provision. Although state funding through taxation dominates funding regimes in many areas (such as education, health and social security), throughout both state and non-state welfare varying mixtures of funding can be found.

Thus the picture presented by a study of the means of paying for welfare is a complex one. It is also a dynamic one. Differing forms of funding and the balance between these in different sectors of welfare provision are constantly changing. For instance, in the 1980s and 90s the role of direct state funding has been transformed into indirect state subsidy through tax allowances and quasi-markets, and by a greater reliance on market-based fees and user charges. Such changes affect the overall structure of welfare provision but, perhaps more importantly, they also affect its impact on individual citizens and households.

The widespread reliance on blanket state funding for universal state services in the early postwar period was based in large part on a belief that this would ensure that equal access to services was provided for all. As research by commentators such as Le Grand (1982) has shown, this has not always been the case, with middle-class users gaining more from certain services such as health and education. Today the reduced role for state funding that has been experienced in the last two decades of the century, and its replacement with fees and charges for service users, may be operating to divide further access to welfare services.

Obviously, where users must pay fees or charges, income inequalities are likely to restrict access to some services – at least for poor citizens. Yet, at the same time that increased reliance on charging has been developing, income inequalities have been growing in the country (Hills, 1995) and the burden of taxation to pay for the reduced state services has been shifting increasingly towards the lower paid (Hills, 1988). These changes may therefore have had the effect of further advantaging the middle classes, and disadvantaging the poor, in access to welfare.

The greater use of means-testing to target reduced state welfare on those with low, or no, incomes, and the existence of rebates to reduce the impact of some charges, may operate to mitigate the effects of increasing inequality by protecting the poor from charges and by directing resources to them. However, as we have mentioned above, means-testing brings with it its own problems in restricting access to welfare services. In particular, many means-tested benefits are not taken up by those who might be entitled to them, thus removing the attraction of targeting; and where means-tested support is provided, it can act to trap people in poverty by removing the practical incentives to improve one's income through earnings, thus increasing reliance on state support.

Changes in the balance of funding for welfare have not, therefore, necessarily resulted in an improvement of welfare services – at least for all. This is because, as we said at the beginning of this chapter, the pursuit of *equity* and *efficiency* in social policy is not based on a simple trade-off between two incompatible goals but rather on the coordination of service planning and financing to achieve both. Shifting the balance of funding in order to achieve only efficiency savings may therefore mean that essential equitable considerations are not met – those who need services may not receive them. At the same time, the continued demand for service delivery may mean that efficiency targets cannot be met – despite government protestations, overall taxation and public spending levels have continued to rise, and the introduction of charges has frequently failed to provide predicted revenue gains. The development of policies for paying for welfare thus cannot be separated from that of policies for determining access to it – and it is to such issues of access to welfare that we turn in Chapter 13.

13

Delivering Welfare

Access to welfare

It is a common assumption, shared especially by the protagonists of state welfare, that the provision of social services will mean that the benefits of such services will be enjoyed by all those who are the intended recipients of them – if health services, for instance, are provided free at the point of demand, those who need health care will go and use them. In the case of universal services, such as the NHS or education, the intention is that all will indeed benefit from such services, and benefit equally from them. As a result of this, attention in the development, and the study, of social policy has concentrated predominantly on the structure and the funding of welfare provision rather than on the access to and use of the services themselves. The focus has thus been rather more on the *producers* than the *consumers* of welfare – a distinction to which we shall return below.

This producer domination is understandable. It reflects both the powerful influence of major service providers within the discipline of social policy and, at the same time, the predominant concern of social policy analysts to influence service provision. During the early development of the discipline, and in particular under the influence of Fabian concerns to ensure the development of public provision for welfare to meet pressing social needs, such an approach was particularly prominent. However, it is in practice only a part of the picture of social policy; it has not prevented a concern among some commentators to question whether service provision is in itself a guarantee of service use or benefit – and this is a concern that has become of growing importance in the last quarter of the twentieth century. What is more, there is an increasing body of evidence to suggest that the provision of welfare – including, in particular, public services provided through the state – does not in reality mean that all do benefit from these services, or benefit equally from them.

Most disturbingly, perhaps, is the evidence that even the most basic, and arguably most important, of state services – social security benefits – are not always taken up by those who are entitled to claim them. In 1992 the Department of Social Security estimated take-up levels for the major means-tested benefit, Income Support, on which over ten million were dependent, at between 77 and 87 per cent, which meant that between one and two million people were not getting the basic benefit to which they were entitled (DSS, 1995). On this basis the total amount of unclaimed means-tested benefits in the mid 1990s was over £2 billion a year. Non-take-up of benefits has been a long-standing and widely recognised problem within social policy. It has also been challenged by policy practitioners in the field of welfare rights, who seek to provide information and encouragement for claimants wishing to pursue their rights. Despite the efforts of welfare rights workers, however, take-up levels remain low for many benefits, suggesting that there is a significant gap between the rhetoric, and the reality, of the protection supposedly provided by the state social security scheme.

Non-take-up of social security affects all potential claimants, although evidence suggests that some groups are more likely to suffer from higher levels of non-take-up than others – for example ethnic minorities are less likely to receive all the benefits to which they may be entitled (Amin and Oppenheim, 1992). As we discussed in Chapter 11, social divisions within society operate to restrict access to welfare services for some groups, or even to exclude them from benefit altogether. Thus services that in theory are provided equally to all are not in practice equally received by all who might benefit from them. Rather, evidence suggests that many (supposedly) universal services are actually used disproportionately by different social groups. Le Grand's (1982) famous study of the use of education and health services revealed that, although in theory these were equally available to all, better-off sections of society were, for a variety of reasons, more likely to use and benefit from them. And in the 1990s a study of public services provided by local authorities revealed that, in general, the better-off benefited more from most of these services too (Bramley and Smart, 1993).

In fact there is substantial evidence that the provision of public services does not guarantee that all potential users will benefit from them. The picture is the same for private and voluntary sector provision too; although here the problem is perhaps less serious as few organisations aim to provide comprehensive services and may even aim to focus their activity on those who choose to purchase their services or on specific target groups or communities. Such targeting, or selection, of service users is a means of avoiding the problem of the unequal take-up of universal services by particular groups, by designing services particularly for such groups or by restricting access only to them. Selectivity is used to target the public provision of services also; and here it is often contrasted with universalism as a means of securing access to services.

- *Universal* services are intended to be used by, and equally available to, all who need, or expect, to benefit from them. State education up to the age of 16 and most NHS services are universal; so, too, are some social security benefits, notably Child Benefit. As Le Grand's (1982) research revealed, however, education and health services are not equally used by all – although it does appear that Child Benefit is claimed by virtually all parents on behalf of their children. Universal services have not, however, only been criticised for unequal usage; it is also argued that in providing for all they are in practice wasting limited resources on many users who could afford to pay for such services privately. This is a criticism that has often been directed at Child Benefit, which, it is claimed, provides unnecessary additional income to wealthy families.

- *Selective* services seek to avoid these problems by restricting access to those identified as having particular needs that could only be provided for by direct access to particular services. Selection can be made in a number of ways, for instance by focusing service provision on a specific geographical area or on a designated social group. Such geographical or social methods of targeting are widely used both by central and local government and by private and voluntary sector providers. However, perhaps the most common form of selectivity in service allocation is the use of *means-testing* to target resources onto those who have undergone some test of their inability to provide for themselves. As we discussed in Chapter 12, means-testing is widely used within the social security system as a means of targeting benefits, and is sometimes contrasted with universal provision, such as Child Benefit, as a more effective device for focusing benefit expenditure – although, as we saw, it is in practice far from effective in securing access to services for target groups and, in social security in particular, it has generally failed to secure receipt of benefits for all of those in need.

Universal and selective allocation of welfare services thus seek to resolve the problem of access to services in different ways. However, they are also the result of different views about the funding of welfare – again, as we saw in Chapter 12, the choice between universalism and selectivity is not just made on grounds of improved access. Of course, both do have their problems in securing access to services; and this is possibly why both remain, and in practice often overlap, in current welfare provision – most notably perhaps in social security. In setting different criteria for access to services, however, universalism and selectivity are operating as means of *rationing* the use of these services and, as Foster (1983) discusses, other means to ration service use are also in operation.

In general terms any procedures that are used to deliver services can act in effect to ration access to them. For example, reception procedures in health care practices may be used to determine, and to prioritise, appointments with medical staff. Here the receptionist is operating as a kind of *gate-keeper* restricting the use of professional resources. Professionals themselves may also operate as gate-keepers, however, both to their own services – putting off some clients and encouraging others – and to the services offered by others. Doctors in general practice act as important gate-keepers to a wide range of NHS services and, as we have seen, social workers, too, increasingly operate a gate-keeping role over both public and private services.

Gate-keeping describes an organised and relatively well-planned way of using the process of application as a means of rationing access to welfare. However, procedural factors operate to ration access much more widely than this, and sometimes in ways that may not have been intended, or predicted, by service providers. Most obviously, the physical location of service delivery points and their structural design may exclude many. For instance, the town centre location of the local social services or housing department may mean that it is out of reach for those whose mobility is restricted by disability or those who simply cannot afford to travel a long distance to make an appointment. Even where it does not keep people at home, physical disability may prevent them from entering certain buildings if appropriate access points are not provided – the grand staircase up to the Town Hall doors, for example, is a barrier to all people in wheelchairs.

Working practices, as well as physical design, can exclude potential service users. Where there is a relatively high demand for enquiries or problems about services, for instance, many organisations operate queuing systems for potential clients. The experience of waiting in seemingly never-ending queues has often been a common one associated with access to services such as hospitals, housing departments and social security offices. Queuing alone may deter some from pursuing potential access but it is particularly problematic where the time spent queuing is preventing someone meeting other needs or is taking them away from paid employment. It is sometimes said that 'time is money', and this is perhaps most keenly felt by the self-employed or by those in insecure and poorly protected employment where absence from work means direct deduction of wages for time lost.

This is a problem that is compounded by service offices and access points which are only open during the working day on a Monday to Friday, and which therefore effectively exclude all those who work these hours and cannot negotiate, or afford, time off. Trips to offices may be avoided, however, by use of telephone access – and telephones are increasingly used as the first point of contact for those enquiring about potential service use. However, even telephone contact is not available to those who do not have access to a telephone or cannot afford to use one. Furthermore, telephone access – and indeed most written information and application procedures too – are also generally only provided in *English*. Those who have difficulty with spoken or written English are likely to be excluded from services by such a language barrier; and evidence suggests that language does operate as a barrier – for example to exclude many members of ethnic minority communities from essential services such as social security (NACAB, 1991).

Thus language, location, design and working practices all operate in practice to restrict, and so to ration, access to welfare services. Unlike targeting and gate-keeping, however, which (although they may be argued to be undesirable) are *intended* as a means of rationing access to services, this latter form of rationing is unplanned and largely unintended – and generally its effects are not monitored or considered. As Le Grand (1982) has argued, it is such unplanned rationing that may in part account for the unequal use of services across social classes and social groups, for it is frequently the better-off and more articulate white middle class who are more able to acquire information about services and negotiate, or browbeat, their way to the providers of them. What these informal rationing devices reveal, therefore, is the failure of many service providers to recognise all the problems that consumers may experience in gaining access to the services that they provide; this is a criticism that has been levelled in particular against public service providers in the last quarter of the twentieth century.

Producers and consumers

The design and implementation of most public services has largely been based on the assumption that both the producers and the consumers of those services would have a coinciding interest in their development and delivery. For instance, teachers would want to teach children useful and important knowledge and children would want to learn everything that teachers had to tell them. To some extent of course this is true; but, as all of us no doubt found during our own school education, this process of teaching and learning was not without its frustrations and conflicts. More recently, critics from both the right and left wing of the ideological spectrum have begun to challenge the assumed conterminous interests of the producers and consumers of public welfare services, and to suggest that the conflicts which sometimes occur here may in fact represent contradictory tensions within the whole process of delivery between the power and control of providers and the needs and rights of users.

Challenges to the alleged producer control in public welfare have certainly been a major feature of New Right criticisms of state welfare services in the 1980s and 90s (Green, D, 1988; Barry, 1990). As we discussed in Chapter 7, the essence of the New Right argument is that market provision of services, including welfare services, is preferable to state provision, because markets provide for choice for consumers and, through the exercise of choice in the market, consumers can acquire sovereignty over providers. The converse of this consumer sovereignty is the producer domination of service provision which the New Right identify within public services, and which Deakin and Wright (1990, p. 1) – not themselves right-wing critics – describe as 'bleak, unresponsive and inefficient bureaucracies'.

The *bureaucratic* structure of state welfare services is in some ways an inevitable consequence of the attempt to develop and maintain national standards and to secure economies of scale through the organisation of service delivery on a large-scale basis. However, as Weber's (1968) classical discussion of bureaucracy first revealed, bureaucratic organisations eventually acquire their own logic, and the internal logic of the bureaucracy can sometimes come to overbalance the external demand for use of its services. For instance, social security claimants or local authority housing tenants seeking to challenge – or even to find out about – the processing of their cases have often experienced immense difficulties in understanding and negotiating the bureaucratic procedures that the officers dealing with them seem to be trapped within. It may seem to the users of these services – perhaps with some justification – that this bureaucracy is often presented as an *excuse* for inaction ('your file has been sent to another section') rather than as an *explanation* of what is – or is not – being done.

It is not, however, just the process of bureaucracy that alienates consumers and perpetuates the power of producers. These bureaucracies employ workers whose job it is to deliver services within the procedures laid down; and these workers thus acquire a vested interest in maintaining their employment – and so indirectly in maintaining the bureaucratic structures and procedures within which they work. Public sector services workers are able to protect their work, and their working practices, in this way through membership of trades unions and through negotiation with their public sector employers. On some occasions at least, therefore, these employers (the departments of central and local government) have been forced into meeting the demands of their workers, even where these may be in conflict with the needs of potential service users – for example in maintaining nine-to-five office hours or in keeping on workers even where service demand has reduced. This is in large part a product of the absence of an active labour-market policy to promote change within public services, and it has sometimes resulted in much-publicised industrial disputes between employers and employees in public welfare services that have often clearly disadvantaged service users – most notably in the so-called 'Winter of Discontent' in 1979 when many public sector workers went on strike to protect their jobs and wages, much to the disgust of New Right commentators and large sections of the popular media.

It is not, however, just ordinary workers and their trades unions that have prevented consumer interest from being exercised in public services. The role of the *professionals* in public service delivery has also had the effect of disempowering the consumer of professional services. Professional power can be seen most clearly in the work of the medical profession – doctors and hospital consultants think they know what their patients need and they expect patients to follow the recommendations they make without question. In fact, of course, doctors may not always know best what is in the best interests of their patients' health; and in some cases patients do challenge the opinions of doctors – for example women who wish to choose their own method of childbirth. In the case of some other welfare professionals the assumption that they always know what is in the best interests of their clients is more obviously open to question. For instance, there are examples of social workers in residential homes deciding what time residents should go to bed or eat their meals, and of housing officers in local authority departments deciding whether to permit council tenants to put up greenhouses in their gardens.

These professionals are, of course, in most cases acting altruistically in making such judgements about their clients' needs, as indeed may be other workers who are defending the procedures within which they work. The problem with this altruism, as New Right critics continually point out, is that in practice it is *paternalistic* in its operation. It is based on the assumption that the bureaucrats or the professionals know best; and therefore that the clients, or the users, should have no say. To adopt the terminology of the American critic, Hirschman (1970), paternalistic state services do not give their users the rights of 'exit' or 'voice'.

There is no right of *exit* for public service users because such services are in most cases a monopoly. The state provides services universally to all (in theory at least); but it is also the only provider of such services. Potential consumers are thus left with a 'take it or leave it' choice to engage with the bureaucracy and follow the professional advice, or to go without. In these circumstances people cannot take their business, or their needs, anywhere else (that is, exit); and so, if they are unable or unwilling to use the state services available, they will fail to secure the welfare services which they need – and to which indeed in theory they are entitled.

The lack of a right of exit from monopoly state services might be more acceptable if there was nevertheless a right for consumers to have a *voice* within them; in other words, if the users of these services were able to influence service provision to ensure that their needs were met in ways that they experienced as appropriate and accessible. However, the paternalism of many state services has militated against the development of any mechanisms for a consumer voice, because of the belief that it is professionals and service providers who know best what potential users need. In paternalistic monopolies, therefore, it is the producers, and not the consumers, who hold the power to determine the structure of service provision. The New Right criticism of the producer domination of state welfare services has often struck a resonant chord among those users who have experienced frustration or disadvantage as a result of this.

This new-found 'consensus' on the criticism of the producer domination of state services is shared by many left-wing commentators on social welfare too – although these critics are not surprisingly less supportive of private markets as a viable alternative to the problems of consumer weakness in welfare. In their introduction to a text in *Consuming Public Services*, Deakin and Wright (1990), criticise state welfare for confusing collectivism with uniformity, for confusing defining needs with meeting needs, and for allowing welfare provision to develop as services *to* the public rather than services *for* the public. Like the New Right critics they point to the effects of bureaucracy and professionalism in excluding service users from any say in the running of the services – which in reality of course they own and pay for – and they quote with endorsement the recommendation of a National Consumer Council (NCC) review of local authority services that all public services should ensure an effective role for the user (National Consumer Council, 1986).

Deakin and Wight also draw attention to the different, and confusing, terminology used to describe the consumers of welfare services, and the different ideas and concepts that are sometimes concealed within these terms. Paternalistic welfare services have often referred to users as *clients*, a term that suggests a supplicant role for users – relying upon the judgement, or even the discretion, of professional providers. More recently, recognition of such paternalism within welfare services has resulted in a shift in terminology with the adoption of the term *customers*. Users as customers suggests a market-based approach to service delivery, where greater politeness, and even deference, is shown to service users – referred to by some providers as 'customer care' – but where the services themselves may remain largely unchanged.

More recently the term *consumer* has begun to displace both client and customer within policy debate and, in its emphasis on the receipt of, and benefit from, services, it is certainly a more generic, and accurate, term than either of the previous two. However, the notion of a consumer of services is also in some ways a rather narrow conception of the use made of public services, because not all services are delivered to – or are of benefit to – only those individuals who consume them. For instance, public health programmes such as immunisation do not benefit only those who are the immediate consumers of them; and, looking more generally, services such as education and social work also have indirect benefit for a wide range of the population beyond those in the classroom or on the social work caseload.

In this sense, therefore, the users of public services are not just the direct consumers of these, but all the *citizens* of a town, city or country. So to focus on the alliterative trend we have identified, it is perhaps as citizens, rather than as clients, customers or consumers, that the users of public services should be given a voice within them if the paternalism of state bureaucracy is to be challenged. This challenge may be taken up by giving citizens more *choice* – or by giving them more *control.*

Choice

The New Right critics of state paternalism point out that it is the lack of choice within state services that prevents many potential users from getting access to the services they need, or want. By contrast, they argue, private markets operate according to the principle of consumer choice and, therefore, are more likely to meet consumer demand. For instance, Bosanquet (1987) argues that choice implies a variety of providers, and that this requires the operation of a market and a pricing mechanism. However, it is precisely the operation of the pricing mechanism within markets that can deny access, and therefore choice, to many would-be consumers if they are unable to afford prices charged for the services they need. This is a criticism that has been taken up trenchantly in recent times by Plant (1988 and 1990) but was also made in the early days of the development of state welfare by Tawney (1931), when he pointed out that inequality would inevitably restrict access to essential services if these were provided only on a market basis.

In any event, the operation of private markets is not a guarantee of protection against monopoly providers, as the operation of the private utility providers of gas, water and electricity has revealed in the 1990s. So despite the example which these provide – or perhaps because of it – market provision of welfare services has tended to operate alongside, rather than as a complete alternative to, public provision through the state. For instance, in education and health private provision allows those who can afford it to opt out of state welfare and choose alternative providers in the private market. This power of opt-out has also been extended to other services, such as social security protection for pensions and council tenants' right to secure house repairs from private contractors.

As we have discussed before, however, market-based choice has also been introduced into state welfare services in the 1990s through the mechanism of quasi-markets. In theory, quasi-markets allow consumers, or those acting on their behalf, to choose between different public providers; and, because the income providers receive depends entirely upon the numbers of people using their services, this should ensure that consumer demand operates to determine the structure of service provision here. Of course, as we have seen, there are problems associated with the use of quasi-markets to secure consumer sovereignty but the idea of extending consumer choice in this way is proposed by many commentators across a wide range of ideological opinion. For instance, Le Grand, who popularised the failure of public services to secure equal access for all users (Le Grand, 1982), has discussed the introduction of *vouchers* into the state education scheme as a way of using the quasi-market principle to permit parents to exercise choice over their children's schooling (Le Grand, 1989). Vouchers, equivalent to the cost of a place at a state school, would permit parents to 'cash in' these to place their child in any school in the public or private sector – and, if desired, increased value vouchers could be targeted on the children of poor parents to make them more attractive to good schools.

If choice is to be extended to consumers across the public and private sectors in this way, some form of subsidy or support for private sector providers, such as that exemplified by education vouchers, would almost certainly be necessary. In practice at present, such subsidies are provided to private providers in areas such as health, education, social security and housing. To extend choice further, however, subsidies also need to be provided to non-profit providers in the voluntary sector. In areas such as community care, choice of service provision extends in theory across the public, private and voluntary sectors; yet to make choices here realistic, public resources are likely to have to be used to support providers in all three – and perhaps even more so to support the informal providers who at present deliver the majority of welfare in the field of social care.

Consideration of the provision of choice in welfare services thus requires examination of the relationship between public provision and the other sectors of the welfare mix, and of the role of public resources in funding or supporting service provision in each of these sectors. It is thus bound up with the consideration of paying for welfare, which we discussed in Chapter 12. This is true of attempts to provide control over services to citizens or consumers too.

Control

Lack of consumer control over the public services provided for them is also largely a product of the paternalistic practices of state welfare. The belief that the providers of welfare could define, as well as meet, the needs of the citizens who used it meant that little or no attention was paid in the construction of state welfare services to the need for any mechanisms for enforcement of, complaint about, or challenge to, service provision. In other words, there was no recognition of the need for consumers to have a voice.

The lack of complaints procedures or appeals mechanisms in public services has been a source of criticism, in particular by lawyers looking at the implementation of social policies (Lewis and Birkinshaw, 1993). For lawyers, recognition of the need for procedural rights and safeguards is almost second nature. Yet it is just such a concern with a legalistic, or rights-based, approach to service delivery that has been absent from much of the growth and development of most welfare services and has resulted instead in reliance upon bureaucratic procedures and professional discretion.

We shall return later to discuss the potential future role for legal rights and safeguards in the delivery of welfare services. However, there have been some developments in the last quarter of the century that have sought to some extent to provide vehicles for consumer evaluation of the operation of public services. One such voice for the perspective of the consumer is provided by the work of the *ombudsmen* (though they may sometimes be women) appointed to pursue consumer complaints over the delivery of local authority or NHS services. The ombudsmen do not have the power to enforce action by, or changes in, service providers but their reports on maladministration are published and can carry significant weight in creating pressure for change. Similar pressure can be brought to bear by the reports of the *Audit Commission*, which is empowered to investigate the spending decisions of public service providers and make judgements about the proper (or improper) use of public funds.

Ombudsmen and the Audit Commission are in effect professionals acting on behalf of the consumers of public services, and (although they are independent of the providers, as well as the consumers, of welfare) in a sense the protection that they provide is still coloured with an element of paternalism. Thus it is not a means of ensuring real consumer control. By contrast, direct involvement in public welfare services by consumers themselves is a more obvious means of consumer empowerment – although examples of this in practice are rare or partial. School governing bodies, which in the 1990s are much more powerful in controlling school resources than they have ever been in the past, are one example of giving the parents of users some say in how their school is organised and run. Similar kinds of user forum have been established by local authorities for some other local services, for example allowing representation by tenants on bodies to discuss the management of local housing estates and the inclusion of local citizens on community health councils.

Deakin and Wright (1990) argue that the accountability of service providers that may result from such user forums is an important means of ensuring greater consumer control over the delivery of welfare services. Democratic control, as they also call this, is one of three themes examined in their concluding chapter – the others being local organisation and access, and the maintenance of quality.

Of course, in a sense, democratic control over public services is already provided by the electoral process through which the members of central and local government are chosen. However, the infrequency of (especially national) elections and the broad range of issues on which they are fought, make them a hopelessly remote vehicle for ensuring any realistic consumer accountability in the delivery of public services. This is compounded by the role of party politics in the electoral process, which means in effect that most elected representatives are unlikely to be swayed by the wishes of particular groups of local or national service users. This insensitivity of party politics to consumer preferences is to some extent confirmed by Bramley and Smart's (1993) study of local government services which revealed that differences in party control of local authorities appeared to make little difference to use of local services.

Mechanisms to ensure accountability to consumers need to extend beyond the ballot box therefore, for example through the use of consumer forums to ensure participation of consumers in the planning of public services. However, such participation is not without its problems. As with access to the services themselves, there is the danger that forums for participation will be dominated by certain groups of users and will thus exclude others; consultative forums may operate only as a means for the articulate middle class to make their own voice heard. Yet even where participation is more open and widespread, there is the danger that it can be tokenistic, especially where relatively ill-informed consumers are expected to monitor complex decision-making processes in which professional influence, and professional jargon, still dominate debate – a situation which is still found on many school governing bodies. The danger of *tokenism* is ever present in moves to extend democratic control over large-scale organisations, and serves as a sharp reminder that the introduction of accountability is no quick fix.

Accountability may, however, be easier to introduce if the scale of organisational structures is not so grand, and if decisions over the delivery of public services can be brought nearer to the local people who are the users and beneficiaries of them. In the eyes of the consumer of public welfare small may often be beautiful, especially where small-scale structures are associated with flexible procedures and close, local access. This has been recognised by a number of local government service providers who have introduced schemes to *decentralise* the access to, and delivery of, local services – for example by placing representatives of all service departments in neighbourhood offices to which local residents have easy access, and delegating decisions over service delivery to them. Such decentralised service delivery also makes it easier to establish and to manage user forums, and to ensure that all local users are genuinely represented on them.

However, the process of decentralisation can have contradictory consequences for the consumers of welfare services, for local control implies local variation in service delivery and perhaps, therefore, variation in service standards. This could result in the residents in one neighbourhood receiving different, and better, services than those in another one – again perhaps with middle-class areas benefiting at the expense of poorer ones. It was to avoid the inequity of such geographical variation that nationalised provision of services such as health and education was introduced in the welfare state reforms of the postwar period; an unchecked return to local flexibility here could mean a return to the kinds of inequalities in service standards that would not be of benefit to all consumers.

It is in part because of such fears that Deakin and Wright (1990) stressed the importance of ensuring service quality as a crucial feature of the expansion of consumer control over public services. In fact concern with *quality control* of public services has become something of an obsession among some service providers in the 1990s, with complex new procedures for monitoring of quality and the setting of 'enforcable' performance targets being introduced into the day-to-day management of organisations such as hospitals, schools and universities. Indeed, ironically, there is a danger that the procedures for quality control can become yet another aspect of the bureaucracy of state service delivery rather than a means of control over it – in particular where it is the service providers themselves rather than the consumers who decide whether quality is being maintained. The new managerialist tendencies within public services, and the increasing emphasis on the 'contract culture' in the measurement and control of all public service delivery, are thus evidence that trends in quality concern and accountability can lead away from, rather than towards, more consumer responsiveness in welfare.

However, this does not mean that mechanisms to monitor and measure the performance of public servants should not be an important element of the attempt to ensure that control is exercised over them, especially where the results of such monitoring can be made publicly available to the users of these services. Public evaluation of public services ought to be a central feature of welfare provision within a democracy, so that all citizens can examine and assess the performance of those who are working for them. If this knowledge is to be turned into control, however, citizens must also be provided with the right to act on it to secure the services that they need or want.

Rights and citizenship

We should, therefore, conceive the users of welfare services as citizens and not only as consumers; and when we approach welfare services from the perspective of *citizenship* it is clear that, because of its dominant focus upon the provision of services, social policy has largely failed to address the problems of the delivery of these. This is a criticism that appears to be shared by a wide range of ideological perspectives and political opinions in the 1990s. There also seems to be widespread agreement on the action that should flow from such criticism – a concern with the successful delivery of welfare services, it is argued, requires the empowering of the users of those services. In other words, the paternalism and professionalism of public service needs to be replaced by a *bottom-up* pressure for responsiveness and accountability to the felt needs and desires of citizens.

However, as Plant (1990, pp. 20–1) argues in his discussion of citizenship in welfare services, in these circumstances power is a 'positional good' – that is, it cannot just be *extended* to citizens but must be *transferred* to them. Therefore an increase in the power of users will only lead to change if it is accompanied by a decrease in the power of providers. This is an obvious point but an important one – and one that is perhaps not fully appreciated by all those who criticise current welfare provision. The divesting of power by service providers in order to give citizens a real voice is likely to lead to change and conflict among well-established, and influential, interests; and those who stand to lose their power in this may well seek in practice to create some distance between the *rhetoric* of empowerment and the *reality* of any genuine delegation. It also means that empowerment is not just a process of involving users from the bottom up; it is also a process of securing commitment to reform among providers – from the *top down*.

Empowerment of citizens is thus about the restructuring of welfare services bottom-up and top-down. It concerns both policy development and the policy process. In other words, change is needed not just in the aims of welfare service provision but also in the procedures adopted to put those aims into practice. It is at this procedural level where some of the earliest concerns about user control and accountability were voiced, and where some of the most significant practical challenges to the producer domination of welfare services have been mounted. This procedural challenge can be seen in the politics, and the practice, of welfare rights.

Welfare rights is the term used to describe the activity of providing independent advice and advocacy to the users of welfare services in order to encourage and assist them to pursue the delivery of services they are entitled to, but are not currently benefiting from. Welfare rights activists adopt a legalistic perspective to the delivery of social services, although few of them are actually lawyers themselves. They operate on the premise that the users of welfare services have a right to benefit from the delivery of these services. So, where this delivery is not happening to the satisfaction of users, these users can be advised of their rights and can be assisted to complain to providers or, where possible, to appeal against decisions that may have excluded or disadvantaged them.

The operation of this advice and advocacy role can be seen most clearly in the area of social security benefits. Here the right to benefit is usually clearly defined in law and, where benefits are not in payment or have been wrongly refused, formal rights of challenge and appeal generally apply. Welfare rights workers are skilled at identifying non-take-up of social security benefits by potential beneficiaries and at challenging the legal interpretation of entitlement criteria at appeal. In the 1980s and 90s, in particular, the size and scale of such welfare rights activity in the social security benefits field has grown dramatically (Berthoud *et al.*, 1986). However, although much of the focus of welfare rights work is on social security take-up, the rights-based challenge to service delivery (or non-delivery) has also been used in other areas – for instance to challenge local authority housing departments on failure to provide adequate repairs, or social services departments on failure to secure proper services for people with chronic sickness or disability.

The welfare rights challenge to service delivery arose primarily at the time of growing discontent with state welfare services in the 1970s and 80s; and much of this early welfare rights work was motivated by a left-wing desire to improve services through procedural challenge. This could be seen in particular in the work generated in the project-based schemes set up by central government to provide a new focus of support on some of the most deprived parts of Britain's declining urban areas, such as the Community

Development Projects (CDPs) of the 1970s (Loney, 1983; Alcock, 1993, Ch. 15). The CDPs were set up to use community work support to help challenge local decline and deprivation. They quickly found, of course, that there was little that a small community project could do to arrest such broader-based problems; but they also found that they were able to use their community work skills to provide advice and advocacy for local people in challenging some of the failings of public sector agencies in meeting the rights to benefits and services of poor local people (Bradshaw, 1975).

The 'independent' advice and advocacy that the CDP workers were able to provide in the few communities where they were based in the 1970s has since been taken up and expanded by a range of independent advice and community development organisations. The most well-known of these agencies is probably the national network of Citizens Advice Bureaux (CABs), but there are many more. There are also national bodies providing specialist support for the welfare rights work carried out by local agencies. The CABs have their own national association (NACAB) which produces an extensive guide to rights and procedures across a wide range of services; the Child Poverty Action Group (CPAG) provides specialist advice and publishes detailed handbooks on social security rights; and other organisations (such as Shelter for the homeless) provide specialist support in other areas.

In addition to these independent agencies in the voluntary sector, welfare rights workers are also now employed by a large number of local authorities to assist local people to pursue their rights to services (Berthoud *et al.*, 1986; Fimister, 1986). Here one aspect of the state (local government) is helping citizens to challenge another aspect (central government departments such as social security). Of course, local authority welfare rights workers do not just assist local citizens to challenge central government departments; they provide support for challenges to other sections of local government too. In such circumstances the providers of services in the departments challenged by welfare rights activity may sometimes question local government support for such activity – accusing rights workers of 'biting the hand that feeds them'. However, this criticism has probably encouraged rather than restricted the growth in such rights work; in practice the welfare rights challenge to public service is now widely and variously established both within the public sector and across the voluntary sector too.

Furthermore, the focus on procedural challenge to secure service delivery on which welfare rights is based is not restricted only to public services, it also provides a potential source of challenge, and change, to inadequate service provision across the voluntary and private sectors. In his pamphlet outlining the left-wing case for a democratic review of welfare services to provide both exit and voice for users, Plant (1988) focuses on the importance of rights in securing enforcement of welfare provision and links the concept of welfare rights directly to need for empowerment and accountability in service delivery. Plant also links an enhanced role for welfare rights in service delivery with a rethinking of the concept of *citizenship* in directing the attention of policy makers and policy practitioners towards those who should be the beneficiaries of policy development. In simple terms, Plant's argument is that it is only when we conceive of welfare as being something to which we all have a right as citizens that power over the provision of welfare will begin to pass from the producers to the consumers of these services.

This notion of citizens' rights to services has also been taken up from a different perspective by the Conservative government of the 1990s, under John Major, in the development of *citizens' charters* covering access to a range of public and privatised services. The idea behind the citizens' charters is that they can be a formal expression of the expectations of service delivery which citizens can have of different service providers; and that, where these service providers fail to meet such expectations, citizens have a formal right of complaint – and compensation. Critics of the citizens' charters have pointed out that they often provide only a rather bland and generalised expression of service delivery needs and that the limited rights of compensation that they guarantee do not act as effective means of enforcing service delivery standards. Despite their practical ineffectivity, however, the principle of the formal charter of rights to delivery is an important means of expressing, and realising, the consumer interest in publicly provided services, in particular because these are not subject to the private enforcement mechanisms of the law of contract. They combine the concern with a consumer voice with the legal concept of enforceability in much the same way as Plant (1988) also seeks to link citizenship and rights in providing a new model for welfare.

It is important to recognise, however, that, despite their universal appeal, the concepts of rights and citizenship can frequently operate in practice to exclude some citizens from the benefits of welfare rather than to guarantee access to them. Taylor (1989) makes the point that, in the nationalistic and socially divided context in which welfare rights often in practice operate, their effect can be to remove or restrict the legal rights and welfare needs of marginalised or excluded groups. For instance, when linked to discriminatory immigration controls and practices of institutionalised racism, citizenship and rights can readily become concepts that are available, and beneficial, only to some.

Nevertheless, these practical problems of exclusion and marginalisation, while they must be recognised and challenged by policy makers, do not contradict the principle of citizenship and rights as a means of re-addressing the problems of user choice and user control over welfare service that have been identified by the critics of public welfare in the 1980s and 90s. Because of their focus on consumers rather than providers in determining rights of access to services, these principles can be applied to private and voluntary sector providers too. Indeed, citizenship and rights provide a potentially valuable vehicle for adapting concerns with choice, control and quality to operate across the mixed economy of welfare that we have identified as occupying such a central position in social policy development at the end of the twentieth century (Alcock, 1991).

At the end of the century therefore, concerns with delivery and accountability in welfare have significantly shifted the focus of debate and analysis within social policy. In the earlier part of the century, and in particular during the postwar years of the welfare state, the focus was on the importance of guaranteeing the provision of universal services to all who needed them. It was a concern to establish a *welfare state* to respond to the *need* for welfare. At the end of the century, however, the critics of the past – and the policy makers of the future – have pointed to the failure of such universal services to secure access to welfare for all and have argued instead for a concern to establish a *welfare mix* in which the emphasis lies not on the idea of need – but rather on the concept of *right* to welfare.

SECTION FIVE

Conclusion

14

The Future of Social Policy

Discipline boundaries

Any assessment of the future development of social policy in Britain, both as a feature of social structure and as an academic discipline, must focus first on the boundaries between social policy and other aspects of the social world and academic discourse. As we discussed in Chapter 1, the history of the implementation of social policy has been one of changing boundaries and of changing relationships. In particular there have been changes in the economic contexts and social structures within which policies have been developed and applied; and the academic boundaries between social policy and economic policy and sociology have been both blurred and shifting. In Chapter 1 we suggested that some of these changes could be encapsulated in the change of title which the discipline has seen from *social administration* to *social policy*. This is seen by some as a broadening out of the concern of the discipline to include a concern with the context, as well as the content, of policy development. In general terms such a broadening of outlook is to be welcomed – it is also likely to continue to develop.

As we have seen, the early concern of social policy was on the introduction and implementation of state welfare services to meet the social needs that could not be catered for within a capitalist market economy. However, it is now recognised that state welfare services have only ever been a part of welfare provision within Britain, or indeed within other welfare capitalist countries. Private markets have provided welfare on a commercial basis, for some at least; and such market-based provision has in practice expanded, not declined, since state services became established. Voluntary sector activity has also continued – and continued to grow. Informal welfare support, through families and communities, has consistently been the basis upon which many of the most basic of social and individual needs have been provided for. As we stressed, therefore, social services provision consists of a *welfare mix* rather than a *welfare state*; and social policy analysis has increasingly begun to recognise this.

Identification of a welfare mix has also directed attention to the different means by which service provision is paid for and supported. The assumption that social services are provided out of public expenditure, drawn from direct taxation, has always been a very partial picture of complex and interlocking ways in which public and private funding for welfare operate together, and of the different ways in which resources are both collected and distributed. Paying for welfare encompasses financial and non-financial contributions from a wide range of sources and involves a mixture of fees, charges, contributions and rebates that in practice govern access to services in both pubic and private sectors. What is more, in recent years this complex mixture of funding sources and models of resource distribution has become still more complicated as market principles have been imported into the state sector and independent providers have grown in scale. Social policy analysts must look to a wide range of funding mechanisms when they seek to understand how welfare services are supported, and how they can be developed.

The focus on the redistribution of public resources through state social services as the main feature of social policy is also, in another sense, a narrow one. It has to some extent led the discipline to identify the *redistribution* of resources as the main goal of social policy activity, either through the payment of benefits to people or through the provision of services to them (the 'social wage'). Recognition of the economic and social context of individual needs, on the other hand, focuses our attention also on the role that policy may play in influencing the initial *distribution* of resources from which many individual needs flow, and on the *production* of the resources which may be available to meet such needs. When we focus on these, too, the policy field broadens to include the control of wages and employment protection, and the control of wealth holding and capital movement; and analysis is extended to include economic trends and investment decisions affecting the growth and development of the wider economy.

Criticisms of this narrow focus of social policy have been made by both the Marxist theorists of the New Left and the neo-liberals on the New Right. They are criticisms that became more telling when the economic growth, upon which much of the expansion of state welfare in the postwar period had been predicated, came to an end in the mid 1970s, forcing both policy makers and policy analysts to reassess the priority to be accorded to economic growth and social protection in a declining economy.

Analysis of the achievement of welfare goals in the latter quarter of the twentieth century has been challenged from other perspectives too, both within and beyond social policy. The focus on the redistribution of resources through state welfare services has been argued to have resulted in an emphasis on the role of service providers in the distribution of such resources to meet social needs, within which concern over the provision of social services was equated with effective enjoyment of them. As we saw in Chapter 13, however, the provision of social services has not always resulted in the effective delivery of appropriate services to those who might have been the intended recipients of them. And, as we discussed in Chapter 11, the intentions of service providers have not always matched the real circumstances, and real needs, of different social groups in a diverse – and conflictual – social structure.

As a result of this, social policy has extended its concern to include analysis of the access to, and delivery of, social services from a range of different providers to the potential users of those services. Policy analysts increasingly recognise the importance of examining the social differences and social divisions among service users – consumers and citizens – and the means of inclusion, or exclusion, which result in support or protection being provided, or not. Policy makers are also more aware of the diverse communities and individuals who may need, or want, access to the provision which they develop; and they are increasingly under pressure from users and their representatives to ensure that the processes of policy development and implementation take account of social difference by responding to demands from the *bottom up* as well as the *top down*.

These challenges and changes have all forced the discipline boundaries of social policy both to expand and to become more opaque, as the wider context and more complex structure of welfare services is recognised and understood. However, we should be careful not to characterise earlier policy analysts as narrow-minded, or shortsighted, servants of state welfare providers. Although public welfare may have dominated debate, social policy has been concerned throughout the twentieth century with much more than state welfare and the welfare state and policy development has always extended much beyond the redistribution of public resources to those in need.

As we look to the future of social policy in the twenty-first century, therefore, it is clear that concerns of our discipline will build on this broadening base to examine and to analyse the socioeconomic context and political climate within which policies continue to change and develop. Social policy will thus overlap ever more with economics, sociology and politics; but the boundary changes will not stop there. Social policy analysts are also challenging the boundaries in areas such as law and accountancy. In 1995 a textbook was published bringing together social housing law and policy (Hughes and Lowe, 1995); and, following the devolution of budgetary powers in organisations such as hospitals and schools, accountancy skills have become an important feature of the education and training of social policy managers and administrators.

In the twenty-first century social policy students will study economics, politics, sociology, psychology, law, and more, alongside the more traditional aspects of the discipline. Social policy researchers will look at econometric analysis of distribution and redistribution, make statistical comparison of whole populations across international boundaries, and examine the interpersonal relationships of family members sharing caring responsibilities – indeed, they already do these different things, and more. And policy makers will be working from within state departments, private companies, community action groups, and even their own homes.

Geographical boundaries

Throughout much of its development social policy analysis in Britain has focused upon the policy context, and the policy decisions, of the national state; and policy makers have largely been involved in developing and implementing the policies of the national government within the country. At the end of the twentieth century, however, it is increasingly clear that neither the British government nor British social policy operate only within such a narrow national context. Of course, national policy decisions have always been affected by wider international pressures and concerns – and in the case of Britain in the earlier twentieth century by its imperial domination of other nations throughout the world. However, at the end of the century the international context of economic and social policy making is undoubtedly both more extensive, and more intensive, than at any previous time. In Britain, that international context is made all the more acute, and its influence more pervasive, by our membership of the European Union.

Membership of the EU constrains and directs the policy parameters of the British government and Parliament, as we discussed in Chapter 9. Although this may be regretted, and even resisted, by some in Parliament, its control over policy development in Britain will become ever more extensive and direct over the foreseeable future. In particular, the EU is now a single market, thus economic planning and economic policy increasingly take on a European-wide context – for instance many major private investors now regard the EU as one single economic entity and place their investments within it accordingly. This process of economic harmonisation is also likely to be accentuated further by the development and implementation of a single European currency, which will require national economic planning to take on a Union-wide dimension.

Social policy development in all member nations must respond to this supranational economic context and most European national governments now actively recognise this. In addition to the economic pressure, however, will be the expanding role of the EU, and the Commission acting on its behalf, in direct determination of social policy across national boundaries within the Union. EU social policy initiatives are already quite extensive, as we discussed in Chapter 9; the pressure, both from the Commission and from member states, will be for them to extend much further in the future. Thus social policy in Britain will be determined by what happens in Brussels and Strasbourg, as well as what is decided in Westminster and Whitehall.

EU influence on policy development in Britain in this century and the next will thus be direct, and irresistible; but it will not be the only international influence on policy development – or on policy debate. We live in a world where the distances between nations have been much reduced, both practically and symbolically, by improved transport and communication links. We know instantly what is happening anywhere on the globe, and could get there within

twenty-four hours. Thus the lessons that can be learnt from developments in other countries are both more immediate and much easier
to assess. In such a context all countries are likely to take up ideas
and influences from others with whom they can make comparisons
about social contexts or social needs. For instance, as we have seen,
policy initiatives have been imported into Britain in the 1970s, 80s
and 90s from the USA and from Australia.

Furthermore, if models of policy development are being taken
across international boundaries, policy analysis must be prepared to
cross these boundaries too. The comparative study of social policy in
different countries is now a central feature of the curriculum of all
social policy study; and international comparison is also increasingly
driving the research agenda of policy analysis. Much policy research
is now based on comparison of policy developments in different
national contexts and this has been considerably assisted by the
growth of international databases that can be accessed by researchers
from a range of different countries, such as the Luxembourg Income
Study (LIS) (Smeeding *et al.*, 1990).

Comparative study of social policy will increasingly broaden the
empirical, or *descriptive,* base of social policy – we know more and
more about what is happening in policy development in other
countries. This will also strengthen the *prescriptive* role of social
policy in influencing policy making; for lessons from abroad provide
powerful arguments that things can be done differently – and
therefore that changes should perhaps be made here, too.

The international boundaries of social policy are thus becoming
closer, and more fluid, at the end of the twentieth century. However,
they are not the only geographical boundaries within the discipline
that are changing. Within the nation state, internal boundaries
between regions, localities, and neighbourhoods or communities are
also shifting. It has never been true to suggest that all social policy
planning in Britain takes place at a national level – much is delegated
to the local level, as we discussed in Chapter 10. But the designation
of local areas, and the power and autonomy to be devolved to them,
are also all changing.

The role of the central state in Britain is in any case more complex
than in many other countries because of our status as a 'United
Kingdom'. Thus policy development and implementation in a
number of areas is delegated to the *subnations* of Scotland, Wales and
Northern Ireland, although the model of delegation is different for

each of these. Further devolution of power to these subnations has been a significant feature of political debate in the last quarter of the century, and has been given added impetus by the political pressure for 'complete' devolution from the Nationalist political parties – and, more recently, by the impact of the peace process in Ireland. The future development of policy making in Britain will almost certainly see further devolution of some powers, and resources, to Scotland, Wales and Northern Ireland – although the aspirations of the Nationalists for separation are perhaps less likely to be realised.

Devolution of more power to the subnations may also increase pressure within England for some devolution of policy development and implementation to the various *regions* within the country. During the 1980s and 90s the socioeconomic differences between regions in England – and in particular between the declining industrial regions of the North and Midlands and the developing service sectors of the South and East – have been accentuating; thus the importance of developing policy at a regional level to respond to these different circumstances and needs has been growing (Balchin, 1990).

Regionalism has also been given something of a push, however, by supranational policy development within the EU. EU policy makers, too, have become acutely aware of the growing discrepancies between the development, or decline, of different regions throughout the Union and have sought to focus policy resources upon regions in need, often deliberately bypassing national governments in order to target resources more closely. Although the British government is one of those which has been most resistant to EU Commission attempts to direct resources within member nations (and perhaps against national development priorities), the impact of such regional development has become ever more important across Europe, and within the UK, and seems set to develop further in the foreseeable future.

As regions become more important, it might be anticipated that local areas, and *local government*, will decline in influence, in particular given the reduction in the powers and resources that have been allocated to local authorities in Britain since the attack on local government in the 1980s. While local government may have been in relative decline in the 1980s and 90s, however, it has hardly been facing a demise (Cochrane, 1993). Indeed, in many ways the role of local government in the broader context of social and economic policy development has been enhanced by the moves towards a more enabling, and strategic, role within the local area. It is change, rather than decline, that faces local government in the twenty-first century. This has been accentuated by the effects of the review of local government boundaries and responsibilities undertaken in the mid 1990s, whereby a number of new authorities were created and existing powers redistributed. This has resulted in the most extensive restructuring of local democracy since 1974; and, in many areas therefore (including the whole of Scotland and Wales) it is a radically new local government which faces the policy challenges of the next century.

Finally at the *community* level, too, changes are taking place. The association of community activity and organisation with small geographical neighbourhoods has always been a rather partial and inaccurate picture, as we discussed in Chapter 6. Community organisation frequently extends beyond neighbourhood boundaries, and this is likely to be an accelerating process as communication and transport links improve. Neighbourhoods are also themselves, of course, in a state of change. In many urban areas inner city redevelopment and the demolition of housing provision constructed sometimes only twenty years earlier is rapidly reconstructing city communities; and in rural areas, especially in the southeast and Home Counties, the drift towards new town development and home working is reconstituting village and town life.

Changes at the community and neighbourhood level are also accentuated by the increased emphasis within policy making and delivery on community development and bottom-up accountability in service provision. The criticism of, and the challenges to, statism within welfare provision have resulted not just in a growing distrust of state bureaucracy to deliver national service but also in a further encouragement of devolution in policy debate and the development of a bottom-up emphasis community planning – even though it is frequently unclear quite what is meant by this in practice. The role of the nation state in social policy is thus under attack both from *above* and from *below*, as boundaries are shifting both globally and locally.

Ideological boundaries

From consensus to dissensus

Throughout much of its early development during the first half of the twentieth century the discipline of social policy was largely dominated by the influence of the Fabian tradition. As we discussed in Chapter 1, this culminated in the apparent success of Fabianism in securing the introduction of the welfare state in Britain in the postwar years of the late 1940s. In practice, of course, the welfare state reforms of the 1940s owed their origins to much more than the policy prescriptions of a few Fabian academics and their political allies; and supposed political agreements of the postwar years were far from a universal meeting of minds on the inevitability, and desirability, of state intervention within a capitalist economy.

Nevertheless, many politicians and commentators during these early postwar years saw in the welfare state the product of a political and ideological consensus over the role of public provision for social need. In the fifty years since the introduction of the British welfare state, ideological support for the role of public welfare within a capitalist economy (encapsulated in the concept of *Butskellism*) has in fact remained high across a range of public and political opinion.

Despite this support, however, the Butskellite consensus of the 1940s and 50s has been under mounting challenge from ideological perspectives from a wide and diverse range of political positions. In particular from the 1970s on, critics on both the New Left and the New Right have rejected the premise that growing welfare protection is necessarily conterminous with continued economic development – although their prescriptions for what to do about this mismatch between growth and welfare are of course rather different.

The limitations of state welfare have also been attacked by other new, and increasingly diverse, perspectives on social policy. From feminists, anti-racists, greens, and others, the failure of postwar welfare provision to treat all social groups equally and respond to the differing needs of each has been roundly, and sometimes vehemently, condemned. If the aim of state welfare protection, and redistribution, was to ensure the development of a *strategy of equality* (and, despite the hopes of early Fabians, some have argued quite cogently that it was *not* – for example Hindess, 1987, Ch. 6), the conclusion drawn by many is that this has failed. Rather, new inequalities and divisions within the welfare state have developed (and been subject to closer scrutiny) and existing inequalities have been accentuated rather than reduced.

In the 1990s supporters of the consensus on state welfare and the success of the strategy of equality are thus few and far between in social policy circles – and beyond. The failure of state welfare is widely condemned from a range of new, and old, ideological positions – even though most would probably agree that this failure is in practice a partial one, for many achievements still remain. As a result, social policy in the 1990s is a discipline characterised by theoretical and ideological diversity, not consensus.

From dissensus to consensus

Despite the challenges and the new policy prescriptions of the critics of the welfare state (from the left, the right, and elsewhere) public provision for social protection and redistribution remains a major feature of social policy practice in Britain in the 1990s – as, indeed, it does in most other welfare capitalist countries too. What is more, opinion survey evidence continues to demonstrate public support for state welfare provision (Taylor-Gooby, 1991); and politicians in both major parties, most notably the party leaders (Major and Blair), continue to provide political support for public social services.

Indeed, it is the case that the broader ideological and political debate over state welfare, which has been taking place in the late twentieth century, has ironically had the effect of fostering the development of a renewed belief in its permanency. The collapse of the state socialist regimes of the USSR and Eastern Europe have exposed the failure of total welfare statism and have undermined the claims of some on the left for a more rigorous dose of collectivism. At the same time, however, the free market reforms pursued in Britain, to some extent at least during the Thatcher years of the 1980s, have also been revealed to have led to growing social divisions and social exclusion, and to the renewal of concerns for the need for a strategy of social integration within a divided market economy.

In the mid 1990s, therefore, the extreme critics of the left and right themselves came under attack – as did the record of the Thatcher governments in promoting a 'rolling back' of the boundaries of state welfare. The evidence of the *Rowntree* research on growing social inequalities in the 1980s (one hundred years after Rowntree's own original research) provided social policy once again with empirical evidence of mounting poverty and deprivation within a divided society (Barclay, 1995; Hills, 1995); and the report of the *Borrie Commission* on social justice articulated strategies for the renewal of policies for social justice within a developing market economy (Borrie Commission, 1994). If the aim of the social policy goals of the 1980s was the pursuit of a *strategy of inequality*, in the belief that the advantages that this would produce would eventually 'trickle down' to benefit even the poorest in society (and it is at least debatable whether this draconian model of development was shared by all in government during this time), the conclusion to be drawn on this strategy, too, is that it has been quite unable to deliver to those in most need.

In the 1990s social policy occupies as central a place on the political agenda as at any time earlier in the twentieth century. At all levels (national, local and supranational) policies for the future of economic growth and development are now automatically placed alongside policies for social integration, social regeneration and social justice. Across a wide range of political and academic debate the question being addressed is not *whether* to pursue market-based economic growth *or* public social protection, but *how* to harness *both* together and to ensure that concentration on the one does not prevent securing achievement of the other.

As we have discussed throughout this book, however, this central role for social policy in future social and economic development is no longer a role focused only upon support for, and development of, state welfare protection – indeed, it has never in reality occupied such narrow ideological ground. Social policy in the 1990s, and into the future beyond in the twenty-first century, encompasses both theoretical diversity and organisational heterogeneity. It is the social policy of the *welfare mix*, not the *welfare state* – and, while it generates *consensus* over the need for continued prescriptions for the development of social services, it also enjoys healthy *dissensus* over how these services should develop in practice.

Bibliography

ABBOT, E and BOMPAS, K (1943) *The Woman Citizen and Social Security*, K Bompas.

ABEL-SMITH, B and TOWNSEND, P (1965) *The Poor and the Poorest*, G Bell and Sons.

ABERCROMBIE, N, WARDE, A *et al.* (1994) *Contemporary British Society*, 2nd edn, Polity Press.

ADDISON, P (1975) *The Road to 1945: British Politics and the Second World War*, Jonathon Cape.

ALCOCK, P (1991) Towards Welfare Rights, in Becker, S (ed.) *Windows of Opportunity: Public Policy and the Poor*, CPAG.

ALCOCK, P (1993) *Understanding Poverty*, Macmillan.

ALCOCK, P, CRAIG, G, DALGLEISH, K and PEARSON, S (1995) *Combating Local Poverty: The Management of Anti-Poverty Strategies by Local Government*, Local Government Management Board.

ALCOCK, P, GAMBLE, A *et al.* (eds) (1989) *The Social Economy and the Democratic State: A new policy agenda for the 1990s*, Lawrence and Wishart.

AMIN, K and OPPENHEIM, C (1992) *Poverty in Black and White: Deprivation and Ethnic Communities*, CPAG.

ARBER, S, GILBERT, N and EVANDROU, M (1988) Gender, household composition and receipt of domiciliary services by elderly disabled people, *Journal of Social Policy*, **17**(2).

ATKINSON, A (1990) *A National Minimum? A History of Ambiguity in the Determination of Benefit Scales in Britain*, WSP/47, STICERD, LSE.

ATKINSON, A (1991) *Poverty, Statistics and Progress in Europe*, WSP/60, STICERD, LSE.

BACON, R and ELTIS, W (1976) *Britain's Economic Problem: Too Few Producers*, Macmillan.

BAGGOTT, R (1994) *Health and Health Care in Britain*, Macmillan.

BALCHIN, P (1990) *Regional Policy in Britain: The North–South Divide*, Paul Chapman.

BALDOCK, J and UNGERSON, C (1994) All our futures: becoming a consumer of care in old age, Paper to SPA Annual Conference 1994.

BALDWIN, P (1990) *The Politics of Social Solidarity*, Cambridge University Press.

BALDWIN, S, PARKER, G and WALKER, R (eds) (1988) *Social Security and Community Care*, Avebury.

BALL, S (1896) *The Moral Aspects of Socialism*, Fabian Tract No. 72.

BARCLAY, Sir P (1995) *JR Foundation Inquiry into Income and Wealth*, vol. 1, JR Foundation.

BARRY, N (1987) *The New Right*, Croom Helm.

BARRY, N (1990) *Welfare*, Open University Press.

BARTLETT, W (1993) Quasi-Markets and Educational Reforms, in Le Grand, J and Bartlett, W (eds) *Quasi-Markets and Social Policy*, Macmillan.

BARTLETT, W and HARRISON, L (1993) Quasi-Markets and the National Health Service Reforms, in Le Grand, J and Bartlett, W (eds) *Quasi-Markets and Social Policy*, Macmillan.

BEBBINGTON, A and MILES, J (1989) The Background of Children Who Enter Local Authority Care, *British Journal of Social Work*, **19**(5).

BERTHOUD, R, BROWN, J and WILLIAMS, S (1986) *Standing up for Claimants: Welfare Rights Work in Local Authorities*, Policy Studies Institute.

BEVERIDGE, Sir W (1942) *Report on Social Insurance and Allied Services*, Cmd 6404, HMSO.

BEVERIDGE, Sir W (1948) *Voluntary Action*, Allen and Unwin.

BILLIS, D (1989) *The Theory of the Voluntary Sector: Implications for Policy and Practice*, Centre for Voluntary Organisation, LSE.

BLUNKETT, D and GREEN, G (1983) *Building from the Bottom: The Sheffield Experience*, Fabian Society No. 491.

BLUNKETT, D and JACKSON, K (1987) *Democracy in Crisis: The Town Halls Respond*, Hogarth Press.

BODDY, M and FUDGE, C (eds) (1984) *Local Socialism? Labour Councils and New Left Alternatives*, Macmillan.

BOOTH, C (1889) *The Life and Labour of the People*, Williams and Northgate.

BORRIE COMMISSION (1994) *Social Justice: Strategies for National Renewal – The Report of the Commission on Social Justice*, Vintage.

BOSANQUET, N (1987) Buying Care, in Clode, D, Parker, C and Etherington, S (eds) *Towards the Sensitive Bureaucracy*, Gower.

BOYSON, R (1971) *Down with the Poor*, Churchill.

BRADSHAW, J (1975) Welfare rights and experimental approach, in Lees, R and Smith, G (eds) *Action Research in Community Development*, Routledge & Kegan Paul.

BRAMLEY, G and SMART, G (1993) *Who Benefits from Local Services: Comparative Evidence from Different Local Authorities*, WSP/91, STICERD, LSE.

BRENTON, M (1985) *The Voluntary Sector in British Social Services*, Longman.

BREWSTER, I and TEAGUE, P (1989) *European Community Social Policy – Its Impact on the United Kingdom*, Institute of Personnel Management.

BROWN, C (1984) *Black and White Britain: The third PSI survey*, Heinemann.

BUCHANAN, J (1986) *Liberty, Market and the State*, Harvester Wheatsheaf.

BULL, D (1980) *What Price 'Free' Education?*, CPAG.

CAHILL, M (1994) *The New Social Policy*, Blackwell.

CALLAGHAN, J (1987) *Time and Chance*, Collins.

CAMERON, G *et al.* (eds) (1991) The economic outlook for the regions and countries of the European Community in the 1990s, *Cambridge Economic Review*.

CHANAN, G (1992) *Out of the Shadows: Local Community Action and the European Community*, European Foundation for the Improvement of Living and Working Conditions (Dublin).

CLARKE, J (1993) *A Crisis in Care*, Sage.

COCHRANE, A (1993) *Whatever Happened to Local Government?*, Open University Press.

COCKBURN, C (1977) *The Local State*, Pluto Press.

COLE, I and FURBEY, R (1994) *The Eclipse of Council Housing*, Routledge.

CROMPTON, R (1993) *Class and Stratification: An Introduction to Current Debates*, Polity Press.

CROSLAND, C A R (1956) *The Future of Socialism*, Jonathon Cape.

CURWEN, P (ed.) (1992) *Understanding the United Kingdom Economy*, 2nd edn, Macmillan.

CUTLER, T, WILLIAMS, K and WILLIAMS, J (1986) *Keynes, Beveridge and Beyond*, Routledge & Kegan Paul.

DALE, J and FOSTER, P (1986) *Feminists and State Welfare*, Routledge & Kegan Paul.

DALLEY, G (ed.) (1991) *Disability and Social Policy*, Policy Studies Institute.

DAVIS SMITH, J, ROCHESTER, C and HEDLEY, R (eds) (1995) *An Introduction to the Voluntary Sector*, Routledge.

DEACON, A and BRADSHAW, J (1983) *Reserved for the Poor: The Means-Test in British Social Policy*, Basil Blackwell and Martin Robertson.

DEACON, B *et al.* (1992) *The New Eastern Europe: Social Policy Past, Present and Future*, Sage.

DEAKIN, N (1994) *The Politics of Welfare: Continuities and Change*, Harvester Wheatsheaf.

DEAKIN, N and WRIGHT, A (eds) (1990) *Consuming Public Services*, Routledge.

DENNETT, J, JAMES, E, ROOM, G and WATSON, P (1982) *Europe against poverty: the European Poverty Programme 1975–1980*, Bedford Square Press.

DEPARTMENT OF HEALTH (1992) *The Health of the Nation: A Strategy for Health in England*, Cmd. 1986, HMSO.

DEPARTMENT OF SOCIAL SECURITY (1993) *The Growth of Social Security*, HMSO.

DEPARTMENT OF SOCIAL SECURITY (1995) *Income Related Benefits Estimates of Take-Up in 1992*, HMSO.

DONNISON, D (1994) Social policy studies in Britain: retrospect and prospect, in Ferris, J and Page, R (eds) *Social Policy in Transition*, Avebury.

DOYAL, L, HUNT, G and MELLOR, J (1981) Your life in their hands: migrant workers in the National Health Service, *Critical Social Policy*, **1**(2).

DUNLEAVY, P (1984) The Limits of Local Government, in Boddy, M and Fudge, C (eds) *Local Socialism? Labour Councils and New Left Alternatives*, Macmillan.

DUNLEAVY, P and HUSBANDS, C (1985) *British Democracy at the Crossroads*, Allen and Unwin.

DUTTON, D (1991) *British Politics Since 1945: The Rise and Fall of Consensus*, Basil Blackwell.

ELCOCK, H (1982) *Local Government: Politicians, Professionals and the Public in Local Authorities*, 2nd edn, Methuen.

ESPING-ANDERSEN, G (1985) *Politics Against Markets: the social democratic road to power*, University of Harvard Press.

ESPING-ANDERSEN, G (1990) *The Three Worlds of Welfare Capitalism*, Polity Press.

FIMISTER, G (1986) *Welfare Rights Work in Social Services*, Macmillan.

FINCH, J (1989) *Family Obligations and Social Change*, Polity Press.

FINCH, J and GROVES, D (eds) (1983) *A Labour of Love: Women, Work and Caring*, Routledge & Kegan Paul.

FINLAYSON, G (1994) *Citizen, State and Social Welfare in Britain 1830–1990*, Clarendon Press.

FOSTER, P (1983) *Access to Welfare: An Introduction to Welfare Rationing*, Macmillan.

FRANKENBERG, R (1966) *Communities in Britain*, Penguin.

FRIEDMAN, M (1962) *Capitalism and Freedom*, University of Chicago Press.

GAMBLE, A (1992) *Britain in Decline*, 2nd edn, Macmillan.

GARNHAM, A and KNIGHTS, E (1994) *Putting the Treasury First: The truth about child support*, CPAG.

GEORGE, V and PAGE, R (eds) (1995) *Modern Thinkers on Welfare*, Harvester Wheatsheaf.

GEORGE, V and WILDING, P (1976) *Ideology and Social Welfare*, Routledge & Kegan Paul.

GEORGE, V and WILDING, P (1994) *Welfare and Ideology*, Harvester Wheatsheaf.

GILMOUR, I (1978) *Inside Right*, Quartet.

GINSBURG, N (1979) *Class, Capital and Social Policy*, Macmillan.

GINSBURG, N (1991) *Divisions of Welfare: A Critical Introduction to Comparative Social Policy*, Sage.

GLENDINNING, C (1992) *The Costs of Informal Care: Looking Inside the Household*, HMSO.

GLENDINNING, C and MILLAR, J (eds) (1992) *Women and Poverty in Britain: The 1990s*, Harvester Wheatsheaf.

GLENNERSTER, H (1988) Requiem for the Social Administration Association, *Journal of Social Policy*, **17**(1).

GLENNERSTER, H (1992) *Paying for Welfare: The 1990s*, Harvester Wheatsheaf.

GORDON, P and NEWNHAM, A (1985) *Passport to Benefits: Racism in Social Security*, CPAG/Runnymede Trust.

GORZ, A (1982) *Farewell to the Working Class*, Pluto Press.

GOUGH, I (1979) *The Political Economy of the Welfare State*, Macmillan.

GRAHL, J and TEAGUE, P (1990) *1992 – The Big Market: The Future of the European Community*, Lawrence and Wishart.

GREEN, D (1987) *The New Right: The Counter Revolution in Political, Economic and Social Thought*, Wheatsheaf.

GREEN, D (1988) *Everyone a Private Patient*, IEA.

GREEN, H (1988) *Informal Carers: A study carried out on behalf of the DHSS as part of the 1985 General Household Survey*, HMSO.

HADLEY, R and HATCH, S (1981) *Social Welfare and the Failure of the State: Centralised Services and Participatory Alternatives*, George Allen and Unwin.

HALSEY, A, HEATH, A and RIDGE, J (1980) *Origins and Destinations: family, class and education in modern Britain*, Clarendon Press.

HAM, C (1993) *Health Policy in Britain*, Macmillan.

HAM, C and HILL, M (1993) *The Policy Process in the Modern Capitalist State*, 2nd edn, Harvester Wheatsheaf.

HANTRAIS, L (1995) *Social Policy in the European Community*, Macmillan.

HARRIS, J (1989) The Webbs, The Charity Organisation Society and the Ratan Tata Foundation: Social policy from the perspective of 1912, in Bulmer, M, Lewis, J and Piachaud, D (eds) *The Goals of Social Policy*, Unwin Hyman.

HATCH, S (1980) *Outside the State: Voluntary Organisations in Three English Towns*, Croom Helm.

HAYEK, F (1944) *The Road to Serfdom*, Routledge & Kegan Paul.

HAYEK, F (1960) *The Constitution of Liberty*, Routledge & Kegan Paul.

HAYEK, F (1982) *Law, Legislation and Liberty*, Routledge & Kegan Paul.

HEADLAM, S (1892) *Christian Socialism*, Fabian Tract No. 42.

HILL, M (1990) *Social Security Policy in Britain*, E Elgar.

HILL, M (1993a) *Understanding Social Policy*, 4th edn, Blackwell.

HILL, M (1993b) *The Welfare State in Britain: A Political History Since 1945*, E Elgar.

HILLS, J (1988) *Changing Tax: How the tax system works and how to change it*, CPAG.

HILLS, J (ed.) (1990) *The State of Welfare: The Welfare State in Britain Since 1974*, Clarendon Press.

HILLS, J (1993) *The Future of Welfare: A Guide to the Debate*, JR Foundation.

HILLS, J (1995) *JR Foundation Inquiry into Income and Wealth*, vol. 2, JR Foundation.

HINDESS, B (1987) *Freedom, Equality and the Market: Arguments on Social Policy*, Tavistock.

HIRSCHMAN, A (1970) *Exit, Voice and Loyalty: Responses to decline in firms, organisations and states*, Harvard University Press.

HOLMAN, B (1990) *Good Old George*, Lion.

HUGHES, D and LOWE, S (1995) *Social Housing Law and Policy*, Butterworths.

HUHNE, C (1990) *Real World Economics: Essays on Imperfect Markets and Fallible Governments,* Penguin.

HUMPHRIES, R (1995) *Sin, Organised Charity and the Poor Law in Victorian England,* Macmillan.

JOHNSON, N (1987) *The Welfare State in Transition: The Theory and Practice of Welfare Pluralism,* Wheatsheaf.

JOHNSON, N (1990) *Reconstructing the Welfare State: A Decade of Change 1980–1990,* Harvester Wheatsheaf.

JONES, K and FOWLES, A (1984) *Ideas on Institutions: Analysing the literature of long term care and custody,* Routledge & Kegan Paul.

JOSHI, H (1988) *The Cash Opportunity Costs of Childbearing,* Discussion Paper 208, Centre for Economic Policy Research.

JOSHI, H (1992) The Cost of Caring, in Glendinning, C and Millar, J (eds) *Women and Poverty in Britain: the 1990s,* Harvester Wheatsheaf.

KEANE, J (1988) *Democracy and Civil Society,* Verso.

KEYNES, J M (1936) *The General Theory of Employment, Interest and Money,* Macmillan.

KING, D (1987) *The New Right: Politics, Markets and Citizenship,* Macmillan.

KLEIN, R (1995) *The New Politics of the NHS,* 3rd edn, Longman.

KORPI, W (1983) *The Democratic Class Struggle,* Routledge & Kegan Paul.

KRAMER, R (1990) *Voluntary Organisations in the Welfare State: On the Threshold of the 1990s,* Centre for Voluntary Organisation, LSE.

LARGE, P (1991) Paying for the additional costs of disability, in Dalley, G (ed.) *Disability and Social Policy,* Policy Studies Institute.

LE GRAND, J (1982) *The Strategy of Equality,* Allen and Unwin.

LE GRAND, J (1989) Markets, Welfare and Equality, in Le Grand, J and Estrin, S (eds) *Market Socialism,* Clarendon Press.

LE GRAND, J (1990) Equity Versus Efficiency: The Elusive Trade-off, *Ethics,* **100.**

LE GRAND, J (1993) Paying for or Providing Welfare, in Deakin, N and Page, R (eds) *The Costs of Welfare,* Avebury.

LE GRAND, J and BARTLETT, W (eds) (1993) *Quasi-Markets and Social Policy,* Macmillan.

LE GRAND, J and ESTRIN, S (eds) (1989) *Market Socialism,* Clarendon Press.

LEE, D (1991) Poor work and poor institutions: training and the youth labour market, in Brown, P and Scase, R (eds) *Poor Work: Disadvantage and the Division of Labour,* Open University Press.

LEE, P and RABAN, C (1983) Welfare and Ideology, in Loney, M, Boswell, D and Clarke, J (eds) *Social Policy and Social Welfare*, Open University Press.

LEE, P and RABAN, C (1988) *Welfare Theory and Social Policy: Reform or Revolution*, Sage.

LEIBFRIED, S (1993) Towards a European Welfare State, in Jones, C (ed.) *New Perspectives on the Welfare State in Europe*, Routledge.

LEWIS, J (1995) *The Voluntary Sector, the State and Social Work in Britain*, E Elgar.

LEWIS, N and BIRKINSHAW, P (1993) *When Citizens Complain: Reforming Justice and Administration*, Open University Press.

LEWRG (The London–Edinburgh Weekend Return Group) (1979) *In and Against the State*, Conference of Socialist Economists.

LIPSET, S (1963) *Political Man*, Heinemann.

LONEY, M (1983) *Community Against Government: The British Community Development Project 1968–78*, Heinemann.

LOWE, R (1990) The Second World War: Consensus and the Foundations of the Welfare State, *Twentieth Century British History*, **1**(2).

MACMILLAN, H (1938) *The Middle Way*, Macmillan.

MACNICOL, J (1980) *The Movement for Family Allowances 1918–1945; A Study in Social Policy Development*, Heinemann.

MCGLONE, F (1992) *Disability and Dependency in Old Age: A demographic and social audit*, Family Policy Studies Centre.

MCGLONE, F and CRONIN, N (1994) *A Crisis in Care: The future of family and state care for older people in the European Union*, Family Policy Studies Centre.

MARSHALL, T H (1950) *Citizenship and Social Class*, Cambridge University Press.

MARX, K (1970) *Capital*, vol. 1, Progress Press.

MAUD COMMITTEE (1967) *Report of the Committee on the Management of Local Government*, vol. 1, HMSO.

MAYO, M (1994) *Communities and Caring: The Mixed Economy of Welfare*, Macmillan.

MEANS, R and SMITH, R (1994) *Community Care: Policy and Practice*, Macmillan.

MIDWINTER, E (1994) *The Development of Social Welfare in Britain*, Open University Press.

MISHRA, R (1989) The academic tradition in social policy: The Titmuss years, in Bulmer, M, Lewis, J and Piachaud, D (eds) *The Goals of Social Policy*, Unwin Hyman.

MISHRA, R (1990) *The Welfare State in Capitalist Society*, Harvester Wheatsheaf.

MOORE, R and WALLACE, T (1975) *Slamming the Door*, Martin Robertson.

MORRIS, L (1994) *Dangerous Classes: The Underclass and Social Citizenship*, Routledge.

MURRAY, C (1984) *Losing Ground: American Social Policy 1950–1980*, Basic Books (New York).

MURRAY, C (1990) *The Emerging British Underclass*, IEA.

MURRAY, C (1994) *Underclass: The Crisis Deepens*, IEA.

NACAB (1991) *Barriers to Benefit: Black claimants and social security*, National Association of Citizens Advice Bureaux.

NATIONAL CONSUMER COUNCIL (1986) *Measuring Up: Consumer Assessment of Local Authority Services*, National Consumer Council.

NEWSOM REPORT (1963) *Half our Future: A Report of the Central Advisory Council for Eduction*, HMSO.

NOVAK, T (1988) *Poverty and the State: An Historical Sociology*, Open University Press.

O'CONNOR, J (1973) *The Fiscal Crisis of the State*, St Martin's Press (New York).

OKUN, A (1975) *Equality and Efficiency: the Big Trade-Off*, Brookings (Washington DC).

OLIVER, M (1990) *The Politics of Disablement: A Sociological Approach*, Macmillan.

OPPENHEIM, C (1993) *Poverty: the Facts*, Revised and Updated Edn, CPAG.

PAGE, R (1984) *Stigma*, Routledge & Kegan Paul.

PAHL, J (1989) *Money and Marriage*, Macmillan.

PAPADAKIS, E (1990) Privatisation and the Welfare State, in Hindess, B (ed.) *Reactions to the Right*, Routledge.

PARKER, G (1990) *With Due Care and Attention: a review of research on informal care*, Family Policy Studies Centre.

PASCALL, G (1986) *Social Policy: A Feminist Analysis*, Tavistock.

PEDEN, G (1985) *British Economic and Social Policy: Lloyd George to Margaret Thatcher*, 2nd edn, Philip Allan.

PHILLIPSON, C and WALKER, A (eds) (1986) *Ageing and Social Policy: A Critical Assessment*, Gower.

PLANT, R (1988) *Citizenship, Rights and Socialism*, Fabian Society No. 531.

PLANT, R (1990) Citizenship and Rights, in Plant, R and Barry, N *Citizenship and Rights in Thatcher's Britain: Two Views*, IEA.

PRESCOTT-CLARKE, P (1990) *Employment and Handicap*, Social and Community Planning Research.

QURESHI, H and WALKER, A (1989) *The Caring Relationship: Elderly People and Their Families*, Macmillan.

ROBINSON, V (1990) Roots to Mobility: the Social Mobility of Britain's Black Population, *Ethnic and Racial Studies*, **13**(2).

ROOM, G (1993) *Anti-Poverty Action-Research in Europe*, School of Advanced Urban Studies, University of Bristol.

ROSSITER, C and WICKS, M (1982) *Crisis or Challenge? Family Care, Elderly People and Social Policy*, Family Policy Studies Centre.

ROWNTREE, B S (1901) *Poverty: A Study of Town Life*, Macmillan.

ROWNTREE, B S (1941) *Poverty and Progress: A Second Social Survey of York*, Longman.

RYAN, P (1978) 'Poplarism' 1893–1930, in Thane, P (ed.) *The Origins of British Social Policy*, Croom Helm.

SARRE, P (1989) Recompostition of the Class Structure, in Hamnett, C, McDowell, L and Sarre, P (eds) *Restructuring Britain: The Changing Social Structure*, Sage.

SAVILLE, J (1983) The Origins of the Welfare State, in Loney, M, Boswell, D and Clarke, J (eds) *Social Policy and Social Welfare*, Open University Press.

SEEBOHM REPORT (1968) *Report of the Committee on Local Authority and Allied Personal Social Services*, Cmnd. 3703, HMSO.

SMEEDING, T, O'HIGGINS, M and RAINWATER, L (eds) (1990) *Poverty, Inequality and Income Distribution in Comparative Perspective: The Luxembourg Income Study (LIS)*, Harvester Wheatsheaf.

SMITH, A, (1776) *An Enquiry into the Nature and Causes of the Wealth of Nations*, Adam and Charles Black.

SMITH, D (ed.) (1992) *Understanding the Underclass*, Policy Studies Institute.

SMITH, G (1988) A Paen for the Social Policy Association: A Response to Glennerster, *Journal of Social Policy*, **17**(3).

SOLOMOS, J (1989) *Race and Racism in Contemporary Britain*, Macmillan.

SPICKER, P (1984) *Stigma and Social Welfare*, Croom Helm.

SPICKER, P (1993) Can European social policy be universalist?, in Page, R and Baldock, J (eds) *Social Policy Review 5*, Social Policy Association.

STOKER, G (1988) *The Politics of Local Government*, Macmillan.

SULLIVAN, M (1992) *The Politics of Social Policy*, Harvester Wheatsheaf.

SWANN REPORT (1985) *Education for All: Report of the Committee of Inquiry into the Education of Children from Ethnic Minority Groups*, Cmnd. 9453, HMSO.

TAWNEY, R H (1931) *Equality*, Allen and Unwin.

TAYLOR, D (1989) Citizenship and social power, *Critical Social Policy*, Issue 26.

TAYLOR-GOOBY, P (1991) *Social Change, Social Welfare and Social Science*, Harvester Wheatsheaf.

TAYLOR-GOOBY, P and DALE, J (1981) *Social Theory and Social Welfare*, Edward Arnold.

TEAGUE, P (1989) *The European Community: the Social Dimension. Labour Market Policies for 1992*, Kogan Page.

THANE, P (1982) *The Foundations of the Welfare State*, Longman.

THERBORN, G and ROEBROEK, J (1986) The irreversible welfare state, *International Journal of the Health Services*, **16**(3).

THOMAS, I and BALLOCH, S (1994) Local Authorities and the Expansion of Credit Unions 1991–3, *Local Economy*, **9**(2).

TINKER, A (1984) *The Elderly in Modern Society*, 2nd edn, Longman.

TITMUSS, R (1956) *The Social Division of Welfare: Some Reflections on the Search for Equity*, Liverpool University Press.

TITMUSS, R (1958) Social Administration in a Changing Society, in Titmuss, R, *Essays on 'the Wefare State'*, Unwin.

TITMUSS, R (1970) *The Gift Relationship*, Pelican.

TOWSEND, P (1962) *The Last Refuge: A survey of residential institutions and homes of old people*, Routledge & Kegan Paul.

TOWNSEND, P (1979) *Poverty in the United Kingdom: A Survey of Household Resources and Standards of Living*, Penguin.

TOWSEND, P, DAVIDSON, N and WHITEHEAD, M, (eds) (1988) *Inequalities in Health: The Black Report and the Health Divide*, Penguin.

TWIGG, J (1989) Models of carers: how do social care agencies conceptualise their relationship with informal carers?, *Journal of Social Policy*, **18**(1).

UNGERSON, C (1987) *Policy is Personal: Sex, Gender and Informal Care*, Tavistock.

WALKER, A (1986) Pensions and the Production of Poverty in Old Age, in Phillipson, C and Walker, A (eds) *Ageing and Social Policy: A Critical Assessment*, Gower.

WALKER, A (1990) Poverty and Inequality in Old Age, in Bond, J and Coleman, P (eds) *Ageing in Society: An Introduction to Social Gerontology*, Sage.

WALKER, A and WALKER, L (1991) Disability and financial need – the failure of the social security system, in Dalley, G (ed.) *Disability and Social Policy*, Policy Studies Institute.

WEBER, M (1968) *Economy and Society*, Bedminster Press (New York).

WILLIAMS, F (1989) *Social Policy: A Critical Introduction*, Polity Press.

WILLMOTT, P (1984) *Community in Social Policy*, Policy Studies Institute.

WILSON, E (1977) *Women and the Welfare State*, Tavistock.

WOLFENDEN REPORT (1977) *The Future of Voluntary Organisations*, Croom Helm.

WRIGHT, K (1987) *The Economics of Informal Care of the Elderly*, Centre for Health Economics, University of York.

Index